高等职业院校"十三五"规划教材

专升本英语教程

陈元红　王　锦 ▇ 主编

中国林业出版社
·北京·

内 容 简 介

本教材依据《云南省专升本英语考试大纲》编写。在编写过程中认真、细致分析了最新大纲中的具体要求,捕捉新考纲和题型变化。本教材在云南林业职业技术学院试用3年,并进行了3次修订,力求使教材信息最新、最全、最实用,使之更好地为考生服务。

全书共两大部分,分为8章,对专升本要求的英语基础语法、考点及题型做了详尽解析。第一部分为基础语法,分为词法和句法2章;第二部分为专升本英语考题解析及训练,共6章。另外,本书还附有专升本英语考试真题、模拟试题等数字资源和词汇表。

图书在版编目(CIP)数据

专升本英语教程 / 陈元红,王锦主编. — 北京:中国林业出版社,2019.12

高等职业院校"十三五"规划教材

ISBN 978-7-5219-0467-3

Ⅰ.①专… Ⅱ.①陈…②王… Ⅲ.①英语-成人高等教育-升学参考资料 Ⅳ.①H319.39

中国版本图书馆CIP数据核字(2020)第014997号

中国林业出版社·教育分社

责任编辑:曾琬淋

电话:(010)83143630   传真:(010)83143516

数字资源

出版发行	中国林业出版社(100009 北京市西城区德内大街刘海胡同7号)	
	E-mail:jiaocaipublic@163.com 电话:(010)83143500	
	http://www.forestry.gov.cn/lycb.html	
经　　销	新华书店	
印　　刷	固安县京平诚乾印刷有限公司	
版　　次	2020年1月第1版	
印　　次	2020年1月第1次	
开　　本	787mm×1092mm 1/16	
印　　张	13.75	
字　　数	332千字	
定　　价	42.00元	

未经许可,不得以任何方式复制或抄袭本书之部分或全部内容。

版权所有　侵权必究

《专升本英语教程》编写人员

主　　编：陈元红　王　锦

副 主 编：李思蓓　李青芮　刘妍敏　兰　燕

编写人员：（按姓氏拼音排序）

　　　　　陈军军　陈明艳　陈元红　兰　燕　李青芮

　　　　　李思蓓　刘妍敏　秦　婷　陶思润　汪华仙

　　　　　王　锦　许义婕　晏　林

FOREWORD 前言

专升本考试是大学专科层次学生进入本科层次阶段学习的选拔考试。随着社会的发展，对人才的要求越来越高，高职院校毕业生参加专升本考试的人数剧增。英语作为专升本的考试科目之一，是决定考生能否顺利进入高层次学习的一门重要科目。于是，我们组建了《专升本英语教程》编写团队，在各方领导的支持下，编写了本教材，为高职学生参加专升本考试提供帮助。

本教材依据《云南省专升本英语考试大纲》编写。在编写过程中，认真、细致分析了最新大纲中的具体要求，捕捉新考纲和题型变化，对专升本要求的英语基础语法、考点及题型做了详尽解析。本教材在云南林业职业技术学院试用3年，并进行了3次修订，力求使教材信息最新、最全、最实用，使之更好地为考生服务。

全书共两大部分，分为8章。第一部分为基础语法，分为词法和句法2章；第二部分为专升本英语考题解析及训练，共6章。另外，本书还附有专升本英语词汇表及专升本英语考试真题、模拟试题等数字资源。

本教材的编写人员均为云南林业职业技术学院的一线英语教师，具体分工如下：陈元红、王锦共同负责全书的框架结构设计和前言；第一章第一至第三节、第七至第九节由王锦编写；第一章第四至第六节和第二章由陈元红编写；第三章由陈元红、刘妍敏、李青芮、李思蓓共同编写；第四章由李青芮编写；第五章由李思蓓和兰燕共同编写；第六章和附录由刘妍敏编写；第七章和第八章由李思蓓编写；王锦和李青芮提供数字资源中的真题、模拟试题及解析；晏林、汪华仙、陶思润、陈军军、许义婕、陈明艳、秦婷等提供部分章节专项练习中的部分习题。

本教材在编写过程中参阅和借鉴了该领域的许多英语语法著作和教材，在此，特向原著者表达敬意和感谢！同时感谢支持教材编写和出版的各位领导、专家以及云南林业职业技术学院的全体英语教师！特别感谢李红艳、孙丽娟、李章、许吉平和张俊文等老师的大力支持！

由于编者的水平有限，书中可能存在不足之处，恳请使用该书的教师、学生和英语爱好者提出宝贵意见和建议，使本书的编写更加完善。

最后，衷心祝愿各位考生备考顺利，在考试中取得优异成绩！

编者
2019年10月

前言

第一部分 基础语法

第一章 词法 ………………………………………………………………………… 2
- 第一节 名词 ……………………………………………………………………… 2
- 第二节 冠词 ……………………………………………………………………… 7
- 第三节 数词 ……………………………………………………………………… 11
- 第四节 代词 ……………………………………………………………………… 17
- 第五节 形容词与副词 …………………………………………………………… 25
- 第六节 介词与连词 ……………………………………………………………… 34
- 第七节 动词 ……………………………………………………………………… 45
- 第八节 动词的时态和语态 ……………………………………………………… 57
- 第九节 虚拟语气 ………………………………………………………………… 66

第二章 句法 ………………………………………………………………………… 72
- 第一节 基本句型结构 …………………………………………………………… 72
- 第二节 陈述句、疑问句、祈使句和感叹句 …………………………………… 79
- 第三节 并列句 …………………………………………………………………… 84
- 第四节 名词性从句 ……………………………………………………………… 87
- 第五节 定语从句 ………………………………………………………………… 92
- 第六节 状语从句 ………………………………………………………………… 97
- 第七节 倒装句与强调句 ………………………………………………………… 102
- 第八节 主谓一致 ………………………………………………………………… 108

第二部分 专升本英语考题解析及训练

第三章 词汇与语法结构 …………………………………………………………… 114
第四章 完形填空 …………………………………………………………………… 137

第五章　阅读理解 …………………………………………………………………… 147

第六章　翻译 ………………………………………………………………………… 184

第七章　词义辨析 …………………………………………………………………… 191

第八章　多选题 ……………………………………………………………………… 196

参考文献 ………………………………………………………………………………… 198

附录　专升本英语词汇表 ……………………………………………………………… 199

PART 1

第一部分
基础语法

第一章　词法

第二章　句法

第一章 词法

第一节 名词

一、名词的分类

英语名词(noun)可以分为专有名词(proper nouns)和普通名词(common nouns)两大类。

1. 专有名词

专有名词特指人或事物的名称，包括人名、地名、书名、月份、机构等，首字母必须大写。例如：China、Mary、the Great Wall、Bill Gates 等。

2. 普通名词

普通名词是一类人或东西或是一个抽象概念的名称。普通名词可分为个体名词、集体名词、物质名词和抽象名词4类。

个体名词：表示某类人或事物中的个体。例如：teacher、monkey、factory、train 等。

集体名词：表示若干个体组成的集合体。例如：people、class、army、family 等。

物质名词：表示无法分为个体的实物。例如：water、cotton、grain、air 等。

抽象名词：表示动作、状态、品质、感情等抽象概念。例如：health、happiness、freedom、work 等。

二、名词的数

(一)可数名词和不可数名词

一般来说，个体名词和集体名词可以用数目来计算，称为可数名词(countable nouns)。物质名词和抽象名词一般无法用数目来计算，称为不可数名词(uncountable nouns)。

(1)有些名词既可用作不可数名词，又可用作可数名词，但意义有所不同。

①一些不可数的物质名词可以用作可数的个体名词。例如：

物质名词(不可数)	个体名词(可数)
glass(玻璃)	a glass(一个玻璃杯)
copper(铜)	a copper(一枚铜币)

②一些不可数的抽象名词可以用作可数的个体名词。例如：

抽象名词(不可数)	个体名词(可数)
beauty(美)	a beauty(一个美人)
exercise(运用)	an exercise(一个练习)

(2)不可数名词一般没有复数形式，也不能和不定冠词 a(an)或数词连用。如果表示数量，可以用"of 词组"。of 前面表示单位的名词根据情况用单数或复数。of 后面如果是不可数名词，用单数；of 后面如果是可数名词，用复数。例如：

a glass of milk   a piece of bread
two cups of coffee   three bowls of rice
a basket of eggs   two boxes of apples

(二)可数名词的复数形式

1. 可数名词的复数形式

一般由词尾加-s 或-es 构成，其规则如下所列：

可数名词复数形式的一般规则

类　　别	构成法	读音	例词
一般情况	加-s	在清辅音后读/s/	maps, books
		在浊辅音及元音后读/z/	cars, photos
		在/t/后读/ts/	cats, students
		在/d/后读/dz/	beds, guards
		在/dʒ/后读/iz/	bridges, ages
以字母 s、x、ch、sh 结尾的词	加-es	在/s/、/z/、/ʃ/、/tʃ/后读/iz/	classes, brushes
以辅音字母+y 结尾的词	将 y 改成 i，加-es	读/z/	factories, stories
以字母 o 结尾的词	一般加-es	读/z/	potatoes, tomatoes
	少数外来词或缩略词加-s	读/z/	radios, pianos
以字母 f 或 fe 结尾的词	一般加-s	读/s/	roofs, chiefs
	少数将 f、fe 改为-ves	读/vz/	shelves, knives
	有些加-s 或改为-ves 均可	读/s/或/vz/	scarfs/scarves

2. 可数名词复数形式的不规则变化

英语中有一部分名词由于历史或词源等原因，其复数形式的构成法是不规则的。这种情况主要有：

(1)内部元音字母变化。例如：

foot—feet   man—men   woman—women
tooth—teeth   goose—geese mouse—mice

(2)词尾加-en 或-ren。例如：

child—children   ox—oxen

(3) 单复数同形。例如：
sheep—sheep　　　fish—fish　　Chinese—Chinese
Japanese—Japanese　　deer—deer
(4) 以-an结尾或其他形式结尾的表示民族、国家的人的名词变复数时在词尾加-s。例如：Americans，Asians，Russians，Australians，Italians，Germans等。

> **注　意**
>
> 以-man、-woman构成的表示民族、国家的人的复合名词变复数时，将-man和-woman变成复数。例如：Englishman—Englishmen，Frenchman—Frenchmen。

3. 复合名词的复数形式变化
(1) 主体名词变成复数形式。例如：
son-in-law—sons-in-law　　　editor-in-chief—editors-in-chief
looker-on—lookers-on　　　　passer-by—passers-by
boy friend—boy friends　　　 tooth-brush—tooth-brushes
(2) 两个词都变成复数形式。由man或woman作为第一部分的复数名词，两个组成部分皆变为复数形式。例如：
woman doctor—women doctors　　man driver—men drivers

4. 其他特殊情况
(1) 有些表示由两部分构成的事物和部分学科的名词总以复数的形式出现。例如：
glasses(眼镜)，shorts(短裤)，trousers(裤子)，mathematics(数学)，physics(物理学)，politics(政治学)

Maths is the language of science. 数学是科学的语言。

No news is good news. 没有消息就是好消息。

(2) 有些名词在形式上是单数，但通常当作复数名词用。例如：
people，youth，police
The Chinese people are great people. 中国人民是伟大的人民。

(3) 物质名词是不可数名词，没有复数形式，但有时以复数形式出现，表示类别。例如：
teas(各种茶)，fruits(各种水果)

(4) 有些复数形式的名词表示特别的意义。例如：
papers(文件)，manners(礼貌)，goods(货物)，times(时代)，conditions(环境，情况)，looks(外貌)，sands(沙滩)

(5) 有些名词在习惯用语中一定要用复数形式。例如：
make friends with(与……交朋友)
shake hands with(与……握手)

三、名词所有格

名词所有格是指一个名词与另一个名词之间存在所有关系时所用的形式。

1. 所有格形式的构成

(1)由名词末尾加's构成，多用来表示有生命的东西。放在另一名词之前，作定语用。

①单数名词后加's，其读音与名词复数结尾的读音相同。例如：

the girl's father(女孩的父亲)

②以 s 结尾的复数名词后加'。例如：

two hours' walk(两个小时的步行)

③不以 s 结尾的复数名词后加's。例如：

the children's holiday(孩子们的节日)

④以 s 结尾的人名，可以加's，也可以只加'。例如：

Thomas's brother(托马斯的兄弟)

Charles' job(查尔斯的工作)

⑤表示各自的所有关系，不是共有的，则要分别在名词末尾加's；若表示共有的，则在最后一个名词的末尾加's。例如：

John's and Mary's rooms(约翰和玛丽各人的房间)

John and Mary's room(约翰和玛丽合住的房间)

(2)由介词 of 加名词构成，多用来表示无生命的东西。例如：

the title of the book(书名)

the legs of the table(桌子的腿)

2. 特殊用法

(1)表示有生命者的名词，有时也与 of 构成短语表示所有关系。例如：

The son of my boss(我老板的儿子)

(2)'s 所有格常表示有生命的东西，但也可表示无生命的东西。例如：

表示时间：today's newspaper(今天的报纸)

表示自然现象：the moon's rays(月光)

表示国家、城市机构：Shanghai's industry(上海的工业)

表示度量衡及价值：twenty dollars' value(20 美元的价值)

表示度量衡及价值：five miles' distance(5 英里的距离)

专项练习

(一)写出下列名词的复数形式

1. tooth   2. crisis   3. word   4. sheep   5. son-in-law
6. knife   7. child   8. key   9. radio   10. woman teacher
11. watch   12. photo   13. class   14. month   15. mouse
16. house   17. goose   18. Chinese   19. life   20. girl friend

(二)单项选择

1. Guitar is a popular _____.
   A. machine   B. instrument   C. equipment   D. tool
2. The doctor said that mental _____ is the major cause of her sleeping problem.
   A. tension   B. sadness   C. anger   D. relaxation
3. I'll have a cup of coffee and _____.
   A. two toasts
   B. two pieces of toasts
   C. two piece of toasts
   D. two pieces of toast
4. The train arrived two hours behind _____.
   A. date   B. plan   C. time   D. schedule
5. This is not my book. It's _____.
   A. my daughter's   B. of my daughter's   C. of my daughter   D. to my daughter
6. Keep in _____ that all people are different and some may progress faster than others.
   A. head   B. brain   C. heart   D. mind
7. Can you guess her _____ to the news that her parents will come back tomorrow?
   A. impression   B. reaction   C. comment   D. opinion
8. Over-working can be a _____ on both body and mind.
   A. task   B. burden   C. bother   D. weight
9. ——Why couldn't they meet us at six o'clock?
   ——Because they were delayed by _____.
   A. heavy traffic   B. heavy traffics   C. crowded traffic   D. crowded traffics
10. We had a long telephone _____ yesterday afternoon.
    A. dialogue   B. conversation   C. talk   D. call
11. This is _____. She wrote her name on the first page.
    A. a Sherry's book
    B. a book of Sherry
    C. a book of Sherry's
    D. Sherry's a book
12. You can't find many _____ in a hospital.
    A. man nurse   B. men nurse   C. men nurses   D. man nurses
13. Jim got a _____ of $20,000 from the bank to buy a new car.
    A. loan   B. choice   C. pay   D. option
14. The boy made a _____ to his parents that he would try to earn his own living after graduation.
    A. promise   B. present   C. plan   D. decision
15. In summer, the most popular _____ is swimming.
    A. work   B. action   C. game   D. sport
16. A year after the war, schools in the country returned to _____.
    A. normal   B. condition   C. instruction   D. education

17. In my sister's bedroom, there is a pair of scissors, a stack of books and _____ flowers on her desk.
    A. a piece of   B. a pocket of   C. a slice of   D. a bunch of
18. I like that daughter of _____.
    A. Tom's sister   B. Tom sister's   C. Tom's sister's D. sister's Tom's
19. At weekends, she often helps her mother pick _____ in the field.
    A. cotton   B. a cotton   C. cottons   D. some cottons
20. The _____ are a hard-working people.
    A. Germen   B. Germany   C. Germans   D. German

第二节 冠词

冠词是一种虚词，用在名词或名词词组的前面，表示名词是特指或是泛指。冠词可分为不定冠词和定冠词两种形式。不定冠词有 a、an，定冠词有 the。

一、不定冠词的用法

a 用在发音以辅音音素开头的名词之前，而 an 则用在发音以元音音素开头的名词之前。例如：

a teacher, a house, a university

an hour, an umbrella, an example

(1) 表示某一类人或某事物中的任何一个。经常用在第一次提到某人或某物时，例如：

I gave him a book yesterday. 我昨天给了他一本书。

I am reading an interesting story book. 我在读一本有趣的故事书。

I have got a ticket. 我有一张票。

There is a tree in front of my house. 我的屋前有一棵树。

(2) 表示人或事物的某一种类，强调整体，即以其中的一个代表一类。例如：

A horse is useful to mankind. 马对人类有用。

A bird can fly. 鸟会飞。

A steel worker makes steel. 炼钢工人炼钢。

(3) 用于表示时间、速度、价格等意义的名词之前，表示"每一"。例如：

We often go to school two times a day. 我们常常一天去两次学校。

I went to the library once a week at least. 我一星期至少去一次图书馆。

The potato is sold at about 3 yuan a kilo. 土豆卖三元一千克。

(4) 用来指某人某物，但不具体说明任何人或任何物。例如：

A boy came to see you a moment ago. 刚才有一个小孩来找你。

I got this tool in a shop. 我在商店买的这件工具。

We need a car now. 我们现在需要一辆车。

She is ill, she has to see a doctor. 她病了,她得去看医生。

(5)用来表示"一"这个数量,相当于 one。例如:

The river is about a thousand kilometers long. 这条河大约有一千千米长。

I have a sister and two brothers. 我有一个姐姐和两个哥哥。

(6)用在姓名前,表示"某一个""某位",也可表示"一位"。例如:

A Professor Zhou applied for the post. 某位周教授申请了这个职位。

A Mr. Thomson is waiting for you in the yard. 一位汤姆森先生在院子里等你。

(7)用于某些固定词组。例如:

a few(几个,一些)   a little(有点)
a lot of(许多)   a long time(很长时间)
a moment ago(刚才)   have a look(看一看)
get a cold(感冒)   make a living(谋生)

二、定冠词的用法

(1)特指某(些)人或某(些)事物,以区别于同类中其他的人或事物。例如:

The bag in the desk is mine. 桌子里的书包是我的。

Is this the book you are looking for? 这是你要找的书吗?

Do you know the man in black? 你知道穿黑色衣服的人是谁吗?

It is not the car we are looking for. 这不是我们要找的车。

The man has found his child. 那个人找到了他的孩子。

(2)用来指上文中已提到过的人或事物。例如:

I bought a book from Xinhua Bookstore. The book costs 15 yuan. 我从新华书店买了一本书。这本书花了十五元。

I saw a film yesterday. The film was ended at eight o'clock. 我昨天看了一场电影。电影八点钟结束。

Lucy bought a radio yesterday, but she found something was wrong with the radio. 露西昨天买了一台收音机,但是她发现收音机有问题。

(3)用于表示世界上独一无二的事物或用于自然界现象之前。例如:

the sun(太阳),the moon(月亮),the earth(地球),the sky(天空),the world(世界),the winter night(冬天的夜晚)

The sun is bigger than the moon. 太阳比月亮大。

I can see a bird in the sky. 我能看到天空中有一只小鸟。

I like to have a walk with the bright moon light in the evening. 我喜欢晚上在明亮的月光下散步。

(4)定冠词与单数名词连用,表示某一类人或物。例如:

The dog is not too danger. 犬不太危险。

The cat is an animal. 猫是一种动物。

The umbrella in the shop is very cheap in this season. 这个季节商店里的雨伞很便宜。

(5)定冠词与某些形容词连用，使形容词名词化，表示某一类人或物。例如：
the poor(富人)，the rich(穷人)，the wounded(伤员)，the sick(病人)
The wounded were brought to the hospital. 受伤者被送到了医院。
He always helps the poor. 他经常帮助穷人。
The deaf can go to this special school. 耳聋者可以进这所特殊学校上学。
(6)用在序数词、形容词最高级和表示方位的名词前。例如：
This is the biggest city in China I have ever visited. 这是我在中国参观过的最大的城市。
I saw a plane coming from the east. 我看见一架飞机从东方飞来。
He is the last one to help me. 他不会来帮助我的。
(7)用在演奏乐器和文艺活动、运动场所的名称前。例如：
The little girl likes to play the violin. 小女孩喜欢拉小提琴。
They are going to the cinema tonight. 他们今晚要去电影院看电影。
The theater was on fire last week. 剧院上周着火了。
(8)定冠词用在报刊、杂志的名称之前。例如：
I am reading the *China Daily* now. 我现在正读《中国日报》。
Have you got the Evening Paper yet? 你拿到晚报了吗？
The *Times* is a foreign newspaper. 《时代》是一家外国报纸。
The *Peking Review* is on the desk. 《北京周报》在桌子上放着。
(9)用在江河、海洋、山脉、群岛等的名称之前。例如：
We live near the Yellow River. 我们住在黄河边上。
The Changjiang River is the biggest one in China. 长江是中国最大的河。
The Himalayas is located in Tibet. 喜马拉雅山位于西藏。
(10)定冠词用在姓名复数之前，表示一家人。例如：
The Greens is very kind to us. 格林一家人待我们很好。
The Whites like the classic music. 怀特一家喜欢古典音乐。

三、不用冠词的情况

(1)大多数专有名词、泛指的抽象名词和物质名词之前一般不用冠词。例如：
I think water is a kind of food. 我认为水是一种食物。
Cotton feels soft. 棉花摸起来柔软。
(2)表示日常餐食名词之前不用冠词。例如：
It's time for breakfast. 该吃早饭了。
What do you have for lunch? 你午饭吃点什么？
(3)在表示季节、月份、星期、节日等时间的名词之前，以及表示球类运动、棋类游戏和娱乐活动的名词之前不用冠词。例如：
Summer is hot and winter is cold here. 这儿夏天热冬天冷。
New Year's Day is coming. 新年就要到啦。
Today is the first day of May. 今天是五月的第一天。

We are going to play basketball this afternoon. 今天下午我们要去打篮球。

We don't like bridge very much. 我们不太喜欢桥牌。

(4)语言的名称前不用冠词。例如：

Can you speak English? 你会讲英语吗？

It's difficult to learn Chinese well. 要学好中文很难。

Tom knows English but he doesn't know French. 汤姆懂英语但不懂法语。

(5)名词前已有作定语用的物主代词、指示代词、不定代词时不用冠词。例如：

This is my book. 这是我的书。

I want to buy this dress. 我想买这条裙子。

(6)在表示某一类人或事物的复数名词前不用冠词。例如：

I don't approve of cousins marrying. 我不赞成堂兄的婚姻。

She likes reading books. 她喜欢读书。

(7)在称呼语、表示头衔和职务的名词前不用冠词。例如：

What are you doing now, Mummy? 妈妈，你在做什么？

He is chairman of the Students' Union. 他是学生会主席。

(8)某些固定词组中不用冠词。例如：

by air(乘飞机), on foot(步行), at night(在晚上), after school(放学后), at home(在家), go to class(去上课), in fact(事实上), from morning till night(从早到晚)

I'm going to Chicago by air next week. 下周我要乘飞机去芝加哥。

I go to school on foot. 我步行去学校上学。

In fact, I don't know him at all. 实际上，我一点也不认识他。

He is at home today. 他今天在家。

专项练习

单项选择

1. When you're ready, I'll take you to _____ airport.
   A. /　　　　B. the　　　　C. a　　　　D. an

2. Tom and Sara aren't _____ cousins; they are _____ brother and _____ sister.
   A. the; the; the　B. /; /; /　　C. /; the; /　　D. /; the; the

3. I began to learn _____ Japanese in _____ 1990.
   A. the; the　　B. /; /　　　　C. /; the　　　D. the; /

4. Peter is studying _____ chemistry.
   A. /　　　　B. a　　　　　C. the　　　　D. an

5. Do you think this is _____ most beautiful scenery you've ever seen, _____ Mr. King?
   A. /; the　　B. a; the　　　C. a; /　　　　D. the; /

6. I saw _____ boy going into the room. I don't know who _____ boy was.

A. /; the   B. the; a   C. a; the   D. a; a

7. How about taking _____ short break? I want to make _____ call.

A. the; a   B. a; the   C. the; the   D. a; a

8. He stays _____ till twelve o'clock every morning.

A. in bed   B. in a bed   C. in the bed   D. on the bed

9. _____ doctor told me to take _____ medicine three times _____ day, stay in _____ bed, then I would be better soon.

A. /; a; a; the   B. A; the; the; /
C. The; the; a; /   D. A; /; a; /

10. He likes _____ music. He can play _____ piano very well.

A. /; /   B. /; the   C. the; the   D. the; a

11. There is _____ picture on _____ wall. I like _____ picture very much.

A. /; the; /   B. the; a; /   C. the; a; a   D. a; the; the

12. We always have _____ rice for _____ lunch.

A. /; /   B. the; /   C. /; a   D. the; the

13. Spain is _____ European country and Japan is _____ Asian country.

A. a; an   B. an; a   C. a; a   D. an; an

14. Before _____ December 20 she posted _____ Christmas card to him.

A. /; a   B. the; /   C. /; /   D. a; /

15. We often go to _____ playground to play _____ football in _____ afternoon.

A. a; the; the   B. the; /; the   C. /; /; an   D. the; the; an

16. It took me _____ hour and _____ half to finish _____ work.

A. a; a; a   B. an; a; a   C. an; a; the   D. an; a; /

第三节　数词

表示"多少"和"第几"的词叫作数词。

一、基数词

表示"多少"的词叫作基数词。例如：one、ten。

1. 基数词的基本表示方法

（1）基本的基数词。英语中最基本的基数词是表示其他基数词的基础，借助这些基础的基数词，可以表示出任何需要的基数词。

zero（零）　　　one（一）　　　two（二）　　　three（三）　　　four（四）
five（五）　　　six（六）　　　seven（七）　　　eight（八）　　　nine（九）
ten（十）　　　eleven（十一）　　　twelve（十二）　　　thirteen（十三）　　　fourteen（十四）
fifteen（十五）　　　sixteen（十六）　　　seventeen（十七）　　　eighteen（十八）　　　nineteen（十九）

twenty(二十)　　thirty(三十)　　forty(四十)　　fifty(五十)　　sixty(六十)
seventy(七十)　　eighty(八十)　　ninety(九十)

(2)二十以上的两位数的表示方法。先说"几十"，再说"几"，十位与个位之间用连字符连接。例如："82"可表示为 eighty-two，"43"可表示为 forty-three。

(3)三位数的表示方法。先说"几百(hundred)"然后加 and，再说"几十几"。例如："185"可表示为 one hundred and eighty-five。

(4)四至六位数的表示方法。先说"几千(thousand)"，再说"几百(hundred)"，再加 and，最后说"几十几"。例如："6522"可表示为 six thousand, five hundred and twenty-two。

(5)七至九位数的表示方法。先说"几百万(million)"，然后再按四至六位数的表示方法。例如："12345678"可表示为 twelve million, three hundred and forty-five thousand, six hundred and seventy-eight。

2. 基数词的用法

(1)作主语。例如：

Two of them joined the army last year. 他们中的两个人去年参军了。

Three plus six is nine. 三加六等于九。

(2)作宾语。例如：

Please give me four. 请给我四支笔。

——How many pens did you buy yesterday? 昨天你买了几支笔？

——I bought five. 五支。

(3)作表语。例如：

He is just seven. 他只有七岁。

She was seventeen when she went to college. 当她去上大学的时候有十七岁。

(4)作定语。例如：

There are thirty students in our class. 我们班上有三十名学生。

He borrowed five books from the library yesterday. 她昨天从图书馆借了五本书。

> **注　意**
>
> (1)基数词表示计量时，它所修饰的名词要用复数形式。例如：
>
> The bridge is about 500 meters long. 这座桥大约有500米长。
>
> This piece of meat weights two pounds. 这块肉有2磅重。
>
> (2)带有数词的名词作定语时，一般用单数形式。例如：
>
> a four-month baby(一个四个月大的孩子)，a three-hour drive(一段三小时的路程)

二、序数词

表示"第几"的词叫作序数词。例如：first、twentieth。

1. 表示序数词的基础词汇

first(第一)　　second(第二)　　third(第三)　　fourth(第四)
fifth(第五)　　sixth(第六)　　seventh(第七)　　eighth(第八)

ninth（第九）　　　　tenth（第十）　　　　　eleventh（第十一）　　　twelfth（第十二）
thirteenth（第十三）　　　fourteenth（第十四）　　　　　fifteenth（第十五）
sixteenth（第十六）　　　seventeenth（第十七）　　　　eighteenth（第十八）
nineteenth（第十九）　　　twentieth（第二十）　　　　　thirtieth（第三十）
fortieth（第四十）　　　　fiftieth（第五十）　　　　　　sixtieth（第六十）
seventieth（第七十）　　　eightieth（第八十）　　　　　ninetieth（第九十）
hundredth（第一百）　　　thousandth（第一千）　　　　millionth（第一百万）
billionth（第十亿）

2. 序数词的用法

(1) 作主语。例如：

The first is not so good as the second. 第一个不如第二个好。

Four girls come in. The second is my little sister. 四个女孩走了进来。第二个是我的小妹妹。

(2) 作宾语。例如：

She was among the first to arrive. 她是最先到达的人之一。

Please give me the first. 请把第一个给我。

(3) 作表语。例如：

Sam is always the first to go to school in the morning. 萨姆总是早上第一个去上学的人。

(4) 作定语。例如：

China belongs to the third world. 中国属于第三世界国家。

His father died in the Second World War. 他的父亲死于第二次世界大战。

> **注 意**
>
> 序数词前面常用定冠词 the，但下列 4 种情况不用冠词。
> (1) 序数词前已有物主代词或名词所有格时，不能再用冠词。例如：
> This is Tom's second visit to China. 这是汤姆第二次访问中国。
> (2) 表示比赛或考试的名次时，通常省略定冠词。例如：
> He was (the) second in the English exam. 在这次英语考试中他得了第二名。
> (3) 序数词被用作副词时不用冠词。例如：
> I have to finish my homework first. 我得先完成作业。
> (4) 在某些习惯用语中不用冠词。例如：
> at first（起初），first of all（首先），at first sight（乍一看）

三、分数、小数和百分数

1. 小数

小数由整数部分、小数点和小数 3 个部分组成。小数点读作 point，小数点前面的数词按基数词读出，小数点的后面的数依次按数字读出。例如：

12.297 读作 twelve point two nine seven。
0.5 读作 zero point five。
3.751 读作 three point seven five one。

> **注 意**
>
> 如果一个名词受到大于1的小数修饰，那么该名词要用复数，例如："1.3毫米"说成英语是 1.3 millimeters，不是 1.3 millimeter。

2. 分数

(1) 用英语表示分数的方法是：先说分子，后说分母；分子用基数词，分母用序数词；当分子超过"一"时，分母用复数形式。例如：

"三分之二"可表示为 two thirds。

Only about one-third of the class is going to make it next year. 班里明年会升级的人大约只有三分之一。

Two-fifths of the machines on display were new items. 展出的机器五分之二是新产品。

> **注 意**
>
> 有些分数的表示比较特别，例如：
>
> "二分之一"通常说成 a (one) half。
>
> "四分之一"通常说成 a quarter。
>
> Three quarters of the theatre was full. 剧院的座位坐满了四分之三。
>
> The proportion rose from a quarter to a half. 比率从四分之一上升到了二分之一。

(2) 有时还可以用"分子(用基数词)+in/out of +分母(用基数词)"这样的形式。例如：

"十分之六"可表示为 six in ten/six out of ten。

Eight out of ten of us suffer this miserable condition at some time in our lives. 在我们的生活中的某个时候，10个人有8个经受过这种可悲的情况。

> **注 意**
>
> 当分子及分母都非常大时，可直接读"分子(基数词)+over +分母(基数词)"，例如：
>
> "86/98"可表示为 eighty-six over ninety-eight。

3. 百分数

英语的百分数通常用"基数词 +percent"来表示。例如：

Ten per cent of the apples are bad. 这些苹果中有10%是坏的。

The price was reduced by 18 per cent. 价格降低了百分之十八。

"82%"可表示为 eighty-two percent，其中，percent 也可分开写成 per cent。percent 的符号形式为%，如 45 percent 可写成 45%。注意英语与汉语表达词序的不一样，如汉语说"百分之六十"，英语是"60 per cent"。

四、数词的其他用法

1. 表示时刻

(1)英语的时刻一般用基数词表示。例如：
"12点"可表示为 twelve (o'clock)。

(2)若表示几点过几分(不超过半个小时)，则一般用"分钟数+past+点钟数"表示。例如：
"6点15分"可表示为 fifteen past six。

(3)若表示几点差几分(不超过半个小时)，一般用"分钟数+to+点钟数"表示。例如：
"8点50分"可表示为 ten to nine。

(4)有时也可直接用基数词读点钟数和分钟数。例如：
"9点20分"可表示为 nine twenty。
"11点50分"可表示为 eleven fifty。

2. 表示日期

(1)年份。四位数以下的年份，按基数词的读法读，如"(公元)432年"直接读成 four hundred and thirty-two；满四位数的年份，一般是两位两位地读，即读作"几十几，几十几"，如"1978年"通常读作 nineteen seventy-eight。

若是整百的年份，通常读作"the year+几十几+hundred"，如"1900年"读作 the year nineteen hundred；若是整千的年份，通常读作"the year+几千"，如"2000年"读作 the year two thousand。类似地，"2010年"可读作 two thousand and ten。

(2)日期。日期用"the+序数词"表示，前面用介词 on。例如：
(on) the first, (on) the twenty-second

(3)月份。月份的首字母必须大写，缩写形式由前3个字母构成，前面用介词 in。例如：
(in) January/Jan., (in) October/Oct.

(4)年代。年代用"the+整十位数基数词的复数形式"表示。例如：
The thirties (1930s/1930's), the eighties of the last century

专项练习

单项选择

1. _____ of dollars have gone into the building of this factory.
   A. Three millions   B. Million   C. Millions   D. Three million

2. Mary was _____ in the exam.
   A. a first   B. first   C. the first   D. one

3. Over _____ of China's inhabitants belong to the Han nationality.
   A. nine-tenths   B. nine-tenth   C. ninth-ten   D. ninths-ten

4. _____ of March is my sister's birthday.

A. The twenty-one   B. Twenty-one   C. The twenty-first   D. Twenty-first

5. Shortly after the accident, two _____ police were sent to the spot to keep order.

A. dozens of   B. dozens   C. dozen   D. dozen of

6. The foreign guest stayed in _____ last night.

A. Room 204   B. the Room 204   C. the 204 room   D. 204 the room

7. There are fifty-five students applying for the position, _____ are girls.

A. two-third of whom   B. second-thirds of them

C. second-threes of whom   D. two-thirds of whom

8. _____ new products have been successfully trial-produced.

A. A great deal   B. A large amount of

C. A plenty of   D. A large number of

9. Almost _____ of the population of this country is literate.

A. ninth-tenths   B. nine-tenth   C. nine-tenths   D. ninth-ten

10. The exam will be on the first half of the book. That means we'll have to finish _____.

A. fifteenth chapter   B. fifteen chapter

C. chapter fifteen   D. chapter fifteenth

11. Please go to _____ to pick up your ID card.

A. third window   B. the window three

C. window third   D. the third window

12. He cut the cake _____.

A. in halves   B. in half   C. into halves   D. into half

13. Who is that man, _____ in the front row?

A. one   B. the one   C. first   D. the first

14. We have produced _____ this year as we did in 1993.

A. as much cotton twice   B. as twice much cotton

C. much as twice cotton   D. twice as much cotton

15. The earth is about _____ as the moon.

A. as fifty time big   B. fifty times as big

C. as big fifty time   D. fifty as times big

16. The population of many Alaskan cities has _____ in the past three years.

A. more than doubled   B. more doubled than

C. much than doubled   D. much doubled than

17. The moon is about _____ in diameter as diameter as the earth.

A. one-three as large   B. one three as large

C. one-third as large   D. one third as large

18. Five hundred yuan a month _____ enough to live on.

A. is   B. are   C. is being   D. has been

19. _____ of the buildings were ruined.

A. Three fourth 　　B. Three four 　　C. Three-fourths 　　D. Three-four

20. Consult _____ for questions about earthquakes.

A. the six index 　　　　　　　　　　B. index six

C. sixth index 　　　　　　　　　　　D. index numbering six

第四节　代词

代词是代替名词、形容词和数词的词。大多数代词具有名词和形容词的功能。英语中的代词，按其意义、特征及在句中的作用分为：人称代词、物主代词、反身代词、指示代词、相互代词、疑问代词、关系代词和不定代词9种。

一、人称代词

表示我、你、他、我们、你们、他们等的词称为人称代词。人称代词不仅指人，也可以指物，有人称、数和格的变化。

人　称	单　数		复　数	
	主格	宾格	主格	宾格
第一人称	I	me	we	us
第二人称	you	you	you	you
第三人称：他	he	him	they	them
第三人称：她	she	her	they	them
第三人称：它	it	it	they	them
不定代词	one	one	ones	ones

1. 人称代词在句中的作用

(1)主格作主语，放在句首。例如：

I am Chinese. 我是中国人。

He is my friend. 他是我的朋友。

(2)宾格作宾语，放在及物动词或介词之后，有时还可以在口语中用作表语。例如：

I don't know her. 我不认识她。（作动词宾语）

What's wrong with it? 它怎么了？（作介词宾语）

It's me. 请开门，是我。（作表语）

2. 人称代词并列用法的排列顺序

(1)单数人称代词并列作主语时，其顺序为：

第二人称→第三人称→第一人称

即：you and I；he/she/it and I；you, he/she/it and I。

(2)复数人称代词作主语时，其顺序为：

第一人称→第二人称→第三人称

即：we and you；you and they；we, you and they。

二、物主代词

表示所有关系的代词称为物主代词。物主代词可分为形容词性物主代词和名词性物主代词两种，列表如下。

数	人 称	形容词性物主代词	名词性物主代词
单数	第一人称	my	mine
	第二人称	your	yours
	第三人称	his	his
		her	hers
		its	its
复数	第一人称	our	ours
	第二人称	your	yours
	第三人称	their	theirs

1. 形容词性物主代词

起形容词的作用，用在名词前作定语。例如：

I love my country. 我热爱我的国家。

Is this your car? 这是你的汽车吗？

Someone is looking for you, his name is Tom. 有人找你，他的名字是汤姆。

> **注　意**
>
> (1)如果名词前用了形容词性物主代词，就不能再用冠词(a、an、the)、指示代词(this、that、these、those)等修饰词了。例如：
>
> 这是他的书桌。
>
> 误：This is his a desk.
>
> 正：This is his desk.
>
> (2)与形容词一起修饰名词时，形容词性物主代词要放在形容词的前面。例如：
>
> his English books(他的英语书)；their Chinese friends(他们的中国朋友)
>
> (3)汉语中经常会出现"我妈妈""你们老师"等这样的语言现象，虽然代词用的是"我""你们"，但实际意义仍是"我的""你们的"，所以在汉译英时，注意要用形容词性物主代词"my""your"。例如：
>
> 你妈妈在家吗？
>
> 误：Is you mother at home?
>
> 正：Is your mother at home?
>
> (4) it's 与 its 读音相同，he's 与 his 读音相似，但使用时需注意它们的区别：it's 和 he's 分别是 it is 和 he is 的缩略形式，但 its 和 his 却是形容词性物主代词。例如：
>
> It's a bird. Its name is Polly. 它是一只鸟。它的名字叫波利。
>
> He's a student. His mother is a teacher. 他是一名学生。他妈妈是一位教师。

2. 名词性物主代词

起名词的作用，可用作主语、宾语、表语。

（1）作主语。例如：

May I use your pen? Yours works better. 我可以用一下你的钢笔吗？你的比我的好用。

（2）作宾语。例如：

I love my motherland as much as you love yours. 我爱我的祖国就像你爱你的祖国一样深。

（3）作介词宾语。例如：

You should interpret what I said in my sense of the word, not in yours. 你应当按我所用的词义去解释我说的话，而不能按你自己的去解释。

（4）作表语。例如：

The life I have is yours. It's yours. It's yours. 我的生命属于你，属于你，属于你。

三、反身代词

反身代词是一种表示反射或强调的代词。它的基本含义是：通过反身代词指代主语，使施动者把动作在形式上反射到施动者自己，如我自己、你自己、他自己、我们自己、你们自己、他们自己等。因此，反身代词与其所指代的名词或代词形成互指关系，在人称、性、数上保持一致。反身代词第一、第二人称构成是由形容词性物主代词加"-self"（复数加"-selves"）构成。第三人称反身代词是由人称代词宾格形式加"-self"（复数加"-selves"）构成。

1. 作宾语

数	第一人称	第二人称	第三人称	第三人称	第三人称
单数	myself	yourself	himself	herself	itself
复数	ourselves	yourselves	themselves	themselves	themselves

例如：

Please help yourself to some fish. 请你随便吃点鱼。

I could not dress (myself) up at that time. 那个时候我不能打扮我自己。

You should be proud of yourself. 你应为自己感到骄傲。

有些动词后不跟反身代词，如 get up, sit-down, stand up, wake up 等。

2. 作同位语

反身代词可用作宾语、表语及主语的同位语，加强被修饰词的语气，表示强调"本人""自己"。此时反身代词要重读，可紧放在被修饰名词后或句末。例如：

The box itself is not so heavy. 箱子本身并不重。（作主语同位语）

Martin himself attended the sick man. 马丁亲自照顾病人。（作主语同位语）

Don't trouble to come over yourself. 你不必费神亲自来了。（作主语同位语）

You yourself said so. / You said so yourself. 你自己是这样说的。（作主语同位语）

You should ask the children themselves. 你应该问一问孩子们自己。（作宾语同位语）

四、指示代词

指示代词包括：this、that、these、those。

(1) this 和 these 一般用来指在时间或空间上较近的事物或人，that 和 those 则指时间和空间上较远的事物或人。例如：

This is a pen and that is a pencil. 这是钢笔，那是铅笔。

We are busy these days. 这几天我们很忙。

In those days the workers had a hard time. 在那些日子里，工人们过着艰苦的生活。

(2) 有时 that 和 those 指前面讲到过的事物，this 和 these 则是指下面将要讲到的事物。例如：

I had a cold. That's why I didn't come. 我感冒了。这就是我没来的原因。

What I want to say is this：pronunciation is very important in learning English. 我想说的是：发音在英语学习中非常重要。

(3) 有时为了避免重复提到的名词，常可用 that 或 those 代替。例如：

Television sets made in Beijing are just as good as those made in Shanghai. 北京制造的电视机和上海制造的一样好。

(4) this 在电话用语中代表自己，that 则代表对方。例如：

Hello! This is Mary. Is that Jack speaking? 你好！我是玛丽。你是杰克吗？

五、相互代词

相互代词只有 each other 和 one another 两个词组，它们表示句中动词所叙述的动作或感觉在涉及的各个对象之间是相互存在的。例如：

It is easy to see that the people of different cultures have always copied each other. 显而易见，不同文化的人总是相互借鉴的。

1. 作动词宾语

People should love one another. 人们应当彼此相爱。

2. 作介词宾语

Dogs bark，cocks crow，frogs croak to each other. 犬吠、鸡鸣、蛙儿对唱。

六、疑问代词

疑问代词用于特殊疑问句中。疑问代词一般放在句子的最前面，在句中可用作主语、宾语、表语、定语。疑问代词有下列几个：who(谁，问人)、whose(谁的，问所有者)、whom(谁，问人，是 who 的宾格)、which(哪一个)、what(什么，问东西)等。疑问代词在句中没有性和数的变化，除 who 之外也没有格的变化。例如：

Who will join us? 谁愿意加入我们？（who 作主语）

Who is the man carrying a brown suitcase? 那个提着棕色手提箱的人是谁？（Who 作主语补语）

Whom did she marry? 她嫁给了谁？（whom 作宾语）

With whom did she dance the Waltz? 她跟谁跳的华尔兹舞？（whom 作介词 with 的宾语）

Which do you prefer，beer or whiskey? 你喜欢啤酒还是威士忌？（which 作宾语）

七、关系代词

关系代词有 who、whom、whose、which、what、that。关系代词用来引导名词性从句和定语从句。它代表先行词，同时在从句中作一定的句子成分。关系代词有主格、宾格和属格之分，并有指人与指物之分。that 的用法最广，that 可指人，也可指物。例如：

Do you know what her name is? 你知道她叫什么名字吗？（引导宾语从句，what 在从句中作主语补语）

Tell me which is better. 告诉我哪个好一些。（which 引导宾语从句，在从句中作主语）

This is the pencil whose point is broken. 这就是那个折了尖的铅笔。（whose 指物，在限定性定语从句中作定语）

He came back for the book which he had forgotten. 他回来取他落下的书。（which 指物，在限定性定语从句中作宾语，可以省略）

八、不定代词

不定代词即不指明代替任何特定名词或形容词的代词，常用不定代词有 all、both、every、each、either、neither、more、little、few、much、many、another、other、any、one、no、some、something、anything、everything、somebody、someone、anybody、anyone、nothing、nobody、no one、none、everybody、everyone 等。一般来讲，修饰不定代词的词要置于其后。不定代词大部分可以代替名词和形容词，在句中作主语、宾语、表语、定语和状语。

（一）不定代词的功能与用法

1. 作主语

Both of them are teachers. 他们两人都是教师。

2. 作宾语

I know nothing about this person. 我对这个人一无所知。

3. 作表语

This book is too much difficult for a child. 这本书对一个小孩来说太难了。

4. 作定语

There is a little water in the glass. 玻璃杯里有一些水。

5. 作状语

I can't find my book anywhere. 我在任何地方都不能找到我的书。

上一句也可以表示成：

I can find my book nowhere. 我在任何地方都不能找到我的书。

（二）几组不定代词的区别

1. 不定代词 some 与 any 的用法区别

都表示"一些，几个"作形容词时，后面可以接不可数名词+单数动词，或可数名词+

复数动词。一般来说，不定代词 some 用于肯定句中，any 用于否定句和疑问句中。但是，在表示请求、邀请或征求意见的句子中，通常要用 some 而不用 any。any 有时也用于肯定句中，此时表示"任何"。例如：

Would you like some cake? 吃点蛋糕吗？

Shall I get some chalk for you? 要我帮你拿些粉笔来吗？

Any colour will do. 任何颜色都行。

Come any day you like. 随便哪天来都可以。

2. 不定代词 many 与 much 的用法区别

不定代词 many 和 much 都表示"许多"，但 many 修饰或代替可数名词(复数)，与 few(少数)相对；而 much 用来修饰或代替不可数名词(单数)，与 little(少量)相对。在口语中两者主要用于非肯定句中。例如：

Did you see many people there? 你在那儿看见许多人了吗？

We don't have much time. 我们没有许多时间。

在肯定句中，一般用 a lot of、lots of、plenty of 等代之。但在正式文体中，有时也用于肯定句中。另外，若用作主语或主语的定语，或其前有 how、too、as、so、a good、a great 等修饰，也可用于肯定句中。例如：

Many of us left early. 我们有许多人离开得很早。

Much work has been done. 许多工作都已经做了。

You've given me too much. 你已给我太多了。

Take as many (much) as you want. 你要多少拿多少。

I asked her a great many questions. 我问了她许多问题。

3. 不定代词 few、a few 与 little、a little 的用法区别

(1) 不定代词 few 和 a few 后接可数名词的复数形式。few 表示数量很少或几乎没有，强调"少"，含有否定意义；a few 表示数量虽然少但毕竟还有，强调"有"，含有肯定意义。例如：

It is very difficult, and few people understand it. 它很难，没有几个人能懂。

It is very difficult, but a few people understand it. 他虽难，但是有些人懂。

(2) little 和 a little 之后接不可数名词，其区别跟 few 和 a few 之间的区别相似。例如：

Unfortunately, I had little money on me. 很不巧，我身上没带什么钱。

Fortunately, I had a little money on me. 幸好我身上带着一点钱。

4. 指两者和三者的不定代词

有的不定代词用于指两者(如 both、either、neither)，有的不定代词用于指三者(如 all、any、none、every)，注意不要弄混：

Both of my parents are doctors. 我的父母都是医生。

All of the students are interested in it. 所有的学生对此都很感兴趣。

There are trees on any side of the square. 广场的每一边都种有树。

He has two sons, neither of whom is rich. 他有两个儿子，都不富有。

He has three sons, none of whom is rich. 他有三个儿子，都不富有。

> **注 意**
>
> each 可用于两者、三者或三者以上，而 every 只用于三者或三者以上，因此用于两者时只能用 each，不能用 every。例如，不能说"There are trees on every side of the road"。

5. 复合不定代词

复合不定代词包括 something、somebody、someone、anything、anybody、anyone、nothing、nobody、no one、everything、everybody、everyone 等。它们在句中可用作主语、宾语或表语，但不能用作定语。something、someone 等和 anything、anyone 等的区别与 some 和 any 的区别一样，前者一般用于肯定句，后者一般用于否定句、疑问句或条件句（参见 any 和 some）。具体使用时应注意以下几点：

(1) 复合不定代词受定语修饰时，定语应放在它们后面。例如：

There is nothing wrong with the radio. 这收音机没有毛病。

Have you seen anyone [anybody] famous? 你见过名人吗？

(2) 指人的复合不定代词若用作主语，其谓语动词一般用单数，相应的人称代词和物主代词也用单数 he、him、his（不一定指男性）。但在非正式文体中常用复数代词 they、them、their。例如：

Everyone knows this, doesn't he [don't they]? 人人都知道这一点，不是吗？

If anybody [anyone] comes, ask him [them] to wait. 要是有人来，让他等着。

(3) 指事物的复合不定代词若用作主语，谓语动词只能用单数，相应的人称代词也只能用 it，而不用 they。例如：

Everything is ready, isn't it? 一切都准备好了，是吗？

九、相互代词

英语的相互代词只有 each other 和 one another，它们在句中通常只用作宾语。例如：

We should help each other. 我们应该互相帮助。

They soon fell in love with each other. 他们不久就相爱了。

The sea and the sky seem to melt into each other. 大海和蓝天似乎融为一体。

They respect one another. 他们互相尊重（对方）。

You look as though you know one another. 你们看起来像是互相认识。

They were very pleased with one another. 他们相互很喜欢。

专项练习

单项选择

1. There are several pretty girls standing under the tree, but _____ are known to me.
   A. neither   B. none   C. no one   D. all

2. In one year rats eat 40 to 50 times _____ weight.
   A. its   B. and   C. their   D. theirs

3. You'd better continue to use the same spelling of your name as _____ you used in your application.

    A. one   B. the one   C. any   D. some one

4. Sorry, but I have only _____ ink left over.

    A. little   B. few   C. a little   D. a few

5. John can play chess better than _____ else.

    A. the one   B. no one   C. any one   D. another

6. The weight of something is another way of describing the amount of force exerted on _____ by gravity.

    A. it   B. them   C. that   D. one

7. It is one thing to enjoy listening to good music, but it is quite _____ to perform skillfully yourself.

    A. other   B. another   C. some   D. any

8. Children should be taught how to get along with _____.

    A. another   B. other   C. others   D. any other

9. The poor man lived on wild berries and roots because they had _____ to eat.

    A. nothing else   B. anything else

    C. something other   D. nothing other

10. I go to the cinema _____ day, Tuesdays, Thursdays, and Saturdays.

    A. each other   B. every other

    C. this and the other   D. all other

11. One of the properties of light is _____ traveling in wave form as it goes from one place to another.

    A. it   B. it's   C. its   D. their

12. _____ in the world has been asked to do his duty for the human society.

    A. Each of the tramps   B. Every of the tramps

    C. The each tramp   D. The every tramp

13. In some restaurants, food and service are worse than _____ used to be.

    A. they   B. it   C. them   D. that

14. Let the porter take all the baggage out and put _____ in the lobby.

    A. it   B. they   C. them   D. its

15. Everyone who comes to the party is given a wooden apple with _____ own names cut in it as a souvenir.

    A. his   B. her   C. their   D. our

16. Everybody in the class must give in _____ exercise book within the given time.

    A. their   B. our   C. his   D. her

17. During the journey, the boys and girls entertained _____ with songs and games.

    A. themselves   B. theirselves   C. himself   D. itself

18. You'd better buy _____ some fruits when you go on a trip.
A. youself   B. myself   C. yourself   D. you

19. One of them hasn't got _____ lessons prepared.
A. her   B. its   C. one's   D. his

20. Please write on the paper _____ line.
A. each other   B. every other   C. all other   D. this and that

第五节 形容词与副词

一、形容词与副词及其用法

（一）形容词及其基本用法

形容词修饰名词，说明事物或人的性质或特征。形容词在句中作定语、表语、补语。

(1)作定语，一般放在所修饰的词之前。例如：
It's a cold and windy day. 今天天气很冷并且起风了。
但形容词修饰 something、anything、nothing、everything 等复合不定代词时，须放在其后。例如：
Would you like something hot to drink? 你想喝一些热饮吗？

(2)作表语，放在系动词的后面。常和形容词连用构成系表结构的连系动词有：be（是）、look（看起来，看上去）、feel（感觉）、taste（尝起来）、smell（闻起来）、get（变得）、turn（变）、become（成为，变得）、sound（听起来）等。例如：
This film is very interesting. 这部电影很有趣。
She looks younger than her age. 她看上去比她实际年龄要年轻。

(3)放在宾语后作宾语补足语。例如：
We painted the wall white. 我们把墙刷成了白色。
His coming made us happy. 他的到来让我们开心。

(4)用于表示类别和整体。
①某些形容词加上定冠词可以泛指一类人，与谓语动词的复数连接，如 the dead、the living、the rich、the poor、the blind、the hungry 等。例如：
The poor are losing hope. 穷人行将失去希望。
②有关国家和民族的形容词加上定冠词指这个民族的整体，与动词的复数连用，如 the British、the English、the French、the Chinese 等。例如：
The English have wonderful sense of humor. 英国人颇有幽默感。

> **注 意**
>
> (1)表示长、宽、高、深及年龄的形容词，应放在相应的名词之后。例如：
> How long is the river? It's about two hundred metres long. 这条河有多长？大约200米。

(2) 只能作表语的形容词：afraid(害怕)，alone(独自的)，asleep(睡着的)，awake(醒着的)，alive(活着的)，well(健康的)，ill(病的)，frightened(害怕的)。例如：

(正) The man is ill. 这个男的生病了。

(误) The ill man is my uncle.

(3) 只能作定语的形容词：little(小的)，only(唯一的)，wooden(木质的)，woolen(羊毛质的)，elder(年长的)。例如：

(正) My elder brother is in Beijing. 我哥哥在北京。

(误) My brother is elder.

(4) 貌似副词的形容词：lonely(独自的)，friendly(友好的)，lively(生动的)，lovely(可爱的)。

(误) She sang lovely.

(误) He spoke to me very friendly.

(正) Her singing was lovely. 他的歌声很动听。

(正) He spoke to me in a very friendly way. 他很友好地和我说话。

(5) 复合形容词：snow-white(雪白的)，English-speaking(说英语的)，glass-topped(玻璃罩的)，full-time(全日制的)，well-known(众所周知的)，kind-hearted(善良的)，man-made(人造的)，take-away(可以带走的)，ten-year-old(十岁的)。

(6) 多个形容词修饰名词时，其顺序为：限定词(冠词、指示代词、形容词性物主代词、数词)—描绘词(大小，长短，形状，新旧，长幼，颜色)—出处—材料性质—类别—名词。例如：

A small round table(一张小圆桌)

A tall white building(一幢高大的白色建筑物)

A dirty old black shirt(一件又脏又旧的黑色衬衣)

A famous American medical school(一个非常著名的美国医学院)

The weather gets warmer and the trees turn green in spring. 春天，天气变得更暖和了，树也变绿了。

（二）副词及其基本用法

副词主要用来修饰动词、形容词或其他副词，说明时间、地点、程度、方式等。

1. 副词的位置

(1) 修饰动词时，通常位于动词之后。例如：

It is snowing outside, you'd better drive carefully. 外面在下雪，你最好小心驾驶。

(2) 表示否定或频度的副词通常置于谓语动词之前，但要放在助动词、系动词之后。例如：

I always go to visit my parents at weekends. 我总是在周末去看望父母。

(3) 修饰形容词或副词时，通常放在该形容词或副词的前面(enough 例外)。例如：

My sister is much younger than I. 我妹妹比我小得多。

(4) 修饰全句的副词通常位于句首，有时也可以放在句尾。例如：

First, let me ask you some questions. 先让我来问几个问题。

(5)方式副词 well、badly、hard 等只放在句尾。例如：

He speaks English well. 他英语说得好。

2. 副词的分类

(1)副词按意义可分为以下几类。

方式副词：well, fast, slowly, carefully, quickly。

程度副词：very, much, enough, almost, rather, quite。

地点副词：here, there, out, somewhere, abroad, home。

时间副词：today, early, soon, now, then, recently, still。

频度副词：always, often, usually, sometimes, seldom, never。

否定副词：no, not, neither, nor。

其他：also, too, only。

(2)副词按功能可分为以下几类。

句子副词：fortunately, luckily, unexpectedly, surprisingly。

疑问副词：what, when, where, how, why。

关系副词：what, when, where, how, why。

连接副词：therefore, however, otherwise。

3. 副词的构成

(1)本身即为副词，如：now, rather, very, there, how, when, too 等。

(2)与形容词形式相同的副词，如：early, high, wide, deep 等。

(3)由"形容词+ly"构成副词，例如：

slow—slowly quick—quickly brave—bravely clear—clearly

4. 常见副词用法辨析

(1) close 与 closely。close 意思是"近"；closely 意思是"仔细地"。例如：

He is sitting close to me. 他就坐在我边上。

Watch him closely. 盯着他。

(2) late 与 lately。late 意思是"晚"；lately 意思是"最近"。例如：

You have come too late. 你来得太晚了。

What have you been doing lately? 近来好吗？

(3) deep 与 deeply。deep 意思是"深"，表示空间深度；deeply 时常表示感情上的深度，"深深地"。例如：

He pushed the stick deep into the mud. 他把棍子深深插进泥里。

Even father was deeply moved by the film. 爸爸也被电影深深打动了。

(4) high 与 highly。high 表示空间高度；highly 表示程度，相当于 much。例如：

The plane was flying high. 这架飞机飞得很高。

I think highly of your opinion. 你的看法很有道理。

(5) wide 与 widely。wide 表示空间宽度；widely 意思是"广泛地，在许多地方"。例如：

He opened the door wide. 他把门开得大大的。

English is widely used in the world. 英语在世界范围内广泛使用。

(6) free 与 freely。free 的意思是"免费"；freely 的意思是"无限制地"。例如：

You can eat free in my restaurant whenever you like. 无论什么时候，我这餐馆免费对你开放。

You may speak freely, say what you like. 你可以畅所欲言，想说什么就说什么。

(7) already 与 yet。already 用于肯定句句中，表示"已经"；yet 用于否定句句末，表示"还"，用于疑问句句末，表示"已经"。例如：

He had already left when I called. 当我给他打电话时，他已经离开了。

Have you found your ruler yet? 你已经找到你的尺子了吗?

I haven't finished my homework yet. 我还没有完成作业。

(8) very、much 和 very much。very 用于修饰形容词或副词的原级；much 用于修饰形容词或副词的比较级；修饰动词要用 very much。例如：

John is very honest. 约翰非常诚实。

This garden is much bigger than that one. 这个花园比那个大得多。

Thank you very much. 非常感谢你。

(9) so 与 such 的区别。so 修饰形容词或副词，so 修饰的形容词后可有一个单数可数名词，结构为"so+形容词+a/an+可数名词单数"；such 可修饰可数名词单、复数或不可数名词，结构为"such+a/an+形容词+可数名词单数"或"such+形容词+可数名词复数/不可数名词"。例如：

My brother runs so fast that I can't follow him. 我弟弟跑得那么快以至于我跟不上他。

He is such a boy. 他是一个这样的孩子。

(正) It is such cold weather. 这么冷的天气/天气真冷。

(误) It is so cold weather.

(正) They are such good students. 他们是那么好的学生。

(误) They are so good students.

(10) also、too、as well 与 either 的区别。also、as well、too 用于肯定句。also 常用于 be 动词、情态动词、助动词之后，行为动词之前；as well、too 用于句末；either 用于否定句中，置于句末。例如：

My father is a teacher. My mother is also a teacher. 我爸爸是一名老师，我妈妈也是。

=My father is a teacher. My mother is a teacher as well.

=My father is a teacher. My mother is a teacher, too.

I can't speak French, Jenny can't speak French, either. 我不会说法语，詹妮也不会。

(11) sometime、sometimes、some time 与 some times 的区别。

sometime：某一时间，某一时刻(可指将来时，也可指过去时)。

sometimes：有时，不时地。

some time：一段时间。

some times：几次，几倍。

例如：

We'll have a test sometime next month. 下个月的某一时间，我们要进行一次测试。

Sometimes we are busy and sometimes we are not. 有时我们很忙，有时不忙。

He stayed in Beijing for some time last year. 他去年在北京待了一段时间。

I have been to Beijing some times. 我去过北京好几次。

(12) ago 与 before 的区别。ago 表示以现在为起点的"以前",常与一般过去时连用,不可以单独使用。before 指过去或将来的某时刻"以前",也可泛指以前,常和完成时连用,可以单独使用。例如:

I saw him ten minutes ago. 我十分钟之前看到的他。

He told me that he had seen the film before. 他告诉我他以前看过这场电影。

(13) now、just 与 just now 的区别。

now:与一般现在时、现在进行时、现在完成时连用,意为"现在"。

just:与现在完成时、过去完成时连用,表示"刚……"。

just now:与过去时连用,表示"刚才"。

例如:

Where does he live now? 他现在住在哪里?

We have just seen the film. 我们刚看过这场电影。

He was here just now. 他刚才在这里。

二、形容词与副词的比较等级

大多数形容词(性质形容词)和副词有级的变化,即原级、比较级和最高级,用来表示事物的等级差别。原级即形容词的原形,比较级和最高级有规则变化和不规则变化两种。

(一)比较级、最高级的变化

1. 规则变化

(1)单音节词和少数双音节词,加词尾-er、-est 来构成比较级和最高级。

构成法	原级	比较级	最高级
一般在词尾加-er、-est	tall	taller	tallest
以不发音的 e 结尾时,在词尾加-r、-st	nice	nicer	nicest
	large	larger	largest
以一个辅音字母结尾的重读闭音节的单音节词或少数双音节词,双写末尾的辅音字母,再加-er、-est	big	bigger	biggest
	hot	hotter	hottest
以"辅音字母+y"结尾的双音节词,变 y 为 i,再加-er、-est	easy	easier	easiest
	busy	busier	busiest
以-er、-ow 结尾的双音节词,在词尾加-er、-est	clever	cleverer	cleverest
	narrow	narrower	narrowest

(2)多音节词和部分双音节词的形容词的比较级和最高级,需用 more 和 most 加在形容词前面来构成。例如:

slowly—more slowly—most slowly

beautiful—more beautiful—most beautiful

2. 不规则变化

原级	比较级	最高级
good/well	better	best
bad/badly	worse	worst
many/much	more	most
little	less	least
old	older	oldest
old	elder	eldest
far	farther	farthest
far	further	furthest

（二）原级的用法

用来直接描述人物或动作，讲述某人/物自身的情况时，用原级。

（1）基本句型是：

主语(sb./sth)+动词+(very/too/so/quite/rather…)+形容词/副词原级+…

能修饰原级的词有 very、quite、so、too 等。例如：

He is too tired to walk on. 他太累了以至于不能再继续走了。

My brother runs so fast that I can't follow him. 我弟弟跑得那么快以至于我跟不上他。

I am so happy! 我是如此的快乐。

（2）表示两者之间没有差别时，使用句型：

①"甲+be+(倍数)+as+形容词原级+as+乙"，表示"甲和乙程度相同"或"甲是乙的几倍"。例如：

He is as excited as his younger sister. 他和他妹妹一样兴奋。

Lily rode her bike as slowly as an old lady. 莉莉骑车像老太太一样慢。

They picked twice as many apples as the farmers (did). 他们摘的苹果是农民的两倍多。

②"甲+实意动词+(倍数)+as+副词原级+as+乙"，表示"甲和乙程度相同"或"甲是乙的几倍"。例如：

Tom runs as fast as Mike. 汤姆和迈克跑得一样快。

Tom runs twice as fast as Mike. 汤姆跑的速度是迈克的两倍。

（三）比较级的用法

表示两者有差异，第一个人物超过第二个人物时，用比较级。可以修饰比较级的词有 much、a lot、far(……得多)，a little、a bit(……一点儿)，even(甚至)，still(仍然)。

1. 比较级常用的句型结构

（1）"甲+be+(倍数)+形容词比较级+than+乙"，表示"甲比乙……"或"甲比乙……几倍"。例如：

Tom is taller than Kate. 汤姆比凯特高。

This room is three times bigger than that one. 这个房间比那个大三倍。

> **注 意**
>
> (1)要避免重复使用比较级。
> (误) He is more cleverer than his brother.
> (正) He is more clever than his brother.
> (正) He is cleverer than his brother.
> (2)要避免将主语含在比较对象中。
> (误) China is larger than any country in Asia.
> (正) China is larger than any other countries in Asia.
> (3)要注意对应句型，遵循前后一致的原则。
> The population of Shanghai is larger than that of Beijing.
> It is easier to make a plan than to carry it out.
> (4)要注意定冠词在比较级中的使用。
> 比较：
> Which is larger, Canada or Australia?
> Which is the larger country, Canada or Australia?
> She is taller than her two sisters.
> She is the taller of the two sisters.

(2)"比较级+and+比较级"，表示"越来越……"。例如：
He is getting taller and taller. 他变得越来越高了。
The flowers are more and more beautiful. 花儿越来越漂亮。
He does his homework more and more carefully. 他做作业越来越认真了。
(3)"the+比较级，the+比较级"，表示"越……，越……"。例如：
The more careful you are, the fewer mistakes you'll make. 你越认真，犯的错误越少。
(4)"特殊疑问词+be+形容词比较级，甲 or 乙？"例如：
Which is bigger, the earth or the moon? 哪一个大，地球还是月球？
(5)"特殊疑问词+实意动词+副词比较级，甲 or 乙？"例如：
Who draws better, Jenny or Danny? 谁画得比较好，詹妮还是丹尼？

2. 可修饰比较级的词

(1)a bit、a little、rather、much、far、by far、many、a lot、lots、a great deal、any、still、even 等。
(2)还可以用表示倍数的词或度量名词作修饰语。例如：
Lesson One is much easier than Lesson Two. 第一课比第二课容易得多。
Tom looks even younger than before. 汤姆甚至比以前更年轻。
This train runs much faster than that one. 这辆火车比那辆跑得快。
She drives still more carefully than her husband. 她开车仍然比她丈夫还认真。

(四)最高级的用法

对三者或三者以上的人或物进行比较时用最高级。形容词最高级前面要加定冠词 the，副词最高级前可加 the，也可省掉 the；后面可带 of/in 短语来说明比较范围，即"主语+系动词+the+形容词最高级+of 短语/in 短语"。例如：

She is the youngest of all. 她是所有人中年纪最小的。
Linda draws most carefully in her class. 琳达是班上画画最认真的。

1. 最高级常用句型结构

(1)"主语+be+the+形容词最高级+单数名词+in/of 短语"，表示"……是……中最……的"。例如：

Tom is the tallest in his class/of all the students. 汤姆是他们班上/所有学生当中最高的。
This apple is the biggest of the five. 这个苹果是五个当中最大的。

(2)"主语+实意动词+(the)+副词最高级+单数名词+in/of 短语"，表示"……是……中最……的"。例如：

I jump (the) farthest in my class. 我是我们班跳得最远的。

(3)"主语+be+one of the+形容词最高级+复数名词+in/of 短语"，表示"……是……中最……之一"。例如：

Beijing is one of the largest cities in China. 北京是中国最大城市之一。

(4)"特殊疑问词+be+the+最高级+甲，乙，or 丙？"，用于三者以上的比较。例如：

Which country is the largest, China, Brazil or Canada? 哪一个国家最大，中国、巴西还是加拿大？

(5)"特殊疑问词+be+the+副词最高级+甲、乙 or 丙？"，用于三者以上的比较。例如：

Which season do you like (the) best, spring, summer or autumn?

(6)形容词最高级的意义还可以用比较级形式表达。常见的有：

①形容词比较级+than any other+单数名词。例如：

This is more difficult than any other book here. (=This is the most difficult book of all.) 这些书当中这本最难。

②形容词比较级+than the other+复数名词。例如：

Asia is bigger than the other continents on the earth. 亚洲是地球上最大的洲。

专项练习

(一)单项选择

1. You have just read this newspaper. Did you find _____ in it?
   A. interesting anything   B. anything interesting
   C. interesting something   D. something interesting

2. ——How was your final exam?
   ——The English and Maths papers weren't _____ for me. I hope I haven't failed.

A. easy enough						B. difficult enough
C. enough easy						D. enough difficult
3. ——Could you tell me something about the museum?
—— Yes, It was built in 1979, 230 _____ and 220 _____.
A. long meters; wide meters				B. meters long; wide meters
C. long meters; meters wide				D. meters long; meters wide
4. ——What's your present for Kangkang's birthday?
——He likes painting, so I'm going to buy him a _____ paintings.
A. fine little brown French				B. little brown fine French
C. little fine brown French				D. French little brown fine
5. Sally is doing _____ in all her courses.
A. particular good					B. particularly well
C. particularly good					D. particular well
6. Keeping the balance of nature is so _____.
A. easier		B. more difficult	C. important		D. interested
7. The film is not as _____ as you told me.
A. interested		B. more interested	C. more interesting	D. interesting
8. This building is _____ that one over there.
A. as tall as twice					B. as twice as tall
C. so tall as twice					D. twice as tall as
9. We live _____ now because we have changed the way we live.
A. long			B. longer		C. the longest		D. short
10. Art is much _____ than life, but what a poor life without it!
A. less important					B. more important
C. the most important					D. important
11. ——Which shirt is _____, the blue one or the pink one?
——Oh, they are both nice, so it's hard to choose.
A. nice			B. nicer		C. the nicest		D. good
12. The harder you work, the _____ progress you will make.
A. great		B. greater		C. greatest		D. little
13. If you keep playing sports every day you are getting _____.
A. good and good	B. better and better	C. best and best	D. better and best
14. ——Which is Tom?
——He is _____ of the two boys.
A. tall			B. taller		C. the taller		D. the tallest
15. We should go on learning English although it is getting a little _____.
A. easy			B. easier		C. difficult		D. more difficult
16. ——Mum, could you buy me a dress like this?

——Of course. We can buy _____ one than this, but _____ it.

A. a better; better than   B. a popular; as good as

C. a more popular; not as good as   D. a cheaper; as good as

17. These days, the Internet is becoming _____ useful as a search tool.

A. more and more   B. most and most

C. much and more   D. much and much

18. Tom is _____ experienced among the doctors here.

A. less   B. least   C. the less   D. the least

19. The Yellow River is the second _____ river in China.

A. long   B. longer   C. longest   D. as long

20. Beihai is one of _____ beautiful parks in Beijing.

A. the   B. the more   C. the most   D. the less

(二)用括号内所给单词的适当形式填空

1. Please speak _____ (slow) so that we can make full notes.
2. They all come early, but she come _____ (early) of all.
3. He played the piano _____ (success) than we has thought.
4. Whoever is _____ (quick) is going to have the better chance.
5. This radio is even _____ (expensive) than that one.
6. This trip to China has _____ (real) inspired me to relearn my Mandrin.
7. John's handwriting is the _____ (bad) of the three.
8. The most used letter in the English alphabet is "E", and "Q" is the _____ (little) used!
9. Those who eat most are not always _____ (fat); those who read most, not always wisest.
10. The mother is _____ (worry) about her son's safety.
11. I'm going on a diet for I want to become _____ (thin).
12. In my grandfather's time, computers were far _____ (popular) than they are today.
13. So _____ (excite) was the game that I forgot all about the coming finals.
14. Tom is _____ (tall) of all his brothers.
15. This is our _____ (cheap) pen in our shop.

第六节 介词与连词

一、介词

(一)介词概述

介词(preposition,简写 prep.)又称为前置词,一般用于名词或代词前,表示名词、代词等与句中其他词的关系,在句中不能单独作句子成分。介词后面的名词或代词称为介词宾语(若是人称代词,则要用宾格)。介词和它的宾语构成介词词组,在句中作状语、表语、补语或介词宾语。

介词分简单介词和短语介词两种。简单介词指单个介词,如 in、under、on、for、after 等;短语介词指多个单词构成的介词,如 in front of、out of、instead of、far from、apart from 等。

(二)常用介词辨析

1. 表示地点

(1)at, in, on, to。
at 表示在小地方,"在……附近,旁边"。
in 表示在大地方,"在……范围之内"。
on 表示毗邻,接壤,"在……上面"。
to 表示"在……范围外",不接壤;"到……"。
例如:
in the east of China(在中国的东部)
on the east of China(在与中国的东部接壤的地方)
to the east of China(在中国以东)

(2)above, over, on(在……上)。
above 表示一个物体高于另一个物体,不强调是否垂直,与 below 相对。
over 表示一个物体在另一个物体的垂直上方,与 under 相对,但 over 与物体有一定的空间,不直接接触。
on 表示一个物体在另一个物体表面上,并且两个物体互相接触,与 beneath 相对。
例如:
The bird is flying above my head. 这只鸟飞在我的头上。
There is a bridge over the river. 河上有一座桥。
He puts his watch on the desk. 他把他的手表放在桌子上。

(3)below, under(在……下面)。
under 表示"在……正下方"。
below 表示"在……下",不一定在正下方。
例如:
There is a cat under the table. 有一只猫在桌子底下。
Please write your name below the line. 请把你的名字写在线下。

(4)in front of, in the front of(在……前面)。
in front of 表示"在……前面",指甲物在乙物之前,两者互不包括;其反义词是 behind(在……的后面)。
in the front of 表示"在……的前部",即甲物在乙物的内部,反义词是 at the back of(在……范围内的后部)。
例如:
There are some flowers in front of the house. 房子前面有些花卉。

There is a blackboard in the front of our classroom. 我们的教室前边有一块黑板。
Our teacher stands in the front of the classroom. 我们的老师站在教室前。(老师在教室里)
(5) beside, behind, between。
beside 表示"在……旁边"。
behind 表示"在……后面"。
between 表示"在两者之间"。
(6) on the tree, in the tree。
on the tree：长在树上。
in the tree：外来落在树上。

2. 表示时间

(1) in, on, at(在……时)。

in 表示较长时间，如世纪、朝代、时代、年、季节、月及一般(非特指)的早、中、晚等。例如：in the 20th century(在二十世纪)，in the 1950s(在二十世纪五十年代)，in 1989(在 1989 年)，in summer(在夏天)，in January(在一月)，in the morning(在早晨)，in one's life(在某人的一生中)，in one's thirties(在某人三十几岁时)等。

on 表示具体某一天及某一天的早、中、晚。例如：on May 1st(在五月一日)，on Monday(在星期一)，on New Year's Day(在新年那天)，on a cold night in January(在一月一个寒冷的夜晚)，on a fine morning(在一个晴朗的早晨)，on Sunday afternoon(在星期天下午)等。

at 表示某一时刻或较短暂的时间，或泛指节日等。例如：at 3:20(在 3:20)，at this time of year(在一年中的这个时候)，at the beginning of(在……的开始)，at the end of …(在……尽头；在……结束时)，at the age of …(在……岁的时候)，at Christmas(在圣诞节)，at night(在夜晚)，at noon(在中午)，at this moment(此刻)等。

注 意

在 last、next、this、that、some、every 等词之前一律不用介词。例如：
We meet every day. 我们每天见面。

(2) in, after(在……之后)。
"in +一段时间"表示将来的一段时间以后，由 How soon 对其提问。(for+一段时间，动词用延续性动词，由 How long 对其提问)
"after+一段时间"表示过去的一段时间以后。
"after+将来的时间点"表示将来的某一时刻以后。
(3) from, since, for(自从……)。
from 仅说明什么时候开始，不说明某动作或情况持续多久；说明开始的时间，谓语可用过去、现在、将来的某种时态。
since 表示某动作或情况持续至说话时刻，通常与完成时连用。since 表示"自(某具体时间)以来"，常用作完成时态谓语的时间状语。只从某时一直延续至今，后接时间点，主句用完成时。

for 指动作延续贯穿整个过程，后接时间段，主句用完成时。

例如：

since liberation(1980)[自从解放(1980年)以来]

They have been close friends since childhood. 他们从小就是好朋友。

> **注 意**
>
> 关于 since 的使用，须注意：
>
> (1) since the war 是指"自从战争结束以来"，若指"自从战争开始以来"，须说"since the beginning of the war"。
>
> (2) 不要将 since 与 after 混淆。
>
> 比较：
>
> He has worked here since 1965. 自从 1965 年以来，他一直在这儿工作。(指一段时间，强调时间段)
>
> He began to work here after 1965. 从 1965 年以后，他开始在这儿工作。(指一点时间，强调时间点)

(4) after, behind(在……之后)。

after 主要用于表示时间。

behind 主要用于表示位置。

3. 表示运动

(1) across, through, past(通过，穿过)。

across 表示横穿，即从物体表面通过，与 on 有关，为二维。例如：walk across the road(过马路)。

through 表示穿过，即从物体内部穿过，与 in 有关，为三维。例如：walk through the forest(穿过森林)。

past 表示从物体的旁边通过。例如：walk past the bank(从银行旁边经过)。

(2) from…to…(从……到……)。

from my home to my school(从我家到我学校)

(3) to, towards, onto, into, out of。

to 表示到某处去。例如：go to school(到学校去)。

towards 表示朝着某个方向去。

onto 表示放到某物上面。

into 表示进入物体内部。例如：go into a room(进入一个房间)。

out of 表示从物体内部出来。例如：get out of the room(从房间里出来)。

(4) up, down。

up 表示向上。例如：stand up(起立), turn up(将音量调高)。

down 表示向下。例如：sit down(坐下), turn down(将音量调低)。

(5) over，around。
over 表示从上方跃过。
around 表示环绕一圈。
(6) along(沿着)。

4. 表示方位

表示"在……之间"的介词在英语中属于方位介词，如 in front of、behind、on、in、near、under、up。

between 指在两个人或两个事物之间。

among 指在三个或三个以上的人或事物之间。

5. 其他

(1) on，about(关于……)。

on 表示这本书、这篇文章或演说是严肃的或学术性的，可供专门研究这一问题的人阅读。about 表示内容较为普通，不那么正式。

(2) by，with，in(表示方法、手段、工具)。

by 表示"以……方法、手段"或泛指某种交通工具。

with 表示"用……工具、手段"，一般接具体的工具和手段。

in 表示"用……方式""用……语言(语调、笔墨、颜色)"等。

(3) except，besides(除了)。

except 表示"除……之外"，不包括在内。besides 表示"除……之外"，包括在内。例如：

Except for Mr. Wang, we went to see the film.（王先生没去）

Besides Mr. Wang, we also went to see the film.（王先生也去了）

(4) to，for，from。

to 表示"到达……地点(目的地)或方向"。for 表示目的，"为了……"。from 表示"从……地点起"。例如：

Where's Jack? He has gone to London. 杰克上哪了？他去伦敦了。

Do you know what he comes here for？你知道他为什么来这儿吗？

How far is it from London to New York？从伦敦到纽约有多远？

二、连词

(一)连词概述

连词是一种虚词，用于连接单词、短语、从句或句子，在句子中不单独用作句子成分。连词按其性质可分为并列连词和从属连词。并列连词用于连接并列的单词、短语、从句或句子；从属连词主要引出名词性从句(主语从句、宾语从句、表语从句等)和状语从句(时间状语从句、条件状语从句、目的状语从句等)。

(二)并列连词

1. 表示转折关系的并列连词

这类连词主要有 but、yet、or 等。例如：

Someone borrowed my pen, but I don't remember whom. 有人借了我的钢笔，但我不记得是谁了。

He said he was our friend, yet he wouldn't help us. 他说他是我们的朋友，但却不肯帮助我们。

2. 表示因果关系的并列连词

这类连词主要有 for、so 等。例如：

The child had a bad cough, so his mother took him to the doctor. 这孩子咳得很厉害，所以他妈妈带他去看医生。

You are supposed to get rid of carelessness, for it often leads to serious errors. 你们一定要克服粗枝大叶，因为粗枝大叶常常引起严重的错误。

> **注 意**
>
> for 表示结果通常不能放句首，也不能单独使用。

3. 表示并列关系的并列连词

这类连词主要有 and、or、either…or、neither…nor、not only…but (also)、both…and、as well as 等。例如：

He didn't go and she didn't go either. 他没去，她也没去。

The weather is mild today; it is neither hot nor cold. 今天天气很温暖，不冷也不热。

Both New York and London have traffic problems. 纽约和伦敦都存在交通问题。

（三）从属连词的用法

1. 引导时间状语从句的从属连词

主要有 when、while、as、whenever、before、after、since、until、till、as soon as 等。例如：

Don't talk while you're eating. 吃饭时不要说话。

She's been playing tennis since she was eight. 她从八岁起就打网球了。

I'll let you know as soon as I hear from her. 我一接她的信就通知你。

2. 引导条件状语从句的从属连词

这类连词主要有 if、unless、as [so] long as、in case 等。例如：

Do you mind if I open the window? 我开窗你不介意吧？

Don't come unless I telephone. 除非我打电话，否则你别来。

As long as you're happy, it doesn't matter what you do. 只要你高兴，你做什么都没关系。

In case it rains they will stay at home. 万一下雨，他们就待在家里。

> **注 意**
>
> 在条件状语从句中，通常要用一般现在时表示将来意义，而不能直接使用将来时态。有时表示条件的 if 之后可以用 will，但那不是将来时态，而是表示意愿或委婉的请

求(will 为情态动词)。例如:

If you will sit down for a few moments, I'll tell the manager you're here. 请稍坐,我这就通知经理说您来了。

3. 引导目的状语从句的从属连词

主要的有 in order that(为了)、so that(以便)、in case(以防、以备)、for fear 等。例如:

He raised his voice so that everyone could hear. 他提高了嗓音,以便每个人都能听见。

Take your umbrella (just) in case it rains. 带上雨伞,以防下雨。

She repeated the instructions slowly in order that he should understand. 她把那些指示慢慢重复了一遍好让他听明白。

4. 引导结果状语从句的从属连词

主要的有 so that、so…that、such…that 等。例如:

I went to the lecture early so that I got a good seat. 我去听演讲去得很早,所以找了个好座位。

I had so many falls that I was black and blue all over. 我摔了许多跤,以至于全身都是青一块紫一块的。

He shut the window with such force that the glass broke. 他关窗子用力很大,结果玻璃震破了。

5. 引导原因状语从句的从属连词

主要有 because、as、since、seeing (that)、now (that)、considering (that)(由于考虑到)、on condition that 等。例如:

He distrusted me because I was new. 他不信任我,因为我是新来的。

As you are sorry, I'll forgive you. 既然你悔悟了,我就原谅你。

Since we've no money, we can't buy it. 由于我们没钱,我们无法购买它。

Seeing that he's ill, he's unlikely to come. 因为他病了,他大概不会来了。

Now that she has apologized, I am content. 既然她已经道了歉,我也就满意了。

6. 引导让步状语从句的从属连词

主要有 although、though、even though、even if、while、however、whatever、whoever、whenever、wherever 等。例如:

Although they are twins, they look entirely different. 他们虽是孪生,但是相貌却完全不同。

I like her even though she can be annoying. 尽管她有时很恼人,但我还是喜欢她。

You won't move that stone, however strong you are. 不管你力气多大,也休想搬动那块石头。

Whatever we have achieved, we owe to your support. 我们取得的一切成就都归功于你们的支持。

Whoever you are, you can't pass this way. 不管你是谁,你都不能从这里通过。

Whenever I see him, I speak to him. 每当我见到他，我都和他讲话。

7. 引导方式状语从句的从属连词

主要有 as、as if、as though、the way 等。例如：

Why didn't you catch the last bus as I told you to? 你怎么不听我的话赶乘末班公共汽车呢？

He bent the iron bar as if it had been made of rubber. 他将铁棍折弯，仿佛那是用橡皮做成的。

Nobody else loves you the way(＝as) I do. 没有人像我这样爱你。

8. 引导地点状语从句的从属连词

主要有 where、wherever、everywhere、anywhere 等。例如：

The church was built where there had once been a Roman temple. 这座教堂盖在一座罗马寺庙的旧址。

I'll take you anywhere you like. 你想到哪儿我就带你到哪儿。

Everywhere I go, I find the same thing. 不管我走到哪里，我都发现同样的情况。

9. 引导比较状语从句的从属连词

主要有 than、as…as 和 the more the more。例如：

She was now happier than she had ever been. 现在她比过去任何时候都快活。

I glanced at my watch. It was earlier than I thought. 我看了看表，时间比我想像得早。

He doesn't work as hard as she does. 他工作不像她那样努力。

The busier he is, the happier he feels. 他越忙就越快乐。

10. 引起名词从句的从属连词

主要有 that、whether、if 等，它们用于引导主语从句、表语从句、宾语从句和同位语从句。其中，that 不仅不充当句子成分，而且没有词义，在句子中只起连接作用；而 if、whether 虽不充当句子成分，但有词义，表示"是否"。例如：

He replied that he was going by train. 他回答说他将坐火车去。

I wonder if it's large enough. 我不知道它是否够大。

> **注 意**
>
> 使用状语从句时要注意的几个问题：
>
> (1) 在时间和条件(有时也在方式、让步等)从句中，主句是一般将来时，从句通常用一般现在时表示将来。例如：
>
> We'll go outing if it doesn't rain tomorrow. 如果明天不下雨，我们就会出门。
>
> I'll write to you as soon as I get to Shanghai. 我一到上海就给你写信。
>
> (2) 有些时间、地点、条件、方式或让步从句，如果从句的主语与主句主语一致(或虽不一致，是 it)，从句的谓语又包含动词 be，就可省略从句中的主语＋be 部分。例如：
>
> When (he was) still a boy of ten, he had to work day and night. 当他还是一个十岁男孩的时候，他就不得不没日没夜地工作。

If (you are) asked you may come in. 如果你受到邀请，你就可以进来。

If (it is) necessary I'll explain to you again. 如果有必要，我会向你再次解释。

(3) 注意区分不同从句：看引导的是什么从句，不仅要根据连词，还要根据句子结构和句意来判别。以 where 为例，能引导多种从句。例如：

You are to find it where you left it. 你必须在你离开的地方找到它。（地点状语从句）

Tell me the address where he lives. 告诉我他所住的地址。（定语从句，句中有先行词）

I don't know where he came from. 我不知道他从何处来。（宾语从句）

Where he has gone is not known yet. 他去哪了还不知道。（主语从句）

This place is where they once hid. 这是他们曾经躲藏的地方。（表语从句）

专项练习

(一) 单项选择（介词）

1. _____ the afternoon of May, we visited the old man.
A. On   B. At   C. In

2. Many people work _____ the day and sleep _____ night.
A. on ; at   B. in ; in   C. in ; at

3. He speaks Japanese best _____ the boy students.
A. between   B. with   C. among

4. A wolf _____ a sheep skin is our dangerous enemy.
A. with   B. in   C. on

5. Joan hopes to come back _____ three days.
A. after   B. for   C. in

6. They sent the letter to me _____ mistake.
A. by   B. for   C. with

7. He left home _____ a cold winter evening.
A. at   B. on   C. in

8. Shanghai is _____ the east of China.
A. in   B. on   C. to

9. _____ my father's help, I have finished my composition.
A. Under   B. On   C. with

10. He's very strict _____ himself and he's very strict _____ his work.
A. with; in   B. in; with   C. with ; with

11. I really can't agree _____ you.
A. to   B. on   C. with

12. The shop won't open _____ nine in the morning.

A. until	B. at	C. during

13. How about _____ the flowers now?

A. watering	B. are watering	C. watered

14. She spent all his money _____ books.

A. in	B. with	C. on

15. They are talking _____ low voices.

A. with	B. in	C. on

16. It's very kind _____ you to help us.

A. for	B. to	C. of

17. What will you have _____ breakfast this morning?

A. with	B. for	C. by

18. A plane is flying _____ the city.

A. on	B. over	C. above

19. You are free to speak _____ the meeting.

A. at	B. in	C. on

20. Mr. Green will stay in China _____ Friday.

A. to	B. on	C. till

21. It's wrong to play jokes _____ other people.

A. on	B. of	C. with

22. Which color do you like? I prefer blue _____ red.

A. for	B. as	C. to

23. The student will give us a talk _____ how to use our spare time.

A. for	B. on	C. in

24. I paid two hundred yuan _____ that kind of bicycle.

A. in	B. for	C. on

25. The doctor is very kind _____ his patients

A. to	B. on	C. at

(二) 单项选择(连词)

1. I'd get it for you _____ I could remember who last borrowed the book.

A. on condition that	B. now that	C. except that	D. considering that

2. As she _____ the newspaper, Granny _____ asleep.

A. read, was falling	B. was reading, fell

C. was reading, was falling	D. read, fell

3. Strange _____ his behavior may be, there is a very good reason for it.

A. although	B. even if	C. that	D. as

4. We are worried about our son because no one is aware _____ he has gone.

A. the place	B. of where	C. about the place	D. where

5. The professor spoke in a loud voice _____ every one of us could hear him.

A. such that   B. so   C. so that   D. such

6. When he just got off the plane, he gave us a good description of _____ in Spain.

A. what he had seen   B. that he had seen

C. which he had seen   D. he had seen what

7. You will stay healthy _____ you do more exercise, such as running and walking.

A. if   B. how   C. before   D. where

8. I don't know why she's looking at me _____ she knew me. I've never seen her before in my life.

A. as   B. although   C. even if   D. as if

9. You may use room as you like _____ you clean it up afterwards.

A. so far as   B. so long as   C. in case   D. even if

10. It is hard to avoid mistakes. _____ you correct them conscientiously, it will be all right.

A. In the case   B. As long as   C. Although   D. Despite

11. _____, mother will wait for him to have dinner together.

A. However late is he   B. However he is late

C. However is he late   D. However late he is

12. The highest temperature _____ in any furnace on earth is about 10,000 centigrade.

A. we can get   B. that we can get it

C. which we can get it   D. what we can get

13. Although it's raining, _____ are still working in the field.

A. they   B. but they   C. and they   D. so they

14. Sound is conducted through steel in the same manner _____.

A. as in air   B. as through air   C. as air does   D. like air

15. The piano in the other shop will be _____, but _____.

A. cheaper; not as better   B. more cheap; not as better

C. cheaper; not as good   D. more cheap; not as good

16. The police finally caught up with the man _____ was the escaped prisoner.

A. who they thought   B. whom they thought

C. they thought him   D. that they thought him

17. The new secretary is supposed to report to the manager as soon as she _____.

A. will arrive   B. arrives   C. is arriving   D. is going to arrive

18. _____ do you believe is not about to support our plan?

A. Whom   B. Who   C. Whomever   D. Which

19. He didn't know French, _____ made it difficult for him to study at a university in France.

A. that   B. as   C. this   D. which

20. She is a fine singer, _____ her mother used to be
A. like   B. that   C. as   D. which

第七节 动词

一、动词的概念

动词是用来表示主语做什么(即行为动词),或表示主语是什么或怎么样(即状态动词)的词。例如:

The boy runs fast. 这个男孩跑得快。(runs 表示主语的行为)

He is a boy. 他是个男孩。(is 与后面的表语 a boy 表示主语的状态)

二、动词的分类

动词可以按照含义及它们在句中的作用分成四类,即行为动词(也称实义动词)、连系动词、助动词和情态动词。

(一)行为动词

行为动词(实义动词)是表示行为、动作或状态的词。它的词义完整,可以单独作谓语。例如:

I live in Beijing with my mother. 我和我妈妈住在北京。(live,住)

It has a round face. 它有一张圆脸。(has,有)

1. 及物动词与不及物动词

行为动词(即实义动词)按其是否需要宾语,可以分为及物动词和不及物动词。

(1)及物动词,后面必须跟宾语意思才完整。例如:

Give me some ink, please. 请给我一些墨水。

If you have any questions, you can raise your hands. 如果你们有问题,你们可以举手。

(2)不及物动词,后面不能跟宾语,意思已完整。不及物动词有时可以加上副词或介词,构成短语动词,相当于一个及物动词。例如:

He works hard. 他工作努力。

Jack runs faster than Mike. 杰克跑步比迈克要快些。

Please look at the blackboard and listen to me. 请看黑板,听我说。

He got an "A" this time because he went over his lessons carefully. 这次他得了个"A",因为他仔细地复习了功课。

> **难点解释**
>
> (1)许多动词可用作及物动词,也可用作不及物动词,在阅读中必须仔细体会和区别,例如:
>
> Who is going to speak at the meeting? 谁打算在会上发言?(speak,不及物动词)

Few people outside China speak Chinese. 在中国外很少人讲汉语。(speak，及物动词)

(2)要特别注意有些动词英汉之间的差异。某些词在英语中是不及物的，而在汉语中却是及物的。有时则相反。例如：

He is waiting for you. 他在等你。(英语 wait 为不及物动词，汉语"等"为及物动词)

Serve the people. 为人民服务。(英语 serve 为及物动词，汉语"服务"为不及物动词)

2. 持续动词与瞬间动词

英语的行为动词有持续性动词和瞬间性动词之分，使用中应注意两者的区别。

(1)持续性动词。表示一个动作可以持续一段时间或更长时间。常见的有 study、play、do、read、learn、drive、write、clean、sleep、speak、talk、wait、fly、stay、write、sit、stand、lie、keep 等。

(2)瞬间性动词。表示一个动作发生在一瞬间，非常短暂，也称终止性动词。常见的有 begin、start、finish、go、come、leave、find、get up、arrive、reach、get to、enter、hear、stop、open、close、become、buy、borrow、lend、happen、join、lose、renew、die、take away、put up、set out、put on、get on/off 等。

(3)用法。

①以上两类动词都能用于现在完成时，表示动作到现在为止已结束。例如：

He has studied English for three years. 他学英语已有 3 年了。

He has joined the Party. 他已入党了。

Mum isn't at home. She has gone to the library. 妈妈不在家，她去图书馆了。

②持续性动词在完成时中能与表示持续一段时间的状语连用，而瞬间性动词则不能。例如：

My mother has lain in bed for 3 days. 我母亲生病卧床已经三天了。

My parents have lived in Shanghai since 1950. 我父母亲从 1950 年起就住在上海了。

(二)连系动词

连系动词是表示主语"是什么"或"怎么样"的词，它虽有词义，但不完整，所以不能单独作谓语，必须跟表语一起构成合成谓语。例如：

We are in Grade Two this year. 今年我们上二年级。(are，表示"是"，其词义在句子中常常不译出)。

连系动词可具体分为三类：

1. 表示"是"的动词 be

这个词在不同的主语后面和不同的时态中有不同的形式，如 is、am、are、was、were。例如：

He is a teacher. 他是个教师。

He was a soldier two years ago. 两年前他是个士兵。

We are Chinese. 我们是中国人。

2. 表示"感觉"的词

如 look(看起来),feel(觉得,摸起来),smell(闻起来),sound(听起来),taste(尝起来)等。例如:

She looked tired. 她看上去很疲劳。

I feel ill. 我觉得不舒服。

Cotton feels soft. 棉花摸起来很软。

The story sounds interesting. 这个故事听起来很有趣。

The flowers smell sweet. 这些花闻起来很香。

The mixture tasted horrible. 这药水太难喝了。

3. 表示"变""变成"的词

如 become、get、grow、turn,都解释为"变""变得"。例如:

She became a college student. 她成了一名大学生。

He feels sick. His face turns white. 他感到不舒服,他的脸色变苍白了。

The weather gets warmer and the days get longer when spring comes. 春天来了,天气变得暖和些了,白天也变得较长些了。

He grew old. 他老了。

难点解释

注意区别以下一些动词的用法,它们既可以作为行为动词,又可以作为连系动词。

1. look(看,看起来)

He is looking at the picture. 他正在看这图片。(行为动词)

It looks beautiful. 它看上去很美丽。(连系动词)

2. feel(摸,感觉)

I felt someone touch my arm. 我感到有人碰我的手臂。(行为动词)

Are you feeling better today than before? 你今天比以前感到好些了吗?(连系动词)

3. smell(嗅,闻起来)

My little brother likes to smell the apple before he eats it. 我的小弟弟喜欢在吃苹果前闻一闻。(行为动词)

Great! The flowers smell nice. 这些花闻起来多香啊!(连系动词)

4. sound(弄响,发音;听起来)

The letter "h" in hour is not sounded. 在 hour 这个词中字母 h 是不发音的。(行为动词)

The gun sounded much closer. 枪声听起来更近了。(连系动词)

5. taste(辨味,尝起来)

Please taste the soup. 请尝一口汤。(行为动词)

The soup tastes terrible. 这汤尝起来味道太差了。(连系动词)

6. get(得到，获得；变)

There are some bananas on the table. Each of you can get one. 桌上有些香蕉，你们每个人可以拿一个。(行为动词)

It's getting cold. 天变冷了。(联系动词)

7. grow(生长，种植；变)

Do you grow rice in your country? 你们的国家种水稻吗？(行为动词)

It's too late. It's growing dark. 太迟了，天渐渐变暗了。(连系动词)

8. turn(转动，翻动，使变得；变)

The earth turns around the sun. 地球绕着太阳转。(行为动词)

When spring comes, the trees turn green and the flowers come out. 春天来了，树叶变绿了，花儿开了。(连系动词)

上述句子中的动词如 grow、get、turn 等，既可以作连系动词，又可以作行为动词。如何辨别它们呢？有一个最简便的方法，即用连系动词 be 替换句子中的这些动词，若句子仍然成立，则是连系动词；反之，不能替换的，就是行为动词。例如：

The trees turn/are green when spring comes. 春天来临，树叶变绿。

The earth runs around the sun. 地球绕着太阳转。

这第二句句子中的 turn 是行为动词，意为"转动"，无法以 is 替换。

(三) 助动词

这类词本身无词义，不能单独作谓语，只能与主要动词一起构成谓语，表示不同的时态、语态，或表示句子的否定和疑问。例如：

He does not speak English well. 他英语讲得不好。(句中的 does 是助动词，既表示一般现在时，又与 not 一起构成否定形式。)

A dog is running after a cat. 一只犬正在追逐一只猫。(句中的 is 是助动词，和 run 的现在分词一起构成现在进行时。)

Did he have any milk and bread for his breakfast? 他早餐喝牛奶、吃面包吗？(句中的 did 是助动词，既表示一般过去时，又和动词 have 一起构成疑问。)

(四) 情态动词

这类词本身虽有意义，但不完整。它们表示说话人的能力、语气或情态，如"可能""应当"等。这类动词有 can、may、must、need、dare、could、might 等。它们不能单独作谓语，必须与行为动词(原形)一起作谓语，表示完整的意思。例如：

I can dance. 我会跳舞。(can，能，会)

He can't walk because he is a baby. 因为他是个婴儿，不会走路。(can't，不会)

May I come in? 我可以进来吗？(may，可以)

1. 情态动词的主要特征

(1)都有各自的词义，表示能力、可能、允诺、愿意、请求等情态，因词义不完全，不能单独作谓语，只能和动词原形一起构成谓语。

(2)情态动词没有人称和数的变化。构成疑问句时，通常放在主语前面；构成否定句时，not 放在这些情态动词之后，可用它们的缩写形式(can't、cannot、mustn't 等)。

2. 具体用法

(1)can、could 和 be able to。

①表示能力。例如：

I can speak a little Japanese. 我会说一点儿日语。

She couldn't speak Chinese when she came to our school last month. 上月她来我校时还不会说中文。

be able to 代替 can，也可以表示能力。但 can 只有一般现在时和一般过去时(could)，而 be able to 则有更多的时态形式。例如：

You will be able to talk with the foreign teacher in English next week. 下星期你将能与外国老师用英语交谈了。

My little brother has been able to write. 我的小弟弟已会写字了。

②表示"允许，准许"，这时 can 与 may 可以互换。例如：

Can/May I borrow your bike tomorrow? 明天我可以借你的自行车吗？

Yes, of course. You can/may use my bike tomorrow. 当然可以。明天你可以用我的自行车。

You can't smoke here. 你不可以在这儿抽烟。

③表示客观可能性，用在否定句和疑问句中表示说话人的怀疑、猜测或不肯定。例如：

He cannot/can't be there. 他不可能在那儿。

Can this news be true? 这消息真实吗？

④ could 除表示 can 的过去式外，在口语中还常代替 can，表示非常委婉的请求。这时 could 和 can 没有时间上的差别。例如：

Could/Can you tell me if he will go tomorrow? 你能告诉我他明天是否去吗？

Could/Can I ask you something if you are not busy? 如果您不太忙，我能否问您一些事情？

Could/Can you show me the way to the nearest hospital? 您能给我指一下去最近的医院的路吗？

(2)may 和 might。

①表示"准许"和"许可"，这时可与 can 替换。例如：

May (can) I use your dictionary for a moment? 我可以借你的字典用一下吗？

May I take these magazines out of the reading room? 我可以把这些杂志带出阅览室吗？

He asked me if he might go then. 他问我他是否可以走了。

②表示说话人的猜测，认为某事"可能"发生。例如：

Where's John? He may be at the library. 约翰在哪儿？他可能在图书馆。

Mr. Green hasn't talked with her. He may not know her. 格林先生还未曾与她谈过话，他可能不认识她。

> **注　意**
>
> 以上例子中的 may be 是情态动词 may 加 be，与 maybe 完全不同。后者是副词，解释为"或许"。例如：
>
> He may be at home. 他可能在家。
>
> Maybe he was at home. 或许他在家。

③ might 除表示 may 的过去式外，在口语中还常代替 may，表示非常委婉的请示或实现的可能性较小。这时 might 和 may 没有时间上的差异。例如：

Might（May）I speak to you for a few minutes? 我可以与你谈几分钟吗？

Might I have a photo of your family? 我可以要一张你们的合家照吗？

④ 用于从句中表示目的，意为"以便能……""使……可以"。例如：

Open your mouth wide, so that I may see clearly what's wrong with your teeth. 把嘴张大些，以便我能看清楚你的牙齿有什么毛病。

He wrote down my address so that he might remember it well. 他把我的住址写了下来，以便能记牢。

⑤ 在用 may 提问时，否定回答常用 mustn't 或 may not 表示"不行""不可以"。例如：

May I go now? No, you mustn't. 我可以走了吗？不，不可以。

（3）must。

①must 表示说话人的主观意志，表示义务、命令或必要、应当和必须等。现在式与过去式同形。例如：

I must go to school today. 今天我必须上学去。

He told me I mustn't leave until my mother came. 他告诉我，在我母亲来之前我不许离开。

②must 表示推测，"一定是""准是"。例如：

They must be very tired. Let them have a rest. 他们一定是非常疲劳了。让他们休息一会儿吧。

Jack doesn't look well. He must be ill. 杰克看上去气色不太好。他一定是病了。

> **难点解释**
>
> （1）have to 表示"必须""不得不"，它不仅能代替 must，用于现在时和过去时以外的其他时态，表示说话人的主观看法，而且还表示客观上的需要。例如：
>
> If we miss the last bus, we shall have to walk home. 如果我们错过末班车，我们将不得不走回家。
>
> The ship started to go down slowly. We must leave the ship. 船慢慢地开始下沉了，我们必须离开这艘船。
>
> （2）在回答 must 的疑问句时，否定回答常用 needn't 表示"不必"。例如：
>
> Must I return this book to you in two weeks? 这本书我两星期以后必须还你吗？
>
> Yes, you must. 是的。
>
> No, you needn't. 不，不必了。

(4) need 和 dare。need(需要)和 dare(敢于)既可作情态动词，又可作行为动词。

①need 和 dare 作情态动词时，只用于否定句或疑问句。need 无形态变化，dare 的过去式是 dared。例如：

It's warm today. You needn't put on your coat. 今天天气很暖和，你不必穿上大衣。

Need I post your books to you? 要我把书寄给你吗？

How dare you say it's unfair? 你怎么胆敢说这不公平呢？

She dare not go out alone at night. 她晚上不敢一个人出去。

②need 和 dare 作及物动词时，后常跟动词不定式。它们有人称、数和时态等形态变化。在构成否定和疑问形式时与其他及物动词一样，要用助动词 do、does 或 did 等。例如：

You didn't need to go to school today. 今天你不必上学。

They needed an excuse and soon found one. 他们需要借口，不久便找到了一个。

(5) ought to 和 should。

ought to 和 should 作情态动词，都是"应该""应当"的意思。

ought to 语气较强，指客观上有责任、有义务去做某事，或按观念和道理应对某事负责。should 指主观上认为有责任和义务去做，但语意不如 ought to 强烈。

例如：

You ought to respect your teachers. 你们应该尊敬你们的老师。

We should be careful of others' feelings. 我们应该尊重别人的感情。

(6) 相当于情态动词的几个固定词组。以下几个固定词组，也起着与情态动词一样的作用：had better(最好……), Shall I (we)(我/我们可以这样做吗?), would like(非常想), Will/Would you (please)(请你……吗?), used to(过去常常)。例如：

It's late. I'd better go and look for him. 太迟了，我最好去找他。

You'd better not read books in poor light. 你最好不要在微弱的灯光下看书。

Shall we start the meeting at once? 我们立即开会好吗？

Will you get me some chalk? 你拿些粉笔给我好吗？

Would you like some bananas? 来点香蕉好吗？

三、非谓语动词

非谓语动词是指分词(包括现在分词和过去分词)、不定式、动名词三种形式，即 done、to do、doing。它们有各自不同的变化形式，如下表所列：

非谓语形式	语态	一般式	完成式	进行式
不定式	主动	to do	to have done	to be doing
	被动	to be done	to have been done	
现在分词	主动	doing	having done	
	被动	being done	having been done	
过去分词	被动	done		

非谓语动词的共同特点：三种非谓语动词都具有动词的特征，虽然它们没有人称和数

的变化,但是它们都能带自己的状语或有时跟宾语。

非谓语动词各自的特征:分词具有形容词和副词的特征;动名词具有名词的特征;不定式具有名词、形容词和副词的特征。具体来讲,分词在句子中可以作定语、表语、状语或补足语等;动名词在句子中可以作主语、宾语、表语等;不定式在句子中可以作主语、宾语、表语、补足语或状语。

(一)不定式

不定式在句中可充当主语、表语、宾语、补语、定语、状语。

1. 动词不定式作主语

例如:

To finish the work in 10 minutes is hard. 要在十分钟内完成工作很困难。

To see is to believe. 眼见为实。(前后一致)

To swim in the river is dangerous. 在这条河里游泳很危险。

> **注 意**
>
> 不定式作主语时,常用 it 作形式主语。例如:
> It's hard to finish the work in 10 minutes. 很难在十分钟内完成这项工作。
> It is necessary for us to learn from each other. 我们有必要相互学习。

2. 动词不定式作表语

一般用于 be 动词或 seem 等系表动词后面。主语通常是 wish、idea、works、task、job、aim 等词。例如:

My work is to clean the room every day. 我的工作是每天打扫房间。(表语)

My hope is to visit the city. 我的愿望是能够去这座城市。

What we must do is to send for the doctor. 我们必须做的是派医生来。

3. 动词不定式作宾语

具体用法分为两种情况:

(1)一些动词必须接动词不定式作宾语,这类动词有 want(想要)、decide(决定)、ask(问、寻求)、learn(学习)、tell(告诉)、teach(教、讲授)、hope(希望)、plan(计划)、refuse(拒绝)、expect(期待、期望)、afford(负担得起)、warn(警告)、invite(邀请)等。能跟不定式作宾语的动词很多,如 want、like、wish、hate 等。例如:

I want to talk to you. 我想和你谈谈。

They decided to build a bridge over the river. 他们决定在这条河上建座桥。

(2)think、find、feel、make、believe 等动词可用于"动词+it+形容词+to do sth."结构。在此句型中,it 作形式宾语,而真正的宾语是后面的动词不定式。例如:

I find it interesting to study English. 我发现学英语很有趣。

We consider it necessary for him to answer the question. 我们认为对于他来说回答这个问题有必要。

4. 动词不定式作定语

不定式作定语置于被修饰词后，表示将要发生或应该做的动作。

(1)不定式与所修饰词有动宾关系。例如：

I have two letters to write. (two letters 与 to write 构成逻辑上的主谓关系即动宾关系)

(2)不定式与所修饰词有介宾关系。当不定式是不及物的，须加介词构成介宾关系。例如：

I need a pen to write with. 我需要一支钢笔写字。(a pen 与 to write with 构成介宾关系，with 是介词)

I need a house to live in. 我需要一栋房子来住。

5. 状语

(1)目的状语：表示"为了……"。当不定式位于句首时必为目的状语。例如：

To make money, he worked day and night. 为了赚钱，他没日没夜地工作。

(2)结果状语：表示"结果是……"。例如：

He came here to find the train gone。他到了这里结果发现火车开走了。

(3)原因状语：在形容词后的不定式。例如：

I'm nice to meet you。很高兴认识你。

6. 动词不定式作宾语补足语

(1)后接带 to 的不定式作宾语补足语的动词有 ask、want、tell、wish、would like、teach、invite、advise、allow、order、encourage、warn 等。例如：

My friend invited me to join the art club, and I accepted it with pleasure. 朋友邀请我参加艺术社，我欣然接受了。

(2)后接省略 to 的不定式作宾语补足语的动词有：一感(feel)；二听(hear, listen to)；三使(make, let, have)；四看(see, watch, notice, look at)。要注意的是：在被动语态结构中，应还原动词不定式符号 to。例句：

I often see him go to school on foot. 我经常看见他走路上学。

He is often seen to go to school on foot. 人们经常看见他走路上学。

(二) 动名词

英语动名词是从动词变化而来的，所以它保留了动词的某些特征。例如，它能带自己的宾语、状语等。动名词最大的特点是它相当于一个名词，因此，动名词可以在句中作主语、宾语等。

1. 作主语

动名词是由动词变化而来的，所以动名词的意义往往是表示某个动作或某件事情。例如：

Breathing became difficult at that altitude. 在那个海拔高度呼吸变得很困难。

Cheating on an exam ruins one's character. 考试作弊毁坏人的性格。

It takes me ten minutes to get home from my office. 我从办公室回家要花十分钟。

动名词作主语时，对于一些比较长的动名词短语，一般采用"it is"和"there is"两种句式来表示。例如：

It is no use waiting for him any longer. 等他是没有用的。

It is no good learning without practice. 学而不实践是没好处的。

There is no joking about such matters. 这种事开不得玩笑。

2. 作定语

动名词作定语的情况并不是很普遍，一般只限于单个的动名词作定语，表示"用于……的"或表示"处于某件事情中的……"。例如：

swimming pool(游泳池)　　　　reading material（阅读材料）

walking stick(手杖)　　　　　floating needle（浮针）

opening speech(开幕词)　　　listening aid（助听器）

waiting room(候车室)　　　　running water（自来水）

developing countries(发展中国家)　working people（劳动人民）

3. 作表语

动名词作表语的时候，特别要注意不要与正在进行时混淆。动名词作表语，表达的是"某件事"等。例如：

His part-time job is promoting new products for the company. 他的业余工作是为那家公司推销新产品。

Reading is for sure learning, but applying is also learning to a greater extent. 读书当然是学习，然而运用在很大程度上更是学习。

4. 作宾语

(1)动名词跟在及物动词后作宾语。例如：

He managed to escape suffering from the disease. 他设法避免患那种疾病。

Excuse my interrupting you for a while. 请原谅我打扰你一会儿。

(2)在介词后面也要用动名词作宾语。例如：

I'm looking forward to your coming next time. 我期待着您下一次的到来。

They are against using so many animals in experiments. 他们反对用如此多的动物去做试验。

He apologized for interrupting us. 他因打断了我们的谈话而向我们道歉。

（三）分词

分词可分为现在分词和过去分词两种。现在分词的形式同动名词一样，在动词后面加 ing；而过去分词的形式则在动词后面加 ed。分词在句中可起形容词或副词的作用，作定语、状语或表语。

1. 作定语

例如：

China is a developing country. 中国是一个发展中国家。

That's an interesting story. 这是一个有趣的故事。

The girl singing for us is ten years old. 给我们唱歌的女孩十岁了。

（1）作定语的分词要放在被修饰的名词之前，如果是分词词组则放在被修饰的名词之后。如果被修饰的名词是 something、anything、everything、nothing 等，分词放在被修饰名词的后面。例如：

The working people have played a great role in the activity. 工人在这次活动中起主要作用。

The boy hurt by the car was sent to the hospital immediately. 被汽车撞伤的小孩马上被送到了医院。

There is nothing interesting. 没什么有趣的事。

（2）分词和动名词都可以作定语，可以根据它们和被修饰词有无逻辑上的主谓关系来判断是分词还是动名词，有主谓关系的是分词，否则判断为动名词。例如：

a swimming girl（游泳的女孩）（分词）
a swimming pool（游泳的池子）（动名词）

2. 作状语

例如：

Being a student, he likes to help others. 作为一个学生，他喜欢帮助别人。
Wearing a new pair of glasses, she can read easily. 戴了一副新眼镜，她看书就好多了。
She is there waiting for us. 她在那儿等我们呢。
Told by the teacher, she knew she was wrong. 经老师一说，她知道自己不对了。

3. 作表语

例如：

The story is interesting. 故事有趣。
We are interested in computer. 我们对计算机感兴趣。
The glass is broken. 玻璃杯破了。
The water is boiled. 水是开的。

4. 作宾语补足语

可以跟宾语补足语的谓语动词有 see、watch、hear、set、keep、find、have、get 等词。例如：

I saw him walking in the street. 我看见他在街上走。
I heard them singing in the classroom. 我听见他们在教室里唱歌。
We found the boy sleeping. 我们发现小孩睡着了。

have 后面的宾语补足语用过去分词常表示动作不是句子的主语发出的，而是由别人做的。例如：

I have my hair cut. 我理发了。（是别人给我理发）
She has her bike repaired. 她把自行车修理了。（别人修理的）
They have their house rebuilt. 他们重修了房子。

5. 分词的否定形式：not+分词

例如：

Not knowing what to do next, she stopped to wait. 不知道下一步干什么，她停下来等着。

Not having finished the homework, the little girl doesn't dare to go to school. 小女孩没完成作业不敢去学校。

专项练习

(一)判断下列不定式在句中的成分

1. To learn a foreign language is difficult.
2. His wish is to be a driver.
3. Tom wanted to have a cup of beer.
4. The teacher told us to do morning exercises.
5. I have nothing to say.
6. They went to see their aunt.
7. It's easy to see their aunt.
8. I don't know what to do next.
9. I heard them make a noise.

(二)单项选择

1. Most of the people _____ to the party were famous scientists.
   A. invited   B. to invite   C. being invited   D. inviting

2. Mr. Li is a kind-hearted man. Though he is not rich, he always does everything he can _____ the homeless children.
   A. to support   B. support   C. supporting   D. supported

3. She reached the top of the hill and stopped _____ on a big rock by the side of the path.
   A. to have rested   B. resting   C. to rest   D. rest

4. The next morning she found the man _____ in bed, dead.
   A. lying   B. lie   C. lay   D. laying

5. The purpose of new technologies is to make life easier, _____ it more difficult.
   A. to make   B. not to make   C. not making   D. to not make

6. The Olympic Games, _____ in 776 B.C., did not include women plays until 1912.
   A. first playing
   B. to be first played
   C. first played
   D. to be first playing

7. —— You were brave enough to raise objections at the meeting.
   —— Well, now I regret _____ that.
   A. to do   B. to be doing   C. to have done   D. having done

8. The visiting Minister expressed his satisfaction with talks, _____ that he had enjoyed his stay here.
   A. having added   B. to add   C. adding   D. added

· 56 ·

9. _____ a reply, he decided to write again.
   A. Not receiving   B. Receiving not
   C. Not having received   D. Having not received

10. The speaker raised his voice, but he still couldn't make himself _____.
    A. hear   B. to hear   C. hearing   D. heard

（三）用动词的正确形式填空

1. Little Tom should love _____ (take) to the theatre this evening.

2. Paul doesn't have to be made _____ (learn). He always works hard.

3. The computer centre, _____ (open) last year, is very popular among the students in this school.

4. Go on _____ (do) the other exercise after you have finished this one.

5. How about two of us _____ (take) a walk down the garden.

第八节 动词的时态和语态

一、动词的时态

动词的时态是谓语动词所表示的动作或情况发生时间的各种形式。英语动词有 16 种时态，具体如下：

时态	现在时	过去时	将来时	过去将来时
一般	一般现在时 do	一般过去时 did	一般将来时 will do be going to do	一般过去将来时 would do
进行	现在进行时 be doing	过去进行时 was/were doing	将来进行时 will be doing	▲过去将来进行时 would be doing was/were going to do
完成	现在完成时 have done	过去完成时 had done	▲将来完成时 will have done	▲过去将来完成时 would have done
完成进行	现在完成进行时 have been doing	▲过去完成进行时 had been doing	▲将来完成进行时 will have been doing	▲过去将来完成进行时 would have been doing

常用的动词时态有 10 种：一般现在时、一般过去时、一般将来时、现在进行时、过去进行时、现在完成时、过去完成时、过去将来时、现在完成进行时、将来完成时。

1. 一般现在时

（1）一般现在时的普通用法。

①表示经常性、习惯性的动作。常与表示频率的时间状语连用，如 often、usually、

sometimes、every、sometimes、on Sundays 等。例如：

I leave home for school at 7 every morning. 我每天早晨7点离开家去学校。

He goes to school every day. 他每天去上学。

②表示客观事实，普遍真理。例如：

The earth moves around the sun. 地球绕着太阳转。

Shanghai lies in the east of China. 上海位于中国的东部。

③表示格言或警句。例如：

Pride goes before a fall. 骄者必败。

注　意

②③的用法如果出现在宾语从句中，即使主句是过去时，从句谓语也要用一般现在时。例如：

Columbus proved that the earth is round. 哥伦布证明了地球是圆的。

④表示现在时刻的状态、能力、性格、个性。例如：

I don't want so much。我不想那么多。

Ann Wang writes good English but does not speak well. 王安的英文写得很好但说得不好。

（2）一般现在时的特殊用法。

①在时间状语从句和条件状语从句中，用一般现在时表示将来。例如：

If you come this afternoon, we'll have a meeting. 如果你今天下午过来，我们就开个会。

When I graduate, I'll go to countryside. 毕业后我要去乡下。

②有时这个时态表示按计划、规定要发生的动作（句中都带有时间状语），但限于少数动词，如 begin、come、leave、go、arrive、start、stop、return、open、close 等。例如：

The meeting begins at seven. 会议七点开始。

The rain starts at nine in the morning. 上午九点开始下雨。

③表示状态和感觉的动词（be、like、hate、think、remember、find、sound 等）常用一般现在时表示现在进行时。例如：

I like English very much. 我非常喜欢英语。

The story sounds very interesting. 这个故事听起来很有趣。

2. 一般过去时

（1）在确定的过去时间里所发生的动作或存在的状态。时间状语有：yesterday, last week, an hour ago, the other day, in 1982 等。例如：

Where did you go just now? 刚才你上哪儿去了？

（2）表示在过去一段时间内，经常性或习惯性的动作。例如：

When I was a child, I often played football in the street. 我是个孩子的时候，常在马路上踢足球。

Whenever the Browns went during their visit, they were given a warm welcome. 那时，布朗一家无论什么时候去，都受到热烈欢迎。

> **注 意**
>
> (1)用过去时表示现在，表示委婉语气。
>
> ①动词 want、hope、wonder、think、intend 等。例如：
>
> Did you want anything else? 你还有什么事吗？
>
> I wondered if you could help me. 不知你能不能帮我个忙。
>
> ②情态动词 could、would。
>
> Could you lend me your bike? 你能借给我你的自行车吗？
>
> (2)used to / be used to。
>
> ①used to+do："过去常常"，表示过去习惯性的动作或状态，但如今已不存在。例如：
>
> Mother used not to be so forgetful. 妈妈过去不是这样健忘。
>
> Scarf used to take a walk. 斯卡夫过去常常散步。
>
> ②be used to+doing："对……已感到习惯"，或"习惯于"，to 是介词，后需加名词或动名词。

3. 一般将来时

一般将来时表示将来的动作或状态。

(1)其基本表达形式为"will 或 shall+动词原形""be going to"，表示即将发生的或最近打算进行的事。例如：

We will go to Beijing tomorrow.

It is going to rain. 要下雨了。

We are going to have a meeting today. 我们今天要开个会。

(2)"be to+动词原形"，表示按计划进行或征求对方意见。例如：

The boy is to go to school tomorrow. 男孩明天要去上学。

Are we to go on with this work? 我们要继续这项工作吗？

(3)"be about to+动词原形"，表示即将发生的动作，意为"be ready to do sth"，后面一般不跟时间状语。例如：

We are about to leave. 我们正要离开。

(4) go、come、start、move、leave、arrive、stay 等可用进行时态表示按计划即将发生的动作。例如：

I'm leaving for Beijing. 我要离开北京了。

(5)某些动词(如 come、go、leave、arrive、start、get、stay 等)的一般现在时也可表示将来。例如：

The meeting starts at five o'clock. 会议将在五点开始。

He gets off at the next stop. 他要在下一站下车。

(6)be to 和 be going to 的区别。be to 表示客观安排或受人指示而做某事，be going to 表示主观的打算或计划。例如：

I am to play football tomorrow afternoon. 明天下午我去踢足球。(客观安排)

I'm going to play football tomorrow afternoon. 明天下午我想去踢足球。（主观安排）

4. 现在进行时

(1)主要表示说话人的说话时刻正在进行的动作、不断重复的动作或目前这个阶段(不一定是说话时刻)正在进行的动作。例如：

We're having a meeting. 我们在开会。（说话时正在进行的动作）

Be quiet! The baby is sleeping. 安静，小宝宝在睡觉。

He is teaching in a middle school. 他在一所中学教书。（目前阶段在进行的动作）

(2)表示将来。现在进行时表示将来，主要表示按计划或安排要发生的动作。例如：

I'm leaving tomorrow. 我明天走。

They're getting married next month. 他们下个月结婚。

(3)表示感情色彩。现在进行时有时可表示满意、称赞、惊讶、厌恶等感情色彩，通常与 always、forever、constantly、continually 等副词连用。例如：

She's always helping people. 她老是帮助别人。（表示赞扬）

She always helps others. 她总是帮助别人。（陈述一个事实）

The boy is constantly lying. 这男孩老是撒谎。（表示厌恶）

The boy often lies. 这男孩常撒谎。（指出缺点）

5. 过去进行时

(1)过去进行时的构成。过去进行时由"was/were+现在分词"构成。例如：

He fell asleep when he was reading. 他看书时睡着了。

We were expecting you yesterday. 我们昨天一直在等你。

第一句中的"看书"用了过去进行时，是因为当时看书的动作正在进行；第二句中的"等"也用了过去进行时，也是因为"等"这个动作昨天一直在持续。

(2)表示临时性。即表示在过去短期内正在进行的动作或存在的临时情况，这种情况通常不会长期如此。例如：

It happened while I was living in Paris last year. 这件事发生于去年我住在巴黎的时候。

(3)表示委婉语气。动词 hope、wonder 等的过去进行时常用来表示提出要求，虽然表示现在的内容，但语气比一般现在时或一般过去时要委婉。例如：

I was hoping you would give me some advice. 我希望你给我出点主意。

Good morning. I was wondering if you had two single rooms. 早上好，我不知道你们是否有两个单人房间。

6. 现在完成时

现在完成时用来表示之前已发生或完成的动作或状态，其结果的影响现在还存在，也可表示持续到现在的动作或状态。其构成为：have(has)+过去分词。

现在完成时的时间状语：for、since、so far、ever、never、just、yet、till/until、up to now、in past years、always 等不确定的时间状语。

现在完成时用来表示现在之前已发生过或完成的动作或状态，但其结果却和现在有联系。也就是说，动作或状态发生在过去但它的影响现在还存在。例如：

I have spent all of my money.（现在我没有钱花了）
Jane has laid the table.（现在桌子已经摆好了）
Michael has been ill.（现在仍然很虚弱）
He has returned from abroad.（现在已在此地）
用于现在完成时的句型：
（1）It is the first／second time+that，结构中的从句部分，用现在完成时。例如：
It is the first time that I have visited the city. 这是我第一次访问这个城市。
This is the first time（that）I've heard him sing. 这是我第一次听他唱歌。
（2）This is+形容词最高级+that，that 从句要用现在完成时。例如：
This is the best film that I've（ever）seen. 这是我看过的最好的电影。
——Do you know our town at all?
——No，this is the first time I have been here.

7. 过去完成时

过去完成时表示一个动作或状态在过去某一时间或动作之前已经完成或结束，即"过去的过去"，也可以指过去的动作延续到过去的某个时刻。这里的过去时间可以用某个时间状语表示，也可以通过上下文表示。其构成是"had+过去分词"。

（1）表示一个动作或状态在过去某一时间或动作之前已经完成或结束，也有可能早已完成或结束。例如：

When he was in Beijing, he visited places where he had played as a child. 他在北京的时候游览了他儿时曾玩过的地方。

（2）表示一个过去的动作先于另一过去的动作，这种情况多见于宾语从句。例如：

He remembered that he had left the key at home. 他记得他把钥匙落家了。

（3）表示一个动作或状态在过去某时之前已经开始，一直延续到这一过去时间，而且到那时还未结束，仍有继续下去的可能性。例如：

By seven o'clock, the worker had worked for ten hours. 到七点钟为止，那位工人已经工作十个小时了。

8. 过去将来时

过去将来时表示在过去某个时间看来将要发生的动作或存在的状态。过去将来时常用于宾语从句和间接引语中。其构成是"would/should+动词原形"。例如：

I didn't know if he would come. 我不知道他是否会来。

They never knew that population would become a big problem. 他们从来都不知道人口问题将会成为一个大问题。

She didn't tell me where she would go. 她没有告诉我她要去哪儿。

过去将来时有两种表达：

（1）would+动词原形。常表示按计划或安排即将发生的事。例如：

He said he would come to see me. 他说他要来看我。

He told me he would go to Beijing. 他告诉我他将去北京。

（2）was/were+going to+动词原形。常可用来表示按计划或安排即将发生的事。例如：

She said she was going to start off at once. 她说她将立即出发。

I was told that he was going to return home. 有人告诉我他准备回家。

9. 现在完成进行时

表示动作从某一时间开始，一直持续到现在，或者刚刚终止，或者可能仍然要继续下去。现在完成进行时由"have / has+been+现在分词"构成。其用法如下：

(1)表示现在以前这一段时间里一直在进行的动作，这动作可能仍在进行，也可能已停止。例如：

It has been raining since last Sunday. 自上周日以来就一直在下雨。

He's been watching television all day. 他看了一天电视了。

He has been doing this work for three years. 他已干了三年这工作了。

(2)表示过去某种愿望未实现，某种企图、希望落空，含有遗憾、不耐烦等情绪。例如：

She has been telling me. 她一直想告诉我。

They have been going to build a bridge over the lake for years. 数年来，他们一直想在湖上建一座桥。(但未能实现)

(3)表示一个过去动作对现在的影响或造成的结果(相当于现在完成时)。例如：

Who's been insulting you? 谁欺负你了？

The room stinks. Someone's been smoking in here. 屋里有烟味，有人抽烟了。

10. 将来完成时

将来完成时是用来表示在将来某一时间以前已经完成或一直持续的动作。将来完成时由"shall/will have+过去分词"构成。具体用法有：

(1)表示将来某时之前或某动作发生之前已经完成的动作。例如：

I shall have finished it by next Friday. 到下周五我就完成了。

She will have written it tomorrow at noon. 明天中午她就会写好了。

They will have been graduated from the university before he returns from abroad. 在他从国外回来之前他们就会大学毕业了。

(2)表示一个持续到将来某时或某动作发生之前的动作。例如：

By next Monday, she will have studied here for three years. 到下周一，她在这里学习就要满3年了。

The concert will begin at half past eight. They will have played half an hour when you arrive. 音乐会将在8点半开始。你到达时，他们将已经演奏半个小时了。

(3)表示对现在或将来可能已经完成动作的推测，或对过去实况的推测。例如：

He will have arrived by now. 他可能已经到了。

He is a somebody now. He will have forgotten his old friends. 他现在是个要人了，可能把老朋友都忘了。

You'll have heard that China will launch another spaceship. 你可能已经听说了，中国将要发射另一艘宇宙飞船。

二、动词的语态

（一）语态知识概要

语态是动词的一种特殊形式，用以说明主语与谓语动词之间的关系。语态有两种：主动语态和被动语态。主语是动作的发出者为主动语态；主语是动作的接受者为被动语态，被动语态中动作的执行者一般由介词 by 引起的短语来表示。例如：

We often help them.（主动）我们常帮助他们。

They are often helped by us.（被动）他们常被我们帮助。

（二）被动语态

1. 常见时态的被动语态

被动语态由助动词 be+过去分词构成（be+done），时态通过 be 表现出来。被动语态常用的 8 种时态如下。

(1) 一般现在时：You are required to do this.

(2) 一般过去时：The story was told by her.

(3) 一般将来时：The problem will be discussed tomorrow.

(4) 现在进行时：The road is being widened.

(5) 过去进行时：The new tool was being made.

(6) 现在完成时：The novel has been read.

(7) 过去完成时：He said that the work had been finished.

(8) 过去将来时：He said that the trees would be planted soon. 他说树很快就会被种下。

2. 被动语态的用法

(1)当不知道或没有必要指出动作的执行者时，常用被动语态，这时往往不用 by 短语。例如：

The front window in the classroom was broken yesterday. 昨天，教室的前窗被打破了。（不知谁打破的）

They have been poorly paid. 他们的工资太低。（没必要指出工资是谁付的）

How is this word pronounced? 这个单词怎么发音？

(2)突出或强调动作的承受者，如果需要说出动作的执行者，用 by 短语。例如：

The time-table has been changed. 时间表已变动了。（要突出的是"时间表"）

These books are written especially for children. 这些书是专门为孩子们写的。（强调的是"这些书"）

(3)为了使语言得体或圆滑等不愿意说出动作的执行者。例如：

You are requested to make a speech at next meeting. 请您在下次会议上做个发言。

It is said that she is going to be married to a foreigner. 据说她要嫁给一个外国人。

(4)出于修辞的需要，为了使句子更加简练、匀称。例如：

He appeared on the stage and was warmly applauded by the audience. 他出现在舞台上，受

到了观众的热烈鼓掌。

It is generally considered impolite to ask one's age, salary, marriage, *etc*. 问别人的年龄、工资、婚姻状况等通常被认为是不礼貌的。

3. 被动语态中需注意的一些问题

(1) 若宾语补足语是不带 to 的不定式，变为被动语态时，该不定式前要加 to。此类动词为感官动词，如 feel、hear、help、listen to、look at、make、observe、see、notice、watch。

The teacher made me go out of the classroom. 老师让我走出教室。

→ I was made to go out of the classroom (by the teacher). 我是被老师请出教室的。

We saw him play football on the playground. 我看见他在操场踢足球。

→ He was seen to play football on the playground. 他被看见在操场上踢足球。

(2) 表示"据说"或"相信"的词组，如 believe、consider、declare、expect、feel、report、say、see、suppose、think、understand。

It is said that… (据说)

It is reported that… (据报道)

It is believed that… (大家相信)

It is hoped that… (大家希望)

It is well known that… (众所周知)

It is thought that… (大家认为)

It is suggested that… (据建议)

It is taken granted that… (被视为当然)

It has been decided that… (大家决定)

(3) 不及物动词或动词短语无被动语态：appear, die, disappear, end (vi. 结束), fail, happen, last, lie, remain, sit, spread, stand, break out, come true, fall asleep, keep silence, lose heart, take place 等。例如：

(误) The price has been risen.

(正) The price has risen. 价格上涨了。

(误) The accident was happened last week.

(正) The accident happened last week. 事故发生在上周。

专项练习

(一) 单项选择

1. ——Don't drop litter, boy. Look at the sign: "Rubbish _____ into the dustbin."
——Sorry.

A. has thrown   B. was thrown   C. must throw   D. must be thrown

2. After the earthquake in Taiwan on CCTV on December 19th, 2009, lots of people donated money.

A. reports   B. was reported   C. was reporting   D. reported

3. I think computers _____ in everyday life in a few years' time.

   A. will use   B. will be used   C. are used   D. were used

4. —— What's wrong with that boy?

   —— He _____ by a car yesterday.

   A. was hit   B. hit   C. is hit   D. hits

5. ——Your sweater looks nice. Is it wool?

   ——Yes, and it's _____ Inner Mongolia.

   A. made of; made by   B. made of; made in

   C. made by; made for   D. made by; made from

6. This kind of medicine _____ cool, clean and dry according to the instructions.

   A. should be carried   B. must be put   C. should be live   D. must be kept

7. —— What a pity! The old bridge _____ down at last. It had such a long history.

   —— But it had been too dangerous to walk on it, anyway.

   A. breaks   B. was broken   C. has broken   D. had been broken

8. —— Can I play football for some time, Mum?

   —— You can, if your homework _____.

   A. will do   B. does   C. is done   D. will be done

9. After the earthquake, a lot of new schools _____ so that the students can go back to school to continue their studies.

   A. will build   B. have built   C. are building   D. are being built

10. ——What can we do if the rain lasts for another day?

    ——If so, the school sports meeting _____.

    A. will put off   B. have put off   C. will be put off   D. have been put off

(二)用括号中动词的适当形式填空

1. The boy is happy because he _____ (sell) out all the newspapers.

2. The plan _____ (give) up because of the heavy rain.

3. If it _____ (not rain) tomorrow, we _____ (go) fishing.

4. Where _____ you _____ (be) these days?

5. Where is Tom? He _____ (go) to the post office. He said he _____ (come) back soon.

6. Mike says he _____ (want) to be a worker after he _____ (finish) school.

7. The last bus _____ just _____ (leave) when they _____ (get) to the bus stop.

8. She _____ (not go) to bed until she _____ (finish) her work.

9. Light _____ (travel) much faster than sound.

10. I _____ (feel) much better after I _____ (take) the medicine.

11. "Where _____ we _____ (meet)?" "Let's meet outside the park gate."

12. I _____ (be) afraid Mr. Johnson _____ (not visit) out school tomorrow.

13. I _____ (lost) my bike. _____ you _____ (see) it anywhere?
14. _____ this kind of car _____ (produce) in Shanghai?
15. We _____ (see) several members of the family since we _____ (arrive).
16. I found that the students _____ (play) football on the playground.
17. The shop _____ (close) at this time of day.
18. Where _____ your watch _____ (lose)?
19. _____ the doctor _____ (send) for last night?
20. Three children _____ (invite) to the party by Miss Li yesterday.
21. Some children _____ (take) good care by the nurse.
22. Some new houses _____ (build) by the villagers themselves.
23. What language _____ (speak) in Australia?
24. The colour TV _____ (buy) in that shop three days ago.
25. He said he _____ (stay) here for another two days.
26. The doctor said Jim must _____ (operate) on at once.
27. "_____ the bridge _____ (repair) yet?" "Yes, the workers _____ already _____ (repair) it."
28. We are in Grade One this year, so we _____ (teach) physics next year.
29. "Where _____ (be) you last night?" "I _____ (ask) to help Tom at home."
30. The big tree _____ (blow) down in the storm last night.

第九节 虚拟语气

一、语气概说

语气(mood)是一种动词形式,用以表示说话者的态度、意见、感情或评论等。英语中的语气有三种:陈述语气、祈使语气和虚拟语气。

1. 陈述语气

表示动作或状态是客观存在的、确定的或符合事实的,用于陈述句、疑问句和某些感叹句中。例如:

Iraq is an Asian country. 伊拉克是亚洲国家。(肯定句)

The US and British armies did not start the Second Gulf War until March 20, 2003. 美英联军直到2003年3月20日才发动第二次海湾战争。(否定句)

Who was it that they want to help? 他们想要帮忙的人到底是谁呀?(疑问句)

How interesting my stay in China has been! 我在中国的日子过得真有趣!(感叹句)

2. 祈使语气

表示说话人对对方的请求、警告、建议或命令。例如:

Please come over here. 请到这边来。
Would you be so kind as to lend me a hand? 请帮个忙好吗？
Watch your steps! 当心！（走路）
Never be late again! 再也不要迟到了。

3. 虚拟语气

用来表达假设、主观愿望、猜测、建议、可能或空想等非真实情况，或难以实现的情况，甚至表达彻底相反的概念。虚拟语气通过谓语动词的特殊形式来表示。例如：

If I were a bird, I would be able to fly in the air. 如果我是一只小鸟，我就能在空中飞行。
If I were you, I would not go. 我要是你，我就不会去。
I wish I had a lot of money. 要是我有很多很多钱就好了。

二、虚拟语气的用法

1. if 条件状语从句中虚拟语气的用法

if 条件状语从句有真实条件句和非真实条件句。假设条件可以实现的句子为真实条件句，反之为非真实条件句，要用虚拟语气。其形式分为以下三种：

时态类型	主句谓语形式	If 虚拟条件句的谓语形式
与现在事实相反	would/should/could/might+do	动词过去式 did ＊be 动词统一用 were
与过去事实相反	would/should/could/might+have done	动词过去完成式 had done
与将来事实相反	would/should/could/might+do	①动词过去式 ②should+do ③were to+do

（1）与现在事实相反的假设。结构为：从句的谓语动词用过去式，系动词用 were，主句的谓语用"should（would，could，might）+动词原形"。例如：

If I were in your position, I would marry her. 如果我是你，我就娶她为妻。
If I were you, I should study English. 如果我是你，我就该学英语。

（2）与过去事实相反的假设。结构为：从句的谓语动词用"had+过去分词"，主句用"should（would，could，might）+have+过去分词"。例如：

If it had not rained so hard yesterday, we could have played tennis. 如果昨天没有下大雨，我们就能打网球了。
If you had taken my advice, you would not have failed in the test. 如果你接受了我的建议，你就不会在考试中不及格了。

（3）与将来事实相反的假设。结构为：从句的谓语动词用"should（were to）+动词原形"，主句用"should（would，could，might）+动词原形"。例如：

If you should miss the chance, you would feel sorry for it. 如果你错过了这次机会，你会难过的。

> **注 意**
>
> (1) would/should/could/might 主句谓语中的 should 主要用于第一人称后；would 表示结果，还表示过去经常做某事，might 表示可能性，could 表示能力、允许或可能性。比较：
>
> If you tried again, you would succeed. 要是你再试一试，你就会成功的。(would 表示结果)
>
> If you tried again, you might succeed. 要是你再试一试，你可能会成功的。(might 表示可能)
>
> If you tried again, you could succeed. 要是你再试一试，你就能成功了。(could 表示能力)
>
> (2) 错综时间虚拟条件句。即条件从句与主句所指时间不一致，如从句指过去，而主句指的是现在或将来，此时应根据具体的语境，结合上面提到的三种基本类型对时态做相应的调整。例如：
>
> If it had rained last night, the ground would be wet now. 要是昨晚下过雨的话，现在地面就会是湿的。
>
> You would be much better now if you had taken my advice. 假若你当时听我的话，你现在就会好多了。
>
> (3) 省略形式。有时可以把含有助动词、情态动词、be 或 have 的虚拟条件句中的连词 if 省去，而将 had、should、were 等词提到主语之前，即用倒装结构。这时，如果出现 not 等否定词，需放在主语后面。例如：
>
> If she had been here five minutes earlier, she would have seen her old friend. →
>
> Had she been here five minutes earlier, she would have seen her old friend. 如果她早到五分钟，她就会看见她的老朋友了。

2. 宾语从句中虚拟语气的用法

(1) wish 后接宾语从句中的虚拟语气：根据从句的意义来判断。

①表示与现在和将来事实相反的愿望，从句谓语动词用过去时。例如：

I wish they were not so late. 要是他们来得不是这么晚就好了。

I wish that the experiment were a success. 我希望这个实验是成功的。

We wish we had wings. 我们希望有翅膀。

②表示与过去事实相反的愿望，从句谓语动词用过去完成时。例如：

I wished he hadn't done that. 我真希望那件事不是他做的。

I didn't go to the party, but I do wish I had been there. 我没有去参加晚会，但是我真的希望我去过那里。

(2) 表示"要求、建议、命令"等动词后面的宾语从句中的虚拟语气。用于此结构的动词有：advise, direct, agree, ask, demand, decide, desire, insist, order, prefer, propose, request, suggest 等。从句的谓语动词用"should+动词原形"，其中 should 可以省去。例如：

I insisted that he (should) go with us. 我坚持让他和我们一起去。

> **注 意**
>
> 当 insist 表示"坚持认为"、suggest 表示"表明，显示"时，不用虚拟语气。例如：
> He insisted that I had read his letter. 他坚持说我看过他的信。
> He insisted that I should read his letter. 他坚持要我看他的信。
> He suggested that we (should) stay for dinner. 他建议我们留下吃饭。
> I suggested that you had a secret understanding with him. 我觉得你与他心照不宣。

3. 主语从句中的虚拟语气

（1）It be+形容词+that…(should)+verb…。用于该句型的形容词有：necessary, good, important, right, wrong, better, natural, proper, funny, strange, surprising 等。例如：

It's natural that he should feel hurt. 他感到疼是很正常的。

（2）It be+过去分词+that…(should)+verb…。用于该句型中的过去分词是表示"建议、请求、命令"等词的过去分词，如 desired、suggested、requested、ordered、proposed 等。例如：

It is desired that the building of the house be completed next month. 真希望这所房子在下个月就能竣工。

（3）It is time (about time / high time) that…+(过去时或 should+动词原形)…。例如：
It is high time I went home now. = It is high time I should go home. 我该回家了。

4. 表语从句、同位语从句中的虚拟语气

在 suggestion、proposal、order、plan、idea、advice、decision 等表语从句、同位语从句中的名词后要使用虚拟语气，其谓语动词为 should+动词原形，连接从句的 that 不能省略。例如：

My suggestion is that we should go there at once. 我的建议是我们应该马上去那儿。

5. would rather 后句子用虚拟语气

在 would rather、would sooner、would just as soon 后的 that 从句中，句子的谓语习惯上要用虚拟语气，表示"宁愿做什么"，具体用法为：

（1）一般过去时表示现在或将来的愿望。例如：
I'd rather you went tomorrow (now). 我宁愿你明天(现在)去。

（2）用过去完成时表过去的愿望。例如：
I'd rather you hadn't said it. 我真希望你没有这样说过。

6. as if (though) 从句用虚拟语气

以 as if (as though)引导的方式状语从句或表语从句，有时用虚拟语气，与 wish 用法相同。例如：

He acts as if he knew me. 他显得认识我似的。
They treat me as though I were a stranger. 他们待我如陌生人。
He talks as if he had been abroad. 他说起话来好像曾经出过国。

注 意

(1) 从句所表示的内容若为事实或可能为事实，也可用陈述语气。例如：
It looks as if we'll be late. 我们似乎要迟到了。

(2) 注意 It isn't as if 的翻译。例如：
It isn't as if he were poor. 他不像穷的样子(或他又不穷)。

专项练习

单项选择

1. I enjoyed the movie very much. I wish I _____ the book from which it was made.
   A. have read   B. had read   C. should have read   D. are reading

2. You are late. If you _____ a few minutes earlier, you _____ him.
   A. come; would meet   B. had come; would have met
   C. come; will meet   D. had come; would meet

3. The two students talked as if they _____ friends for years.
   A. should be   B. would be   C. have been   D. had been

4. It is important that I _____ with Mr. Williams immediately.
   A. speak   B. spoke   C. will speak   D. to speak

5. He looked as if he _____ ill for a long time.
   A. was   B. were   C. has been   D. had been

6. If the doctor had come earlier, the poor child would not _____.
   A. have laid there for two hours   B. have been lied there for two hours
   C. have lied there for two hours   D. have lain there for two hours

7. I wish that I _____ with you last night.
   A. went   B. could go   C. have gone   D. could have gone

8. Let's say you could go there again, how _____ feel?
   A. will you   B. should you   C. would you   D. do you

9. I can't stand him. He always talks as though he _____ everything.
   A. knew   B. knows   C. has known   D. had known

10. _____ the fog, we should have reached our school.
    A. Because of   B. In spite of   C. In case of   D. But for

11. If you had told me in advance, I _____ him at the airport.
    A. would meet   B. would had met
    C. would have met   D. would have meet

12. Mike can take his car apart and put it back together again. I certainly wish he _____ me how.
    A. teaches   B. will teach   C. has taught   D. would teach

13. I would have told him the answer, had it been possible, but I _____ so busy then.
    A. had been   B. were   C. was   D. would be
14. He's working hard for fear that he _____.
    A. should fall behind   B. fell behind
    C. may fall behind   D. would fallen behind
15. If it _____ another ten minutes, the game would have been called off.
    A. had rained   B. would have rained
    C. have seen   D. rained
16. He suggested that they _____ use a trick instead of fighting.
    A. should   B. would   C. do   D. had
17. My father did not go to New York; the doctor suggested that he _____ there.
    A. not went   B. won't go   C. should not go   D. not to go
18. I would have gone to the meeting if I _____ time.
    A. had had   B. have had   C. had   D. would have had
19. Would you rather I _____ buying a new bike?
    A. decided against   B. will decide against
    C. have decided   D. shall decide against
20. You look so tired tonight. It is time you _____.
    A. go to sleep   B. went to sleep   C. go to bed   D. went to bed
21. ——Why didn't you buy a new car?
    ——I would have bought one if I _____ enough money.
    A. had   B. have had   C. would have   D. had had
22. If she could sew, _____.
    A. she make a dress   B. she would have made a shirt
    C. she will make a shirt   D. she would had made a coat
23. _____ today, he would get there by Friday.
    A. Would he leave   B. Was he leaving
    C. Were he to leave   D. If he leaves
24. His doctor suggested that he _____ a short trip abroad.
    A. will take   B. would take   C. take   D. took
25. I didn't know his telephone number, otherwise I _____ him.
    A. had telephoned   B. would telephone
    C. would have telephoned   D. telephone

第二章 句法

第一节 基本句型结构

句子是由各种词类按照一定的语法规则组成的，可以表达完整的概念。句子开头第一个字母一定要大写，结尾要注明标点符号。句子按使用目的可分为陈述句、疑问句、祈使句和感叹句。句子按其结构可以分为简单句、并列句和复合句。

一、英语句子成分

组成句子的各个部分称为句子的成分。英语的基本成分有7种：主语(subject)、谓语(predicate)、表语(predicative)、宾语(object)、定语(attribute)、状语(adverbial)和补语(complement)。其中，主语和谓语是句子的主体，表语、宾语和宾语补足语是谓语的组成部分，其他成分如定语和状语是句子的次要部分。

1. 主语(subject)

主语为句子说明的人或事物，通常用名词、代词、不定式或相当于名词的词、短语或从句担任。主语要放在句首。例如：

The sun rises in the east. （名词）

He likes dancing. （代词）

Twenty years is a short time in history. （数词）

Seeing is believing. （动名词）

To see is to believe. （不定式）

What he needs is a book. （主语从句）

It is very clear that the elephant is round and tall like a tree. (It 形式主语，主语从句是真正主语)

2. 谓语(predicate)

谓语说明主语的动作、状态和特征，必须用动词表示。谓语和主语在人称和数两方面要一致。谓语通常在主语之后。谓语的构成如下：

(1)简单谓语：由一个动词或动词短语构成。例如：

He practices running every morning. 他每天早上练习跑步。

(2)复合谓语：

①由情态动词或其他助动词加动词原形构成。例如：

You may keep the book for two weeks. 这本书你可以借两个星期。

He has caught a bad cold. 他得了重感冒。

②由系动词加表语构成。例如：

We are students. 我们是学生。

3. 表语(predicative)

表语用于说明主语的性质、特征、身份或状态，可以由名词、形容词、副词、介词和不定式以及相当于名词或形容词的词或短语来担任。表语要放在连系动词之后。常见的系动词有：be，sound(听起来)，look(看起来)，feel(摸起来)，smell(闻起来)，taste(尝、吃起来)，remain(保持，仍是)，feel(感觉) 等。例如：

He is a teacher. 他是一位老师。(表语为名词)

Seventy-four! You don't look it. 74 岁！你看起来根本不是。(表语为代词)

Five and five is ten. 5 加 5 是 10。(表语为数词)

Her voice sounds sweet. 她的声音听起来很甜。(表语为形容词)

His father is in. 他的父亲在。(表语为副词)

The picture is on the wall. 那幅画在墙上。(表语为介词短语)

My watch is gone / missing / lost. 我的手表丢了。(表语为形容词化的分词)

To wear a flower is to say "I'm poor, I can't buy a ring." 戴花是说："我很穷，我买不起戒指。"(表语为不定式)

The question is whether they will come. 问题是他们是否会来。(表语为从句)

4. 宾语

宾语是及物动词所示动作的对象或介词的对象，名词、代词、不定式或相当于名词的词、短语及从句都可以作宾语。宾语要放在谓语动词(及物动词)或介词之后。

(1)动作的承受者——动宾。例如：

I like China. 我爱中国。(宾语为名词)

He hates you. 他讨厌你。(宾语为代词)

How many do you need? We need two. 你们需要多少个？我们需要两个。(宾语为数词)

I enjoy working with you. 我喜欢和你一起工作。(宾语为动名词)

I hope to see you again. 我希望能再次看见你。(宾语为不定式)

Did you write down what he said? 你记下来了他所说的吗？(宾语为从句)

(2)介词后的名词、代词和动名词——介宾。例如：

Are you afraid of the snake? 你害怕蛇吗？

Under the snow, there are many rocks. 雪下有许多岩石。

(3)双宾语——某些及物动词之后要求有双宾语，即直接宾语和间接宾语，其中直接宾语指物，间接宾语指人。这一类动词有 bring、give、pass、tell、hand、show、end、read、leave、teach、find、buy、make、do、get、order、play、promise、pay 等。

I promised her a wonderful present on her birthday. 我答应在她生日那天给她一件很棒的礼物。

She made me a sweater. (= She made a sweater for me.) 她给我织了一件毛衣。

He left her three children. (=He left three children to her)他给她留下三个孩子。

5. 宾语补足语

有些及物动词的后面,其宾语还需要有一个补足语,才能表达完整的意思。名词、形容词、不定式或介词短语都可以作宾语补足语。例如:

We elected him monitor.（名词）

We all think it a pity that she didn't come here.（名词）

We will make them happy.（形容词）

We found nobody in.（副词）

Please make yourself at home.（介词短语）

Don't let him do that.（省 to 不定式）

His father advised him to teach the lazy boy a lesson.（带 to 不定式）

Don't keep the lights burning.（现在分词）

I'll have my bike repaired.（过去分词）

6. 定语

定语指修饰或限制名词或代词的词、词组或句子。可以担任定语的有形容词、代词、名词、数词、名词所有格、副词、不定式、分词和分词短语、介词短语及从句等。定语的位置很灵活,凡有名词和代词的地方都可以有定语。例如:

Ai Yanling is a chemistry teacher. 艾艳林是一名化学老师。（定语为名词）

He is our friend. 他是我们的朋友。（定语为代词）

We belong to the third world. 我们属于第三世界。（定语为数词）

He was advised to teach the lazy boy a lesson. 他被建议给这个懒男孩一个教训。（定语为形容词）

The man over there is my old friend. 在那边的那个男的是我的老朋友。（定语为副词）

The woman with a baby in her arms is my sister. 那个怀里抱着孩子的女的是我姐姐。（定语为介词）

The boys playing football are in Class 2. 那个踢足球的男孩在二班。（定语为现在分词）

The trees planted last year are growing well now. 去年种的那棵树现在长得很好。（定语为过去分词）

I have an idea to do it well. 我有办法把它做好。（定语为不定式）

You should do everything that I do. 你应该做我做的所有事。（定语为从句）

7. 状语

状语用于修饰动词、形容词、副词或整个句子。状语一般由副词、介词短语、分词和分词短语、不定式或相当于副词的词或短语来担当,其一般放在句末,但也可放在句首或句中用来修饰动词、形容词、副词或句子,表示时间、地点、原因、目的、结果、程度、条件、方式和让步。例如:

I will go there tomorrow. 我明天去那儿。（表示时间）

The meeting will be held in the meeting room. 会议将在会议室举行。（表示地点）

The meat went bad because of the hot weather. 因为天气热,肉变坏了。（表示原因）

He studies hard to learn English well. 他努力把英语学好。（表示目的）

He didn't study hard so that he failed in the exam. 他学习不努力，结果考试不及格。（表示结果）

I like some of you very much. 我很喜欢你们中的一些人。（表示程度）

If you study hard, you will pass the exam. 如果你努力学习，你就会通过考试。（表示条件）

He goes to school by bike. 他骑车去学校。（表示方法）

Though he is young, he can do it well. 虽然他很年轻，但他能做好。（表示让步）

二、英语基本句型结构

英语中千变万化的句子归根结底都是由以下五种基本句型组合、扩展、变化而来的。

1. subject（主语）+verb（谓语）

这种句型中的动词大多是不及物动词。所谓不及物动词。就是这种动词后不可以直接接宾语。常见的动词如：work, sing, swim, fish, jump, arrive, come, die, disappear, cry, happen 等。例如：

Li Ming works very hard. 李明学习很努力。

The accident happened yesterday afternoon. 事故是昨天下午发生的。

2. subject（主语）+link. v（系动词）+predicate（表语）

这种句型主要用来表示主语的特点、身份等。其系动词一般可分为下列三类。

（1）be 动词类：am、is、are、was、were。

（2）感官动词类：look、sound、smell、taste、feel 等。例如：

This kind of food tastes delicious. 这种食物吃起来很可口。

He looked worried just now. 刚才他看上去有些焦急。

（3）表示变化。这类系动词有 become、turn、get、grow、go 等。例如：

Spring comes. It is getting warmer and warmer. 春天到了，天气变得越来越暖和。

The tree has grown much taller than before. 这棵树比以前长得高多了。

3. subject（主语）+verb（谓语）+object（宾语）

这种句型中的动词一般为及物动词。所谓及物动词，就是这种动词后可以直接接宾语，其宾语通常由名词、代词、动词不定式、动名词或从句等来充当。例如：

He took his bag and left. 他拿着书包离开了。（名词）

Li Lei always helps me when I have difficulties. 当我遇到困难时，李雷总能给我帮助。（代词）

She plans to travel in the coming May Day. 她打算在即将到来的"五一"外出旅游。（不定式）

I don't know what I should do next. 我不知道下一步该干什么。（从句）

> **注 意**
>
> 英语中的许多动词既是及物动词，又是不及物动词。

4. subject（主语）+verb（谓语）+indirect object（间接宾语）+direct object（直接宾语）

这种句型中，直接宾语为主要宾语，表示动作是对谁做的或为谁做的，在句中不可或缺，常常由表示"物"的名词来充当；间接宾语也被称为第二宾语，去掉之后，对整个句子的影响不大，多由指"人"的名词或代词承担。引导这类双宾语的常见动词有 buy、pass、lend、give、tell、teach、show、bring、send 等。例如：

　　Her father bought her a dictionary as a birthday present. 她爸爸给她买了一本词典作为生日礼物。

　　The old man always tells the children stories about the heroes in the Long March. 老人经常给孩子们讲述长征途中那些英雄的故事。

　　5. subject（主语）+verb（动词）+object（宾语）+complement（补语）

　　这种句型中的"宾语+补语"统称为复合宾语。常见的动词有：tell、ask、advise、help、want、would like、order、force、allow 等。例如：

　　You should keep the room clean and tidy. 你应该让屋子保持干净整洁。（形容词）

　　We made him our monitor. 我们选他当班长。（名词）

　　His father told him not to play in the street. 他父亲告诉他不要在街上玩。（不定式）

　　My father likes to watch the boys playing basketball. 我的父亲喜欢看男孩打篮球。（现在分词）

　　Yesterday I had a picture taken with two Americans. 昨天我和两个美国人合影了。（过去分词）

专项练习

（一）指出下列句子中划线部分的句子成分

1. We always work hard at English.
　　A　B　　C　　D　　E

2. He said he didn't come.
　　A　B　　C　　D

3. They love each other.
　　A　　B　　C

4. What did you buy?
　　A　　B　C　D

5. She watched her daughter playing the piano.
　　A　　B　　　C　　C　　　　E

6. Your job today is to help the old.
　　A　　B　　C　　D

7. Speaking doesn't mean doing.
　　A　　B　　C

8. By the time I got to the station, the train had left.
　　　　　　A　　　　　　　　B　　　C

9. The children bought their parents a car for the 25th anniversary of their marriage.
　　A　　　B　　　C　　　D　　　　E

10. It takes me an hour to get there.
　　 A　 B　　C　　 D　　　　E

（二）指出下面句子分别属于哪种句型

（1）I will spend this summer holiday in the countryside.

（2）In the modern city, there are some problems, such as air pollution, crowdness and noise.

（3）In the countryside I can enjoy a comfortable and quiet life.

（4）There, the air is fresh and the water is clean.

（5）I can hear birds singing in the green trees.

（6）I can also go boating, fishing, and swimming in the lake.

（7）All this will be interesting and good for my health.

（8）So I want to go to the countryside for a change.

1. subject（主语）+verb（谓语）_____
2. subject（主语）+verb（谓语）+object（宾语）_____
3. subject（主语）+link. v（系动词）+predicate（表语）_____
4. subject（主语）+verb（谓语）+indirect object（间接宾语）+direct object（直接宾语）____
5. subject（主语）+verb（谓语）+object（宾语）+complement（补语）_____
6. There be 句型_____

（三）翻译下列句子

1. 基本句型一：主语+不及物动词（subject+verb）

(1) 他昨天早上起床很晚。
_____

(2) 那天晚上我们谈了很多。
_____

(3) 会议将持续两个小时。
_____

2. 基本句型二：主语+及物动词+宾语（subject+verb+object）

(1) 昨晚我写了一封信。
_____

(2) 我父亲能流利地说英语。(fluently)
_____

(3) 你介意我开窗户吗？
_____

(4) 你们必须在两周之内看完那些书。
_____

(5) 他指出我的作文中的错误。(point out, composition)
_____

3. 基本句型三：主语+系动词+表语（subejct+link. v+predicate）

(1) 我的兄弟都是大学生。

_____

(2) 这本书是关于美国历史的书。

_____

(3) 她的工作是在幼儿园里照看儿童。（nursery）

_____

(4) 他失业了。

_____

(5) 树叶已经变黄了。

_____

4. 基本句型四：主语+及物动词+间接宾语+直接宾语（subject+verb+indirect object+direct object）

(1) 奶奶昨晚给我们讲了一个有趣的故事。

_____

(2) 请把那本字典递给我好吗？（dictionary）

_____

(3) 我父亲已经给我买了一辆新自行车。

_____

(4) 我替你叫辆出租车好吗？

_____

(5) 这个学期我已经给父母写过三封信了。

_____

5. 基本句型五：主语+及物动词+宾语+宾语补足语（subject+verb+object+complement）

(1) 我们大家都认为他是诚实的。（consider）

_____

(2) 我们把小偷释放了。（set…free）

_____

(3) 他叫我们参加做游戏。

_____

(4) 我要你把真相告诉我。

_____

(5) 每天早晨，我们都听到他大声朗读英语。

_____

第二节 陈述句、疑问句、祈使句和感叹句

句子按使用目的可分为陈述句、疑问句、祈使句和感叹句。

一、陈述句（declarative sentences）

陈述句用于说明一个事实或陈述一种看法。例如：
Light travels faster than sound. 光比声速度快。（说明事实）
The film is rather boring. 这部电影很乏味。（说明看法）
It being raining heavily, the outing had to be put off. 雨下得很大，郊游不得不推迟。
I was the only person in my office who was invited. 我是我们办公室唯一被邀请的人。

二、疑问句（interrogative sentences）

疑问句用于提出问题。有以下四种。

1. 一般疑问句（general questions）

一般疑问句以一个助动词、情态动词、be 动词或 have 开头。回答一般用 yes 或 no，间或用 sure、certainly、of course、perhaps 等回答。例如：
——Did you have a good time at the party? 晚会上玩得好吗？
——Yes, we enjoyed every minute. 是的，我们一直玩得很好。
——Do you mind my smoking here? 我在这里吸烟你介意吗？
——Not at all, please go ahead. 不介意，请吸吧。
——Can you finish the work in time? 你能及时完成工作吗？

2. 特殊疑问句（w questions；h questions）

特殊疑问句由"疑问代词或疑问副词+一般疑问句"构成，句子要用倒装语序。特殊疑问句直接回答。注意 how many、how much、how often、how old、how long、what、what time、what day、what colour、which、when、who、whose 等疑问词的用法。例如：
——What are you going to do tomorrow? 你明天干什么？
——I am going to see a friend in hospital. 我准备去看一个住院的朋友。
——How soon will you finish writing the book? 还有多久才能写完这本书？
——In a year. 一年以后。

3. 选择疑问句（alternative questions）

选择疑问句就是在一般疑问句后用 or 连接一个选择部分。选择疑问句回答较灵活，可以任选其一回答，可以用 either（两者中的任何一个）回答，可以用 both（两者都）回答，还可以用 neither（两者都不）回答。例如：
——Which do you like, tea or coffee? 你喜欢喝什么？茶还是咖啡？
——Tea, please. 喝茶。
——Do you like the red one or the blue one? 你喜欢红色的还是蓝色的？

——Either will do. 哪一个都行。

4. 反意疑问句(tag questions)

在陈述句之后附上一个简短问句，对陈述句所叙述的事实提出相反的疑问，这种疑问句称为反意疑问句。如果前面陈述句部分是肯定式，后面问句部分一般用否定式；如果前一部分是否定式，后一部分一般用肯定式。前后两部分在人称、数及时态上通常保持一致。

(1) 前半部分肯定，后半部分否定。回答和一般问句相同。例如：

——You are going to Xi'an, aren't you? 你准备去西安，是吗？

——Yes, I am. 是的。

——He has finished the work, hasn't he? 他已经把工作做完了，是吗？

——No, he hasn't. 不，还没有。

(2) 前半部分否定，后半部分肯定。回答可以根据实际情况，肯定就用 Yes，否定就用 No；或前后一致原则，即前面用了 Yes，后边不能加 not，前面用了 No，则后边必须加 not。例如：

——He didn't buy that PC computer, did he? 他没有买那台个人电脑，是吗？

——No, he didn't. 是的，没有买。

——You have no classes tomorrow, do you? 你们明天不上课，是吗？

——Yes, we do. 不，我们上课。

> **注 意**
>
> 关于反意疑问句的几个问题：
>
> (1)如果陈述部分含有否定词 never、nothing、rarely、seldom、hardly、few、little 等，疑问部分用肯定形式。例如：
>
> He said nothing about the accident, did he? 关于那个事故他什么也没说，是吗？
>
> You have never been abroad, have you? 你从来没出过国，是吗？
>
> (2)如果陈述部分的主语是 everyone、someone、anyone、no one、everything、something、anything 等不定代词，疑问部分的主语用 they。例如：
>
> Everything goes very smoothly, don't they? 一切进展得很顺利，是吗？
>
> Everyone is invited to the party, aren't they? 每个人都被邀请参加晚会，是吗？
>
> (3)当陈述部分为"I'm+表语"时，疑问部分用 aren't I。例如：
>
> I am your husband, aren't I? 我是你丈夫，不是吗？
>
> I am a student, aren't I? 我是学生，不是吗？
>
> (4)在 think、suppose、believe 构成的否定句中，当主句主语是第一人称时，反意疑问句根据宾语从句改写；当主句主语是第二、第三人称时，其后的简短问句则应与主句相一致(此时否定只看主句，与从句无关)。例如：
>
> Your sister supposes she needs no help, doesn't she? 你姐姐认为她不需要帮助，是吗？
>
> I don't think he will come this afternoon, will he? 我想下午他不会来，他会吗？
>
> He doesn't believe I can do the work, does he? 他相信我做不了那项工作，是吗？

(5)在使用祈使句询问对方意向时，反问部分的主语和实际主语相一致，并用 shall I/we，或 will you。例如：

Let's go for a walk, shall we? 我们去散步，好吗？

Please don't do that again, will you? 别再那样做了，好吗？

但：

Let us discuss the problem further, will you? 咱们把这个问题再讨论一下，好吗？

Let me carry the box, will you? 让我来拿箱子，行吗？

(6) must 表示对现在情况的推测时，疑问部分助动词用一般现在时。表示对过去情况的推测时，如果有表示过去的时间状语，疑问部分助动词用过去式；如果没有表示过去的时间状语，疑问部分用完成式反问。例如：

He must be in the classroom, isn't he? 他肯定在教室，是吗？

Judging from her clothes, she must have a rich father, doesn't she? 从她的衣着判断，她肯定有一个富有的父亲，是吗？

The ground is wet, it must have rained last night, didn't it? 地面很湿，昨晚肯定下雨了，是吗？

The student must have finished his homework, hasn't he? 那个学生肯定已经做完了作业，是吗？

(7)陈述部分谓语动词为 used to do 时，其疑问部分用 didn't 或 usedn't。例如：

You used to be a student, usedn't/didn't you? 你过去是学生，是吗？

There used to be a temple on the top of the hill, usedn't/didn't there? 山顶过去有一座庙，是吗？

(8)陈述部分谓语为 ought to do 时，疑问部分用"oughtn't＋主语"或"shouldn't＋主语"。例如：

You ought to make a rule and read one serious book a week, shouldn't you? 你应该定个规则，每星期看一本严肃主题的书，是吗？

You oughtn't to have spoken to her in that way, ought you? 你本不该那样对她讲话，是吗？

(9) had better 反问用"hadn't＋主语"，"would rather"和"would like"反问用"wouldn't＋主语"。例如：

You'd better have a rest, hadn't you? 你最好休息一下，好吗？

He'd like to go with us, wouldn't he? 他愿意和我们一起去，是吗？

(10) mustn't 表"禁止"时，反问用 must；must 表示"有必要"时，反问用 needn't。例如：

You must go home right now, needn't you? 你必须回家，是吗？

You mustn't walk on grass, must you? 你不该在草坪上走，是吗？

You are a student, aren't you? 你是学生，对吗？

三、祈使句（imperative sentences）

祁使句用于提出请求，建议或发出命令。

(1)说话对象是第二人称时，多省略主语，但有时可加主语 you。肯定形式用动词原形开头，否定形式用"Don't(Never)＋动词原形"。例如：

Do what the teacher asks you to do. 按照老师要求的去做。

Never judge from appearances. 不要以貌取人。

(2)说话对象是第一、第三人称时。

肯定：Let+宾语+动词原形。

否定：Don't let+宾语+动词原形或Let+宾语+not+动词原形。

例如：

Let him be here by ten o'clock. 让他10点到这儿。

Don't let me have to speak to you again. 别让我再和你说话。

(3)肯定的祈使句前加do，用以加强语气。例如：

Do clean and tidy the classroom every day. 一定要每天打扫和整理教室。

Do be sure to write to me soon. 请一定给我来信。

四、感叹句（exclamatory sentences）

感叹句用于表示说话人惊奇、喜悦、愤怒等情绪。感叹句型如下。

1. What+名词！

What fun！ 多有趣！

What nonsense！ 胡说八道！

2. What+(a/an)+形容词+名词+主语+谓语！

如果名词为可数名词单数，加不定冠词；如果名词为复数或不可数名词，不加不定冠词。例如：

What a good heart you have！ 你的心多好啊！

What bad weather it is today！ 今天天气多糟糕！

3. How+形容词+a/an+名词单数+主语+谓语！

此句型只可用于名词为可数名词单数时。例如：

How lovely a day it is today！ 今天天气多好！

How good a book this is！ 这本书多好！

4. How+形容词或副词+主语+谓语！

How kind you are as to help me with my English！ 你的心多好，帮我学英语！

How fast he runs in the relay race！ 他在接力赛中跑得多快！

5. How+主语+谓语！

How time flies！ 时光飞逝！

How they love each other, the members of this family！ 这一家人多么的互相爱护呀！

专项练习

（一）句型转换

1. He does his homework on Sunday.（改为否定句）

   He_____his homework on Sunday.

2. Dick is watching TV now.（用 sometimes 改写）
Dick ＿＿＿＿＿＿ sometimes.
3. He watches TV three times a week.（就画线部分提问）
＿＿＿＿＿＿ does he watch TV?
4. What is the weather like in Beijing?（改为同义句）
＿＿＿＿＿＿ the weather in Beijing?
5. My father would like to go out for a walk.（就画线部分提问）
Would your father like ＿＿＿＿＿＿?
6. I think I can mend it.（改为否定句）
I ＿＿＿ think I ＿＿＿ mend it.
7. The blue bag is the biggest of all.（就画线部分提问）
＿＿＿＿＿＿ is the biggest of all?
8. Tom is a good student. Mary is a good student, too.（合并为一句）
＿＿＿ Tom ＿＿＿ Mary ＿＿＿ good students.
9. There is little milk in the glass.（改为反意疑问句）
There is little milk in the glass, ＿＿＿＿＿＿?
10. You must put these things into the blender.（改为祈使句）
＿＿＿＿＿＿＿＿＿＿＿＿＿＿＿＿＿＿＿＿＿＿.
11. Chi wants to be an actor.（就画线部分提问）
＿＿＿＿＿ Chi ＿＿＿ to be?
12. My uncle is a reporter.（就画线部分提问）
＿＿＿＿＿＿ your uncle?
13. I think Eliza is the best performer.（就画线部分提问）
＿＿＿＿＿＿ is the best performer?
14. Tina liked playing tennis.（用 play basketball 改选择疑问句）
＿＿＿ Tina like ＿＿＿ tennis ＿＿＿＿＿＿?
15. Jim has stayed in the college for five years.（就画线部分提问）
＿＿＿＿＿＿ has Jim stayed in the college?
16. The twin brothers get on very well.（就画线部分提问）
＿＿＿＿＿＿ the twin brothers get on?
17. My foreign friends will arrive in half an hour.（就画线部分提问）
＿＿＿＿＿＿ will your foreign friends arrive?
18. The car near the river is mine.（就画线部分提问）
＿＿＿＿＿＿ is yours?
19. It's very wet and hot today.（就画线部分提问）
＿＿＿＿ the weather ＿＿＿＿ today?
20. He is looking for a pair of black shoes.（就画线部分提问）
＿＿＿＿ is he ＿＿＿＿?

(二)填入适当的词完成下列感叹句

1. _____ difficult homework we had yesterday!
2. _____ cute dog it is!
3. _____ interesting the story is!
4. _____ bad the weather in England is!
5. _____ honest boy Tom is!
6. _____ tasty smell the cake gave off!
7. _____ good time we had on the beach yesterday!
8. _____ exciting news you've brought us!
9. _____ cool your new car is!
10. _____ scary these tigers are!

(三)单项选择

1. _____ fast the boy ran!
   A. How   B. How an   C. What   D. What an

2. _____ well you sing but _____ badly he dances!
   A. How; how   B. What; what   C. How; what   D. What; how

3. _____ delicious the soup is! I'd like some more.
   A. How   B. How an   C. What   D. What an

4. _____ fools they were! They believed what the man said.
   A. How   B. How an   C. What   D. What an

5. _____ foolish they were! They believed what the man said.
   A. How   B. How an   C. What   D. What an

6. _____ difficult questions they are! I can't answer them.
   A. How   B. How an   C. What   D. What an

7. I miss my friend very much. _____ I want to see her!
   A. How   B. How an   C. What   D. What an

8. _____ lovely weather we are having these days!
   A. How   B. How an   C. What   D. What an

9. _____ beautiful your new dress is!
   A. How   B. How an   C. What   D. What an

10. _____ interesting work it is to teach children!
    A. How   B. How an   C. What   D. What an

第三节 并列句

并列句(compound sentences)是由两个或多个简单句连接而成的。其中的各个简单句并列平行，同等重要，相互之间没有从属关系，能够独立成句。它们之间要用连词连接。并列连词有 and、or、but、both…and、neither…nor、either…or、not only…but also 等。例如：

We love peace but we are not afraid of war. 我们热爱和平但我们并不害怕战争。
Not only does she sing well, but she dances well. 她不仅歌唱得好，而且舞也跳得好。

并列句可分为 3 种：

(1)表示相同关系，用连词或逗号、分号连接构成并列句。常用连词有：and、both…and、not only…but also、neither…nor。例如：

Susan not only runs fast, but also jumps high. 苏姗不但跑得快，而且跳得高。
I could neither swim nor skate. 我既不会游泳，也不会滑冰。

(2)表示转折关系。常用连词有：although、but、however、still、yet、while、or 等。例如：

It was late at night, but he went on doing his homework. 夜已深了，但是他还在继续做作业。
She was busy cooking while they were watching TV. 她忙着做饭，而他们却在看电视。
The film is not perfect, still, it's good. 这部影片虽然不是无可挑剔，但还是好的。

(3)表示选择关系。常用连词为：or、either…or。例如：

The teacher wanted to see either his father or mother. 老师要见一下他的父亲或是母亲。
Either this road or that one can lead you to that hospital. 这条路或那条路都通往那家医院。
Hurry up, or you'll miss the train. 赶紧，否则你赶不上火车了。

专项练习

(一)从下列所给的并列词中选出正确的一个。

and   or   so   but   because   though

1. Open the door _____ let the cool air in.

2. There are few new words in the article, _____ we couldn't understand it.

3. I like beef, _____ my father doesn't like it.

4. We finished the homework quickly _____ it was very easy.

5. Be more careful, _____ you'll have an accident.

6. It's raining very hard, _____ we'd better stay here.

7. Claire wanted to buy a car, _____ he didn't have enough money.

8. He's always very careful, _____ he never makes any mistakes.

9. Take a raincoat with you, _____ you'll get wet.

10. He kept on working outside, _____ it was colder and colder.

(二)单项选择

1. Stand over there, _____ you can see the pandas better.

A. and   B. or   C. but   D. so

2. The harder you _____, the better progress you _____.

A. will work   B. work; have made

C. work; will make   D. will work; make

3. It was raining heavily, _____ we decided to stay at home and watch TV.

A. but   B. or   C. because   D. so

4. It was very windy and cold, _____ they were still working hard in the field.

A. as   B. till   C. but   D. and

5. ——Will you come _____ have a drink with me?

——I'd love to, _____ I'm too busy these days.

A. and, or   B. and, but   C. or, but   D. or, and

6. Everyone tells me I'm a good speaker, _____ I really don't like speaking in public.

A. and   B. but   C. so   D. or

7. Help others whenever you can _____ you'll make the world a nicer place to live.

A. and   B. but   C. or   D. unless

8. ——Could you tell me _____, Mary?

——Of course. Go straight, and you'll see it on your right.

A. where is the cinema   B. where the cinema is

C. where was the cinema   D. where the cinema was

9. ——Finish your homework, _____ you can't go out to play.

——All right, Daddy.

A. but   B. till   C. and   D. or

10. Study hard, _____ you won't pass the exam.

A. or   B. and   C. but   D. though

11. ——How was your school trip?

——It was great, _____ the weather was much too hot.

A. and   B. but   C. so   D. because

12. Stop smoking, _____ your health will get worse soon.

A. and   B. or   C. but   D. so

13. Lucy enjoys playing computer games, but she can't _____ lots of time _____ that.

A. take; doing   B. spend; doing

C. spend; on doing   D. take; to do

14. Joy, what happened to the plane? It _____ at midnight, but it didn't land on the airport on time.

A. took off   B. put off   C. turned off   D. got off

15. The hotel is almost finished, but it _____ needs one or two weeks to get ready for guests.

A. only　　　　B. also　　　　C. even　　　　D. still

16. Tom's a taxi driver, _____ he really wants to be a singer.
A. or　　　　B. and　　　　C. so　　　　D. but

17. Nancy quickly _____ the door and put down her school things.
A. opens　　　B. opened　　　C. has opened　　D. is opening

18. Animals are part of nature. _____ should be well prepared.
A. and　　　　B. or　　　　C. but　　　　D. while

19. Tom misses his brother very much and he is looking forward _____ him.
A. to hear from　B. hearing from　C. to hearing from　D. heard from

20. ——My favorite subject is English. But I don't like Math.
——I like English _____ and I don't like Math _____.
A. too; too　　B. either; either　　C. too; either　　D. either; too

第四节　名词性从句

在句子中起名词作用的句子称为名词性从句(noun clauses)。名词性从句相当于名词词组，它在复合句中能担任主语、宾语、表语、同位语、介词宾语等。因此，根据在句中不同的语法功能，名词性从句又可分别称为主语从句、宾语从句、表语从句和同位语从句。

注　意

学习名词性从句须掌握以下要点：
(1)在名词性从句中，从句都用陈述语序。
(2)引导名词性从句的词称为引导词。引导词可以分为以下几类：
①从属连词that(用于表示肯定含义)、whether、if(表示疑问，意思是"是否")，这3个词只起连接作用，不充当从句中的任何成分，除宾语从句that可省略外，这些词均不可省略。
②连接代词有who、whom、whose、what、which、whoever、whatever、whichever等。这些词在从句中既起连接作用，又充当从句中的成分，如主语、宾语、表语、补语，且不可省略。
③连接副词有when、where、why、how、wherever、however等。它们既起连词作用，本身又作从句中的状语。

一、主语从句

在复合句中充当主语的从句称为主语从句。例如：
What he wants to tell us is not clear. 他要跟我们说什么，还不清楚。
Who will win the match is still unknown. 谁能赢得这场比赛还不得而知。
Where the English evening will be held has not yet been announced. 英语晚会将在哪里举

行还没有宣布。

有时为避免句子头重脚轻，常用形式主语 it 代替主语从句放于句首，而把主语从句置于句末。主语从句后的谓语动词一般用单数形式。常用句型如下：

It+be+名词+that 从句

It+be+形容词+that 从句

It+be+动词的过去分词+that 从句

It+不及物动词+that 从句

> **注 意**
>
> 在主语从句中用来表示惊奇、不相信、惋惜、理应如此等语气时，谓语动词要用虚拟语气"(should)+do"。常用的句型有：
>
> It is necessary (important, natural, strange, etc.) that…
>
> It is suggested (requested, proposed, desired, etc.) that…
>
> 例如：
>
> It is impossible that he should go home. 他不可能会回家去。
>
> It is necessary that I should return it right now. 我有必要马上把它还回去。
>
> It is requested that a vote (should) be taken. 建议付诸表决。
>
> It is settled that you (should) leave us, then? 那么你肯定要离开我们？

二、宾语从句

在复合句中用作宾语的从句称为宾语从句，在句中可以作谓语动词或介词及非谓语动词的宾语。引导宾语从句的关联词与引导主语从句、表语从句的关联词大致一样。由连接词 that 引导宾语从句时，that 在句中不担任任何成分，在口语或非正式的文体中常被省去，但如果从句是并列句，第二个分句前的 that 不可省。例如：

He has told me that he will go to Shanghai tomorrow. 他告诉我他明天要去上海。

We must never think (that) we are good in everything while others are good in nothing. 我们绝不能认为自己什么都好，别人什么都不好。

> **注 意**
>
> (1) 在 demand、order、suggest、decide、insist、desire、request、command、doubt 等表示要求、命令、建议、决定等意义的动词后，宾语从句常用"(should)+动词原形"。例如：
>
> I insist that she (should) do her work alone. 我坚持要她独立工作。
>
> The commander ordered that troops (should) set off at once. 司令员命令部队马上出发。
>
> (2) 用 whether 或 if 引导的宾语从句，其主语和谓语的顺序不能颠倒，仍保持陈述句语序。此外，whether 与 if 在表示"是否"的意思时，在下列情况下一般只能用 whether，不用 if：

①引导主语从句并在句首时；
②引导表语从句时；
③引导从句作介词宾语时；
④从句后有"or not"时；
⑤后接动词不定式时。
(3) 宾语从句中的时态呼应。
①当主句动词是现在时，从句根据自身的句子情况，而使用不同时态。例如：
I know that he studies English every day. 我知道他每天都学习英语。
I know that he studied English last term. 我知道他上学期学过英语。
I know (that) he will study English next year. 我知道他明年将学习英语。
I know (that) he has studied English since 1998. 我知道他从1998年开始学习英语。
②当主句动词是过去时(could、would除外)，从句则要用相应的过去时，如一般过去时、过去进行时、过去将来时等；当从句表示的是客观真理、科学原理、自然现象等，则从句仍用现在时。例如：
We learnt from his letter that he was in Spain. 我们从他的信得知他在西班牙。
He asked me if I was reading the story The Old Man and the Sea when he was in. 他问我当他在的时候我是否在读《老人与海》的故事。
The teacher told us that Tom had left us for America. 老师告诉我们汤姆已经离开我们去美国了。
The teacher told us that the earth is round. 老师告诉我们地球是圆的。
Father told me that practice makes perfect. 父亲告诉我熟能生巧。

三、表语从句

在句中作表语的从句称为表语从句。表语从句位于连系动词后。其基本结构为：主语+系动词+表语从句。例如：
The fact is that we have lost the game. 事实是我们已经输了这场比赛。
That's just what I want. 这正是我想要的。
This is where our problem lies. 这就是我们的问题所在。
That is why he didn't come to the meeting. 那就是他为什么不到会的原因。

whether 可引导表语从句，但与之同义的 if 却通常不用于引导表语从句。

四、同位语从句

同位语从句是对抽象名词进行说明解释。同位语从句的特点是由一个抽象名词+that 从句构成，引导词一般是 that，而且 that 在从句中不充当任何成分。这些抽象名词有 news、idea、fact、doubt、evidence、promise、rumor、hope、truth、belief、message 等。例如：

The news that our football team at last defeated Korea made the fans wild with joy. 我们足球队最终击败韩国队的消息使球迷们欣喜若狂。

I had no idea that you were here. 我不知道你在这里。

She told us her hope that she would become a pianist. 她告诉我们她希望成为钢琴家。

He made a promise that he would never come late. 他承诺他不会再迟到。

专项练习

（一）判断下列各句哪句含有名词性从句，并指出是什么从句

1. China is no longer what it used to be.
2. The truth that the earth turn around the sun is known to all.
3. It was snowing when he arrived at the station.
4. How he persuaded the manager to change the plan is interesting to us all.
5. The news that they had won the game soon spread over the whole school.
6. The news that you told me yesterday was really disappointing.
7. That is where Lu Xun used to live.
8. He spoke as if he understood what he was talking about.
9. Do you remember the teacher who taught us English at middle school?
10. I wonder why she refused my invitation.

（二）用适当的连词填空

1. I can't decide _____ dictionary I should buy.
2. That's _____ he refused my invitation.
3. I am very interested in _____ he has improved his pronunciation in such a short time.
4. _____ we need is more time.
5. The fact _____ she had not said anything at the meeting surprised everybody.
6. _____ and _____ they will meet has not been decided yet.
7. Please tell me _____ you are waiting for.
8. Is that _____ you are looking for?
9. Would you please tell me _____ the nearest post office is?
10. I don't know _____ he will agree to the plan or not.

（三）单项选择

1. _____ makes mistakes must correct them.
   A. What   B. That   C. Whoever   D. Whatever

2. Tell me _____ is on your mind.
   A. that   B. what   C. which   D. why

3. We must stick to _____ we have agreed on.

A. what   B. that   C. /   D. how

4. Let me see _____.

A. that can I repair the radio   B. whether I can repair the radio

C. I can repair the radio   D. whether can I repair the radio

5. Keep in mind _____.

A. that the teacher said   B. what did the teacher say

C. that did the teacher say   D. what the teacher said

6. Could you advise me _____?

A. which book should I read first   B. what book should I read first

C. that book I should read first   D. which book I should read first

7. He was criticized for _____.

A. he has done it   B. what he had done

C. what had he done   D. that he had done it

8. Would you kindly tell me _____?

A. how can I get to the Beijing Railway Station

B. how I can get to the Beijing Railway Station

C. where can I get to the Beijing Railway Station

D. whether can I get to the Beijing Railway Station

9. Mrs. Smith was very much impressed by _____.

A. what had she seen in China   B. that she had seen in China

C. what she had seen in China   D. which had she seen in China

10. We took it for granted _____.

A. that they were not coming   B. that were they not coming

C. they were coming not   D. were they not coining

11. I really don't know _____.

A. I should do next   B. what should I do next

C. what I should do next   D. how I should do next

12. I'm afraid _____.

A. the little girl will have to be operated on

B. that will the little girl have to operate on

C. the little girl will have to operate on

D. that will the little girl have to be operated on

13. She walked up to _____.

A. where did I stand   B. where I stood

C. I stood there   D. where I stood there

14. Can you tell me _____?

A. who is that gentleman   B. that gentleman is who

C. who that gentleman is   D. whom. is that gentleman

15. We'll give you _____.

   A. that do you need   B. what do you need

   C. whatever you need   D. whether do you need

16. They want us to know _____ to help us.

   A. what can they   B. what they can   C. how they can   D. how can they

17. Did you know _____?

   A. who he was looking after   B. who was he looking for

   C. who he is looking for   D. who he is looking after

18. Did she say anything about _____?

   A. that the work was to be done   B. how was the work to be done

   C. that was the work to be done   D. how the work was to be done

19. He was never satisfied with _____.

   A. what she had achieved   B. had what she achieved

   C. she had achieved   D. that she achieved

20. These photographs will show you _____.

   A. what does our village look like   B. what our village looks like

   C. how does our village look like   D. how our village looks like

21. Peter insisted _____ he pay the bill.

   A. on that   B. what   C. that   D. on which

22. He asked me _____ with me.

   A. what the matter is   B. what the mater was

   C. what's the matter   D. what was the matter

23. Excuse me would you please tell me _____.

   A. when the sports meet is taken place

   B. when is the sports meet going to be held

   C. when is the sports meet to begin

   D. when the sports meet is to take place

24. 1 will describe to you _____ I saw when there.

   A. what   B. that   C. which   D. /

25. From _____ I should say he is a good worker.

   A. what 1 know of him   B. that I do know of him

   C. what do I know of him   D. that do I know of him

第五节 定语从句

定语从句在复合句中作定语,用来修饰一个名词、名词词组或者代词。被修饰的名词、名词词组或代词称为先行词,在先行词和定语从句之间起连接作用的词称为引导词。

定语从句中的谓语动词必须在人称和数量上和先行词保持一致。定语从句分为限定性定语从句和非限定性定语从句两种。

一、关系代词引导的定语从句

(1) who 指人,在定语从句中作主语。例如:

The boys who are playing football are from Class One. 正在踢足球的男孩是一班的。

Yesterday I helped an old man who had lost his way. 昨天我帮助了一位迷路的老人。

(2) whom 指人,在定语从句中作宾语,常可省略。例如:

Mr. Liu is the person (whom) you talked about on the bus. 刘先生就是你们在公共汽车上谈论的那个人。

The professor (whom) you are waiting for has come. 你正在等的教授已经来了。

The girl (whom) the teacher often praises is our monitor. 老师经常表扬的那个女孩是我们的班长。

> **注 意**
>
> 关系代词 whom 在口语或非正式文体中常可用 who 来代替,也可省略。例如:
> The man (whom/who) you met just now is my old friend. 你刚才见到的那个人是我的老朋友。

(3) which 指物,在定语从句中作主语或宾语。作宾语时常可省略。例如:

Football is a game which is liked by most boys. 足球是大多数男孩所喜欢的运动。

The factory which makes computers is far away from here. 制造计算机的那家公司离这儿很远。

This is the pen (which) he bought yesterday. 这是他昨天买的钢笔。

(4) That 指人时,相当于 who 或 whom;指物时,相当于 which。在定语从句中作主语或宾语,作宾语时常可省略。例如:

The number of people that/who come to visit this city each year reaches one million. 每年来参观这座城市的人数达一百万。

Where is the man that/whom I saw this morning? 我今天早上看到的那个人在哪儿?

The person that/whom you introduced to me is very kind. 你介绍给我的那个人很友好。

The season that/which comes after spring is summer. 春季后面的季节是夏季。

(5) Whose 通常指人,也可指物,在定语从句中作定语。例如:

I visited a scientist whose name is known all over the country. 我拜访了一个全国知名的科学家。

He has a friend whose father is a doctor. 他有一个爸爸当医生的朋友。

I once lived in the house whose roof has fallen in. 我曾经住在那幢屋顶已经倒塌了的房子里。

> **注 意**
>
> (1) that 和 which 都可指物,二者常可换用,但下列情况除外。
> ① 只用 that 不用 which 的情况:

当先行词被序数词、最高级、不定代词修饰时。

当先行词既有人又有物时。

当先行词带有 the only、the very、the same、the last、the one 等词时。

当主句中有 who 或 which 时，为避免重复，用 that。

当句子是一个特殊疑问句，且引导词为 which 时，最好用 that。

当前面已有一个定语从句，且连接词为 which 时，宜用 that。

②只用 which 不用 that 的情况：

当主句先行词后有介词时，用 which。例如：

This the one of which I'm speaking. 我说的就是这个。

非限定性定语从句，用 which。

描述句中一般用 which。例如：

Beijing, which was China's capital for more than 800 years. 北京是中国 800 多年的首都。

those+复数名词之后，多用 which。例如：

Shopkeeper want to keep a number of those goods which sell best. 店主想保留一些销售最好的产品。

当前面已有一个定语从句，且连接词为 that 时，宜用 which。

(2) who 和 that 都可指人，但下列情况只用 who 不用 that。

①先行词为 one、ones 或 anyone。例如：

The comrade I want to learn from is the one who studies hard and works hard. 我要学习的同志是一个努力学习、努力工作的同志。

Anyone who breaks the law should be punished. 任何违反法律的人都应受到惩罚。

②先行词为 these 时。例如：

These who are going to Beijing are the best students of our school. 这些将要去北京的学生是我们学校最好的学生。

③在 there be 开头的句子中。例如：

There is a student who wants to see you. 有一个学生想要见你。

④一个句子中带有两个定语从句，其中一个定语从句的关系代词是 that，另一个宜用 who，以免重复。例如：

The student that won the first prize is the monitor who works hard. 获得一等奖的学生是学习努力的班长。

二、关系副词引导的定语从句

(1) when 指时间，在定语从句中作时间状语。例如：

I still remember the day when I first came to this school. 我仍然记得我第一次来到这所学校的那一天。

The time when we got together finally arrived. 我们团聚的时刻终于到了。

October 1, 1949 was the day when the People's Republic of China was founded. 1949 年 10

月1日是中华人民共和国成立的日子。

(2) where 指地点，在定语从句中作地点状语。例如：

Shanghai is the city where I was born. 上海是我出生的城市。

The house where I lived ten years ago has been pulled down. 我十年前住的房子已经被拆掉了。

I visited the farm where a lot of cows were raised. 我参观了那个饲养了许多奶牛的农场。

(3) why 指原因，在定语从句中作原因状语。例如：

Please tell me the reason why you missed the plane. 请告诉我你误机的原因。

The reason why he was punished is unknown to us. 他受惩罚的原因我们都不知道。

I don't know the reason why he looks unhappy today. 我不知道他今天为什么看上去不愉快。

三、"介词+关系代词"引导的定语从句

关系代词在定语从句中作介词宾语时，从句常常由"介词+关系代词"引出。例如：

The school (which/that) he once studied in is very famous. 他曾经就读的学校很有名。

The school in which he once studied is very famous. 他曾经就读过的学校很出名。

This is the boy (whom/who/that) I played tennis with yesterday. 这是昨天和我一起打网球的男孩。

This is the boy with whom I played tennis with yesterday. 这是昨天和我一起打网球的男孩。

四、限定性定语从句

限定性定语从句在句中的主要作用是修饰前面的先行词，使先行词的含义更具体、更明确，并且两者之间紧密联系，无逗号。限制性定语从句不能被省略，否则句意不完整。如果出现关系代词是 that 的情况，that 是可以省略的。例如：

The sports meeting will be held tomorrow when all the things are prepared. 明天所有的事情都准备就绪时，便会举行运动会。

We think about the final exam which (that) will become a standard of scores in the semester. 我们都在想着这学期将会作为评分标准的期末考试。

五、非限定性定语从句

非限定性定语从句在句中的主要作用是既可以修饰先行词，也可以修饰前面的主句。有逗号与前面的先行词隔开。如果将非限制性定语从句省去，主句的意义仍然完整。注意在以下几种情况中不可用 that 作为关系词。

1. 修饰前面的整个主句

What a terrible thing! Mary missed the last bus, which let her late for the class. 太糟糕了！玛丽错过了最后一班公交车，使得她上课迟到。

My cousin failed the examination, which made her pretty sad. 我表妹考试失利，这让她非常难过。

2. 修饰前面的先行词

My friend told me she had a nightmare, which scared her a lot. 我朋友告诉我说，她做了一个令她害怕的噩梦。

试比较：

The old man has a son, who is in the army. （此句中，非限定性定语从句是对先行词 son 进行补充、说明。本句所传达的信息是：这位老人只有一个儿子，他在部队工作。）

The old man has a son who is in the arm. （限定性定语从句要对先行词 son 进行限定、修饰。这样一来，句子所传达的信息就变成了：这位老人有一个儿子在部队工作，还有其他的儿子在干别的工作。）

I have a sister who is a doctor. 我有一个当医生的姐姐。（姐姐不止一个）

I have a sister, who is a doctor. 我有一个姐姐，她是当医生的。（只有一个姐姐）

专项练习

（一）单项选择

1. She heard a terrible noise, _____ brought her heart into her mouth.
   A. it　　　　　B. which　　　　C. this　　　　D. that

2. There are lots of things _____ I need to prepare before the trip.
   A. who　　　　B. that　　　　C. whom　　　　D. whose

3. The weather turned out to be very good, _____ was more than we could expect.
   A. what　　　　B. which　　　　C. that　　　　D. it

4. His English, _____ used to be very poor is now excellent.
   A. which　　　　B. that　　　　C. it　　　　D. whom

5. Some of the roads were flooded, _____ makes our journey more difficult.
   A. that　　　　B. it　　　　C. which　　　　D. who

6. I'll find a nice girl, _____ I want to marry.
   A. who　　　　B. whom　　　　C. that　　　　D. which

7. I'll come at ten, _____ I'll be free.
   A. which　　　　B. that　　　　C. when　　　　D. what

8. The house _____ we live is not big.
   A. in which　　　B. which　　　　C. who　　　　D. that

9. This is the factory _____ I visited yesterday.
   A. that　　　　B. which　　　　C. /　　　　D. where

10. I still remember the days _____ I spent in Beijing.
    A. when　　　　B. what　　　　C. that　　　　D. during

(二)用适当的关系词填空

1. I still remember the night _____ I first came to the house.
2. I'll never forget the day _____ we met each other last week.
3. Mr. Black is going to Beijing in October, _____ is the best season there.
4. I will never forget the days _____ I spent with your family.
5. I'll never forget the last day _____ we spent together.
6. This is the school _____ I used to study.
7. Do you still remember the place _____ we visited last week?
8. Do you still remember the place _____ we visited the painting exhibition?
9. Have you ever been to Hangzhou, _____ is famous for the West Lake?
10. The skirt _____ is made of silk is very expensive. I can't afford it.
11. There are lots of things _____ I need to prepare before the trip.
12. I live in Beijing, _____ is the capital of China.
13. There was a time _____ there were slaves in the USA.
14. It is the third time _____ you have made the same mistake.
15. It was in the street _____ I met John yesterday.
16. It was about 600 years ago _____ the first clock with a face and an hour hand was made.
17. The moment _____ I saw you, I recognized(认出) you.
18. This is the dictionary _____ Mum gave me for my birthday.
19. I like the teacher _____ classes are very interesting and creative.
20. Who is the student _____ was late for school today?

第六节 状语从句

状语从句(adverbial clause)是指句子用作状语时,起副词作用的句子,又称为副词性从句。它可以修饰主句或主句的谓语、非谓语动词、定语、状语。根据其作用一般可分为九大类,分别表示时间、地点、原因、目的、结果、条件、让步、比较和方式。状语从句一般由连词(从属连词)引导,也可以由词组引导。状语从句位于句首或句中时通常用逗号与主句隔开,位于句尾时可以不用逗号隔开。状语从句的关键是要掌握引导不同状语从句的常用连接词和特殊的连接词。

1. 时间状语从句

常用引导词:when、as、while、as soon as、whenever、before、after、since、till、until、once(一旦)等。例如:

As they were picking tea, the girls were singing happily. 女孩子们一边唱歌一边摘茶。
I didn't realize how special my mother was until I became an adult. 直到我成为了一个成年

人，我才意识到我的母亲是多么的特殊。

While John was watching TV, his wife was cooking. 当约翰看电视时，他的妻子正在做饭。

No sooner had I arrived home than it began to rain. 还没等我到家就开始下雨了。

Every time I listen to your advice, I get into trouble. 每当我听取你的建议时，我就会惹上麻烦。

> **注 意**
>
> 时间状语从句中，引导词 while 接的动词是持续性动词，如 drink；when 可以接持续性动词或者瞬间性动词；as 强调主句、从句的动作几乎同时发生。

2. 地点状语从句

常用引导词：where、wherever。例如：

Generally, air will be heavily polluted where there are factories. 一般来说，有工厂的地方空气污染就严重。

Wherever you go, you should work hard. 无论你去哪里，你都应该努力工作。

You should have put the book where you found it. 你应该把书放回原来的地方。

3. 原因状语从句

常用引导词：because、since（既然）、as（因为）、for（由于）、now that（既然、由于）、in that（由于）等。例如：

My friends dislike me because I'm handsome and successful. 我的朋友都不喜欢我，因为我既英俊又成功。

Now that everybody has come, let's begin our conference. 既然每个人都到了，让我们开始我们的会议吧。

The higher income tax is harmful in that it may discourage people from trying to earn more. 更高的收入税是有害的，因为它或许会阻碍人们努力赚钱。

4. 目的状语从句

常用引导词：so that、in order that（为了，以便）、in case（以防，万一）、for fear that（唯恐）、lest（以免，以防）、in the hope that（为了，以便）、for the purpose that（为了……的目的）、to the end that（为……起见）等。例如：

The boss asked the secretary to hurry up with the letters so that he could sign them. 老板要求秘书快写函件以便他能在上面签字。

The teacher raised his voice on purpose that the students in the back could hear more clearly. 为了让后面的学生听得更清楚，老师有意地提高了他的声音。

I've brought some sandwiches in case we get hungry. 我带了些三明治，以防我们肚子饿。

5. 结果状语从句

常用引导词：so that（结果，以致）、so…that（如此……以致）、such…that（如此……以致）。例如：

He got up so early that he caught the first bus. 他很早起床以便赶上第一班公共汽车。

It's such a good chance that we must not miss it. 这是一个好机会，千万不能错过它。
The hall was crowed with people so that they couldn't get in. 大厅里挤满了人，他们进不去。

注 意

(1) such 是形容词，修饰名词或名词词组，故结构为 such+adj.+名词+that clause。
(2) so 是副词，只能修饰形容词或副词，故结构为 so+adj./adv.+that clause。
(3) so 还可以与表示数量的形容词 many、few、much、little 连用，形成固定搭配，结构为 so+many/few+复数名词+that clause；much/little+不可数名词。

6. 条件状语从句

常用引导词：if、unless(除非)、as/so long as(只要)、only if、in case that(如果，万一)、on condition that(如果)等。例如：

We'll start our project if the president agrees. 如果总统同意，我们将开始我们的项目。
You will certainly succeed so long as you keep on trying. 只要你继续努力，你一定会成功的。
Provided that there is no opposition, we shall hold the meeting here. 如果没人反对，我们就在这里开会。

7. 让步状语从句

常用引导词：though(虽然)、although(虽然)、even if、even though(即使)、as(尽管，用在让步状语从句中必须要倒装)、while(一般用在句首)、no matter(how、what、where、when)[不管(怎样、什么、哪里、何时)]、whatever(无论什么)、whoever(无论谁)、however(无论怎样)等。例如：

The old man always enjoys swimming even though the weather is rough. 老人都很喜欢游泳，即使天气很恶劣。
No matter how hard he tried, she could not change her mind. 不论他如何努力，她都不会改变她的主意。
He won't listen whatever you may say. 他不会听你说什么。
Much as I respect him, I can't agree to his proposal. 尽管我很尊敬他，我却不同意他的建议。

8. 比较状语从句

常用引导词：as…as(同级比较)、than(不同程度的比较)、the more … the more(愈……愈)。例如：

She is as bad-tempered as her mother. 她和她妈妈一样脾气很坏。
The house is three times as big as ours. 这房子是我们的三倍大。
The more you exercise, the healthier you will be. 你运动得越多，你就越健康。

9. 方式状语从句

常用引导词：as(像……，如同……)、as if/as though(好像)、the way(……的方式)。例如：

When in Rome, do as the Romans do. 入国问禁，入乡随俗。

She behaved as if she were the boss. 她表现得好像她是老板。

Sometimes we teach our children the way our parents have taught us. 有时，我们用父母教导我们的方式教导我们的孩子。

注 意

(1)在以 when、after、as soon as、until 等引导的时间状语从句以及以 if、unless、as long as(只要)等引导的条件状语从句中，如果主句是一般将来时，则从句用一般现在时代替一般将来时，即"主将从现"。当表示将来完成时的意义时，要用现在完成时来代替将来完成时。例如：

I will go to the cinema as soon as I finish my homework. 我一做完作业就去看电影。

When I grow up, I will join the army. 当我长大了，我要去参军。

We will stay at home if it rains tomorrow. 如果明天下雨了，我们就会待在家。

He won't come here unless he is invited. 除非被邀请，否则他不会到这儿来的。

I shall go to see you when I have finished my homework. 我做完作业后就去看你。

We won't start the work until all the preparations have been made. 直到所有的准备工作都做好了，我们才会开始工作。

(2)because 不与 so 连用，表示"因为……所以"，二者只能选择其一；though(although)不与 but 连用，表示"虽然……但是"，二者只能选择其一。

(3)同一引导词可以引导不同种类的从句，如 where。例如：

You'll find it where it was. 你会找到它的。(地点状语从句)

Tell me the address where he lives. 告诉我他住的地址。(定语从句)

I don't know where he came from. 我不知道他来自哪里。(宾语从句)

Where he has gone is not known yet. 他到哪去了还不知道。(主语从句)

This is where they once lived. 这是他们曾经居住过的地方。(表语从句)

since、as、when 也分别可以引导不同种类的从句。

专项练习

单项选择

1. I'll let you know _____ he comes back.
   A. before   B. because   C. as soon as   D. although

2. It was not _____ he took off his dark glass _____ I realized who he was.
   A. when; that   B. until; when   C. when; then   D. until; that

3. We will work _____ we are needed.
   A. whenever   B. because   C. since   D. wherever

4. Read it aloud _____ the class can hear you.
   A. so that   B. if   C. when   D. although

5. _____ you go, don't forget your people.

A. Whenever　　B. However　　C. Wherever　　D. Whichever

6. It is about ten years _____ I met you last.
A. since　　B. for　　C. when　　D. as

7. They will never succeed, _____ hard they try.
A. because　　B. however　　C. when　　D. since

8. _____ still half drunk, he made his way home.
A. When　　B. Because　　C. Though　　D. As

9. _____ she was very tired, she went on working.
A. As　　B. Although　　C. Even　　D. In spite of

10. Busy _____ he was, he tried his best to help you.
A. as　　B. when　　C. since　　D. for

11. I learned a little Russian _____ I was at middle school.
A. though　　B. although　　C. as if　　D. when

12. _____ we got to the station, the train had left already.
A. If　　B. Unless　　C. Since　　D. When

13. _____ the rain stops, we'll set off for the station.
A. Before　　B. Unless　　C. As soon as　　D. Though

14. She was _____ tired _____ she could not move an inch.
A. so, that　　B. such, that　　C. very, that　　D. so, as

15. We didn't go home _____ we finished the work.
A. since　　B. until　　C. because　　D. though

16. I'll stay here _____ everyone else comes back.
A. even if　　B. as though　　C. because　　D. until

17. Although it's raining, _____ are still working in the field.
A. they　　B. but they　　C. and they　　D. so they

18. Speak to him slowly _____ he may understand you better.
A. since　　B. so that　　C. for　　D. because

19. You'll miss the train _____ you hurry up.
A. unless　　B. as　　C. if　　D. until

20. _____ Newton started to do experiments, he forget about the time.
A. When　　B. Once　　C. If　　D. As

21. We'd better hurry _____ it is getting dark.
A. and　　B. but　　C. as　　D. unless

22. I didn't manage to do it _____ you had explained how.
A. until　　B. unless　　C. when　　D. before

23. _____ he comes, we won't be able to go.
A. Without　　B. Unless　　C. Except　　D. Even

24. I hurried _____ I wouldn't be late for class.

A. since　　　B. so that　　　C. as if　　　D. unless
25. _____ I catch a cold, I have pain in my back.
A. Every time　　B. Though　　C. Even　　D. Where

第七节 倒装句与强调句

一、倒装句

在英语句子里，主语通常在谓语动词的前面，这样的语序称为自然语序。如果谓语动词的一部分或全部放在主语前面，这样的语序称为倒装语序。采用倒装语序的句子称为倒装句。

自然语序：The car rushed out. 那辆车冲了出去。

倒装语序：Out rushed the car.

自然语序：We can lose weight only in this way. 我们只能用这种方法减肥。

倒装语序：Only in this way can we lose weight.

上面的第一个倒装句是谓语动词完全放到主语前，称为完全倒装；第二个倒装句只是将谓语的一部分（如助动词、情态动词）移到主语前，称为部分倒装。

倒装语序常在下列情况出现。

(1)疑问倒装。例如：

Did you see the film yesterday? 你昨天看电影了吗？

Can you speak English? 你会说英语吗？

Where have you been? 你到哪儿去了？

(2)There be 句型倒装。例如：

There is a map of China on the wall. 墙上有一张中国地图。

There seemed to be no problem. 好像没有什么问题。

There used to be a factory on that corner. 拐角处曾有一家工厂。

(3)表示祝愿的倒装。例如：

May you succeed! 祝你成功！

Long live the great unit of all nationalities of our country. 全国各族人民大团结万岁！

Merry Christmas bring you good luck! 祝愿圣诞带给你好运！

(4)表示否定的词或词组放在句首作状语时，句子要倒装。这些词或词组主要有：never(永不、从不)、scarcely(几乎不)、hardly(几乎不)、rarely(很少、难得)、little(几乎不，毫不)、few、nowhere(没有任何地方)、no sooner…than(刚一……便)、not only…but also(不仅…而且…)、in no case(任何情况都不)、in no way(绝不)、on no account(绝不)、at no time(任何时候都不)、under (in) no circumstances(任何情况下都不)。

在这些词或者词组引出的倒装句中，倒装到主语前的那部分谓语动词通常是助动词、情态动词或动词 be。例如：

Hardly had he said anything before he had left. 他几乎什么都没说就离开了。

No sooner had Anne arrived there than she fell ill. 安妮一到这里就生起病来。

Rarely did Tom leave his lab those days. 这几天汤姆几乎从未离开他的实验室。

(5) only 引出的状语放在句首时，这种情况下的倒装一般都是部分倒装。例如：

Only then did the doctor realize that his patient needed surgery。只有到了那时，医生才认识到他的病人需要做外科手术。

Only after class was he allowed to raise the question. 只有下课以后他才被允许提出这个问题。

Only when you adjust down your price to some extent can we conclude the business。只有你方将价格降到一定程度我们才有可能做成这笔生意。

注 意

only 修饰主语，仍用自然语序。例如：
Only socialism can save China. 只有社会主义才能救中国。

(6) 句首为 here、there、then、thus 等副词，并且谓语动词为 come、go、be、exist、follow 等不及物动词时，这种情况下的倒装一般为全部倒装。例如：

Here comes the bus. 公交车来了。

There exist two types of flying machines. 有两种类型的飞行器。

Thus arose the division between the developed and developing countries. 由此产生了发达国家和发展中国家的区分。

(7) 句首为 so、nor、neither 等副词，表明前句说明的情况也适用于本句时。例如：

Richard can speak Japanese. So can his sister. 理查德会说日语，他妹妹也会。

Copper is a good conductor. So are many other metals. 铜是一种良好的导体，许多其他金属也是。

He didn't say anything. Nor/neither did his assistant. 他没有说话，他的助手也没说。

The first one wasn't good enough neither was the second. 第一个不够好，第二个也如此。

(8) 虚拟条件句中的倒装。虚拟语气中条件句省去 if 时，助动词 had、should 和动词 were 须放在主语前面形成部分倒装或完全倒装。例如：

Had I known you were coming, I would have stayed at home. 如果知道你要来，我就待在家里了。

Should it rain tomorrow, what could we do? 万一明天下雨，我们能干些什么呢？

Were there no air, there would be no sound. 没有空气，就没有声音。

(9) Not until 引导的时间状语从句放在句首时，主句用部分倒装。例如：

直到他的妈妈回来，他才完成作业。

He didn't finish his homework until his mother came back.

<u>Not until</u> his mother came back <u>did he finish</u> his homework.

(10) 在 hardly/scarcely/…when（一……就）、no sooner…than、not only … but also、

so…that、such…that 的倒装句中，遵循原则为：前倒后不倒。而 hardly/scarcely/ no sooner 后句子的谓语用 had done，when/than 后句子的谓语用一般过去时。例如：

No sooner had I reached the station than bus moved. 我一到达车站公交车就启动了。

(11)某些表语位于句首，要用完全倒装，其结构为：表语+连系动词+主语。

①形容词+连系动词+主语。例如：

Present at the meeting were Professor White，Professor Smith and many other guests. 出席此次会议的有 White 教授、Smith 教授和其他客人。

②过去分词+连系动词+主语。例如：

Gone are the days when they could do what they liked to the Chinese people. 他们可以对中国人为所欲为的日子已经一去不复返了。

③介词短语+be+主语。例如：

Among the goods are Christmas trees，flowers，candles and toys. 在这些物品中，有圣诞树、花、蜡烛和玩具。

二、强调句

强调就是将句中的一个成分或全句所传递的信息通过某种手段加以突出。在书面语中，表示强调的手段主要有词汇手段、语法手段和修辞手段。

1. 词汇手段

(1) 通过 Only、even、alone、just、at all、on earth、in the world、rather、entirely、completely 等单词或词组对其所修饰的内容进行强调。一般放在所强调的成分之前。例如：

You can't live on bread alone. (=You can't live only on bread.)你不能光靠吃面包生活。

I can't even remember the name of that old friend of mine. 我甚至记不住那位老朋友的名字。

It's just two o'clock. 现在正好是两点钟。

What on earth do you want? 你到底想要什么?

(2)通过强调词 ever 放在 when、what 等疑问词后，主要用来加强疑问句，意味"究竟""到底""无论"。例如：

Whenever did you last see your key? 你到底什么时候最后一次看到你的钥匙？

Whatever do you mean by that？你到底是什么意思？

2. 语法手段

(1)反身代词一般放在所强调的词之后。例如：

I showed Mary herself the letter. 我把信给了玛丽本人看。

I myself showed Mary the letter. (=I showed Mary the letter myself.)我亲自把信拿给玛丽看的。

We ourselves will see to it. (We will see to it ourselves.)我们会亲自负责这件事情的。

(2)助动词 do 放在所强调的谓语动词之前。例如：

They do have sufficient food and drink. 他们的确有足够的食物和饮料。

Tom does have regard for others. 汤姆对别人的确非常尊重。

Do be patient! 一定要有耐心!

(3) It is/was+被强调部分(通常是主语、宾语或状语)+that/who(当强调主语且主语指人时)+其他部分。译成汉语时,被强调部分常用"是""正是""就是"等词来表示强调的含义。例如:

I gave Grace a watch at Christmas. 我在圣诞节送给格雷斯一块手表。

→It was I that/who gave Grace a watch at Christmas. (强调主语)

It was Grace that/whom I gave a watch at Christmas. (强调间接宾语)

It was a watch that I gave Grace at Christmas. (强调直接宾语)

It was at Christmas that I gave Grace a watch. (强调状语)

注 意

在"It+is/was+被强调部分+that"强调句型中,构成强调句的 it 本身没有词义;强调句中的连接词一般只用 that,在强调人时才可以用 who 或 whom 代替 that,that、who 不可省略。即使在强调时间、地点、原因等状语时,连接词仍用 that,不能用 where、when 或 why。强调句中的时态只用两种:一般现在时和一般过去时。原句谓语动词是一般过去时、过去完成时和过去进行时,用 It was,其余的时态用 It is。

(4) not … until 句型的强调句。

句型为:It is/was not until+被强调部分+that+其他部分。

普通句:He didn't go to bed until/till his wife came back.

强调句:It was not until his wife came back that he went to bed.

注 意

此句型只用 until,不用 till,但如果不是强调句型,till、until 可通用;句型中 It is/was not 已是否定句,that 后面的从句要用肯定句,切勿再用否定句。

3. 修辞手段

(1) 提前。把按正常语序出现在谓语动词后的成分提前至句首,使之突出,以示强调。例如:

Even the most complicated problems, a computer can solve in a shot time. 即使是最复杂的问题,计算机也能在最短时间内解决。(宾语提前)

Very grateful they were for your help. 他们非常感谢你们的帮助。(表语提前)

Of all the books I have this is the best. 在我的所有书中,这一本是最好的。(用作定语的 of 介词短语提前)

(2) 重复。通过关键词的重复,或者通过同义词或相似表达法的使用,以示强调。例如:

Smith is an old, old man(=a very old man). 史密斯是一个非常老的男士。

This watch is very, very good(=extremely good). 这块手表相当好。

专项练习

(一) 单项选择 (倒装句)

1. Not until I began to work _____ how much time I had wasted.
   A. didn't I realize   B. did I realize   C. I didn't realize   D. I realized

2. Only by practicing a few hours every day _____ be able to master the language.
   A. you can   B. can you   C. you will   D. will you

3. If you don't go, neither _____.
   A. shall I   B. do I   C. I do   D. I shall

4. No sooner _____ to the station _____ the train left.
   A. had I got; when   B. I had got; than
   C. had I got; than   D. did I get; when

5. ——Your father is very strict with you.
   ——_____. He never lets off a single mistake of ours.
   A. So he is   B. So is he   C. He is so   D. So does he

6. _____ today, he would get there by Sunday.
   A. Would he leave   B. Was he leaving
   C. Were he to leave   D. If he leave

7. Never in my life _____ such a thing.
   A. I have heard or have seen   B. have I heard or seen
   C. I have heard or seen   D. did I hear or see

8. —— Here _____! Where is Xiao Liu?
   ——There _____.
   A. comes the bus; is he   B. comes the bus; he is
   C. the bus comes; is he   D. the bus comes; he is

9. Not only _____ a promise, but also he kept it.
   A. he made   B. does he make   C. did he make   D. has he made

10. ——I like football. I don't like volleyball.
    ——_____.
    A. So do I   B. Neither do I
    C. So it is with me   D. So is it with me

11. _____ the expense, I _____ to Italy.
    A. If it were not; go   B. Were it not for; would go
    C. Weren't it for; will go   D. If it hadn't been; would have gone

12. So _____ in the darkness that he didn't dare to move an inch.
    A. he was frightened   B. was he frightened
    C. frightened he was   D. frightened was he

13. —— In modern times, girls like beautiful clothes.
——Yes, _____ and _____ . After all, our life has greatly improved.
A. so do they; so do you
B. so they do; so you do
C. so do they; so you do
D. so they do; so do you

14. —— You have an English class every day except Sunday.
—— _____ .
A. So we have
B. So we do
C. So have we
D. So do we

15. No sooner _____ than it began to rain heavily.
A. the game began
B. has the game begun
C. did the game begin
D. had the game begun

(二)单项选择(强调句)

1. It was not until midnight _____ they reached the camp site.
A. that B. when C. while D. as

2. —— Who's that?
—— _____ Professor Li.
A. That's B. It's C. He's D. This's

3. _____ was Jane that I saw in the library this morning.
A. It B. He C. She D. That

4. —— Have you ever seen a whale alive?
——Yes, I've seen _____ .
A. that B. it C. such D. one

5. How long _____ to finish the work?
A. you'll take B. you'll take it C. will it take you D. will take you

6. It was through Xiao Li _____ I got to know Xiao Wang.
A. who B. whom C. how D. that

7. It was in the rice fields _____ we had our league meeting.
A. where B. that C. in which D. on which

8. It was on October 1st _____ new China was founded.
A. which B. when C. as D. that

9. Was it because he was ill _____ he asked for leave?
A. and B. that C. that's D. so

10. Mary speaks in a low voice; _____ is difficult to know what she is saying.
A. it B. that C. so D. she

11. It was _____ I met Mr. Green in Shanghai.
A. many years that
B. many years before
C. many years ago that
D. many years when

12. _____ is not everybody _____ can draw so well.

    A. It; all   B. It; that   C. There; who   D. There; that

13. Who was it _____ saved the drowning girl?

    A. since   B. as   C. that   D. he

14. She said she would go and she _____ go.

    A. didn't   B. did   C. really   D. would

15. Was it in this palace _____ the emperor died?

    A. that   B. in which   C. in where   D. which

第八节 主谓一致

主谓一致指"人称"和"数"方面的一致关系。在现代英语中，主谓一致基本遵循如下原则：语法一致原则、意义一致原则和就近原则。

一、语法一致原则

语法一致原则即：主语为单数，谓语用单数；主语为复数，谓语也用复数。

(1) 单数主语即使后面带有with, along with, together with, like(象), but、except、besides(除了), as well as, no less than, rather than(而不是), including, in addition to 引导的短语，谓语动词仍用单数。例如：

Air as well as water is matter. 空气和水都是物质。

No one except two servants was late for the dinner. 除了两个仆人外，没有一个人迟来用餐。

(2) 用 and 连接的并列主语，如果主语是同一个人、同一事、同一概念，谓语动词用单数，否则用复数。例如：

The poet and writer has come. 那位诗人兼作家来了。（一个人）

A hammer and a saw are useful tools. 锤子和锯都是有用的工具。（两样物）

用 and 连接的成对名词习惯上被看成是一个整体。例如：bread and butter(黄油抹面包)、knife and fork(刀叉)等作主语时，谓语动词用单数。

(3) 不定式(短语)、动名词(短语)或从句作主语时，谓语动词用单数。例如：

Serving the people is my great happiness. 为人民服务是我最大的幸福。

When we'll go out for an outing has been decided. 我们什么时候出去郊游已决定了。

(4) 并列主语被 each、every 或 no 修饰时，谓语动词用单数。

Every boy and every girl likes to go swimming. 每个男孩和女孩都喜欢去游泳。

No teacher and no student was absent from the meeting. 没有老师也没有学生开会缺席。

Each man and (each) woman is asked to help. 每个男人和女人都被请去帮忙。

(5) each of+复数代词，谓语动词用单数；复数代词+each，谓语动词用单数。例如：

Each of us has something to say. 我们每个人都有话要说。

Each of them has a book. 他们每人有一本书。

They each have a book. 他们都有一本书。

The suites each have their own private entrances. 每个套间都有它们各自单独的入口。

(6)若主语中有 more than one 或 many a/an，尽管从意义上看是复数，但它的谓语动词仍用单数。但 more+复数名词+than one 作主语时，谓语动词仍用复数。例如：

Many a boy likes playing basketball. 许多男生都喜欢打篮球。

More than one student was late. 不止一个学生迟到。

More persons than one come to help us. 不止一个人来帮助我们。

(7)none 作主语时，谓语动词可用单数，也可用复数。但在代表不可数的东西时总是看作单数，因而谓语动词要用单数。例如：

None of us are (is) perfect. 人无完人。

None of this worries me. 这事一点也不使我着急。

(8)名词如 trousers、scissors、clothes、glasses 等作主语时，谓语动词必须用复数。例如：

His clothes are good. 他的衣服很好。

但这些名词前若出现 a pair of，谓语一般用单数。例如：

A pair of glasses is on the desk. 桌上有一副眼镜。

(9)形复意单名词(如 news)、以 ics 结尾的学科名称(如 physics、mathematics、economics)、国名(如 the United States)、报纸名(如 the New Times)、书名(如 *Arabian Night*《天方夜谭》)及 The United Nations(联合国) 等作主语时，谓语动词用单数。

(10) a+名词+and a half、one and a half+名词、the number of+名词等作主语时，谓语动词要用单数。例如：

Only one and a half apples is left on the table. 桌上只剩下一个半苹果。

> **注　意**
>
> one or two+复数名词作主语，谓语动词用复数形式。例如：
> One or two places have been visited. 参观了一两个地点。

(11) the+形容词作主语时，若指一类人，则谓语用复数。例如：

The rich get richer and the poor get poorer. 富者愈富，贫者愈贫。

二、意义一致原则

意义一致原则即从意义着眼处理一致关系。例如，主语形式虽是单数但意义是复数，谓语动词也采取复数形式；而有些主语形式虽是复数但意义上看作单数，谓语动词也采取单数形式。

(1)主语中有 all、half、most、the rest 等，以及"分数或百分数+名词"作主语时，谓语动词单、复数取决于连用的名词。例如：

The rest of the bikes are on sale today. 剩下的自行车今天出售。

Most of the apples were rotten. 大部分的苹果都是烂的。

Most of the apple was eaten by a rat. 这个苹果的大部分被老鼠吃了。

(2)不定数量的词组，如 part of、a lot of、lots of、one of、a number of、plenty of 等作

主语时，谓语动词的单、复数取决于量词后面名词的数。例如：

A part of the textbooks have arrived. 一小部分教科书已运到。

A part of the apple has been eaten up by the pig. 这个苹果的一部分被猪吃光了。

（3）加、减、乘、除用单数。例如：

Fifteen minus five is ten. 15 减去 5 等于 10。

Five and three is eight. 5 加 3 等于 8。

（4）表示时间、金钱、距离、度量等的名词作主语时，尽管是复数形式，它们作为一个单一的概念时，其谓语动词用单数。例如：

Ten miles is a good distance. 十英里是一个合适的距离。

（5）集体名词作主语表示一个整体概念时，谓语动词用单数；强调整体中具体的人或物时，谓语动词则用复数。

①通常作复数的集体名词，包括 police、people、cattle 等。例如：

The British police have only very limited powers. 英国警察的权利非常有限。

②通常作不可数名词的集体名词，包括 equipment、furniture、clothing、luggage 等。

③可作单数也可作复数的集体名词，包括 audience、committee、government、family、enemy、group、party、team、public 等。例如：

The committee has/have decided to dismiss him. 委员会决定解雇他。

（6）从句、动词不定式、-ing 形式作主语时的主谓一致。

①在"主语+系动词+表语"结构中，如果以 what 从句作主语，表语又是单数，主句的谓语动词一般用单数；如果表语是复数，主句的谓语动词一般用复数。若以动词不定式、动词-ing 形式作主语，谓语动词一般用单数。例如：

What caused the accident is a complete mystery. 事故是由什么引起的完全是个谜。

What his father left him are a few English books. 父亲留给他的只是几本英语书而已。

To learn English well is difficult. 学好英语是困难的。

②当 what 从句具有两个或两个以上的动词表示复数意义的并列结构时，主句中的谓语动词多用复数形式。例如：

What I say and think are none of your business. 我说的和我想的都与你无关。

③以 who、why、how、whether 或 that 引导的从句作主语时，谓语动词通常用单数形式。例如：

Why she did this is not known. 她为什么做这件事还不清楚。

④And 连接的两个名词性从句作主语，如果表示两件事情，其谓语动词常用复数形式。例如：

What caused the accident and who was responsible for it remain a mystery to us. 造成事故的原因是什么，谁应对事故负责，对我们来说还是一个谜。

三、就近原则

（1）由 here、there、where 等引导的倒装句中（有时主语不止一个时），谓语动词与靠近它的主语在数上一致。例如：

Here comes the bus. 公共汽车来了。

Here is a pen and some pieces of paper for you. 给你一支钢笔和几张纸。

Where is your wife and children to stay while you are away？你不在这儿的时候，你爱人和孩子在哪儿待呢？

（2）用连词 or、either…or、neither…nor、not only…but also 等连接的并列主语，谓语动词与靠近它的主语在数上一致。例如：

Neither the students nor the teacher knows anything about it. 学生和老师都不知道这事。

He or you have taken my pen. 他或你拿了我的钢笔。

（3）当 There be 句型的主语是一系列事物时，谓语应与最邻近的主语保持一致。例如：

There is a pen, a knife and several books on the desk.

There are twenty boy-students and twenty-three girl-students in the class.

专项练习

单项选择

1. About 60 percent of the students _____ from the south, the rest of them _____ from the north and foreign countries.

 A. are; is   B. are; are   C. is; are   D. is; is

2. Half of the workers here _____ under 30 _____.

 A. is; years   B. are; year old   C. is; years old   D. are; years of age

3. Nobody but Betty and Mary _____ late forclass yesterday.

 A. was   B. were   C. has been   D. have been

4. The number of pages in this dictionary _____ about two thousand.

 A. are   B. has   C. have   D. is

5. Thirty dollars _____ too expensive.

 A. are   B. is   C. were   D. be

6. The audience _____ so large that no seat was left unoccupied in the great hall.

 A. is   B. are   C. was   D. has

7. The league secretary and monitor _____ asked to make a speech at the meeting.

 A. is   B. was   C. are   D. were

8. "If anybody _____, please put down _____ name." Said the teacher to the monitor.

 A. wants to buy the boo; his   B. want to buy the book; their

 C. will buy the book; one's   D. wants to have the book bought; her

9. Nothing but one desk and six chairs _____ in the room.

 A. are   B. is stayed   C. is   D. are left

10. We Chinese _____ a hard-working people.

 A. is   B. are   C. is being   D. are being

11. Between the two roads _____ a TV tower called "Skyscraper Tower".

A. stands   B. standing   C. which stands   D. stand

12. Either of you _____ going there tonight.

A. will   B. was   C. is   D. are

13. You as well _____ right.

A. I are   B. I am   C. as I am   D. as I are

14. All but Dick _____ in Class Three this term.

A. are   B. is   C. were   D. was

15. This pair of shoes _____.

A. is her   B. is hers   C. are hers   D. are her

16. _____ a good enough price for this book.

A. Two yuans are   B. Two yuan are   C. Two yuans is   D. Two yuan is

17. No bird and no beast _____ in the lonely island.

A. are seen   B. is seen   C. see   D. sees

18. Every means _____ prevent the water from _____.

A. are used to; polluting   B. get used to; polluting

C. is used to; polluted   D. is used to; being polluted

19. Each of the _____ in the ship.

A. passenger has his own room   B. passengers have their own room

C. passenger have their own room   D. passengers has his own room

20. What we need _____ good textbooks.

A. is   B. are   C. have   D. has

PART 2

第二部分
专升本英语考题解析及训练

第三章　词汇与语法结构

第四章　完形填空

第五章　阅读理解

第六章　翻译

第七章　词义辨析

第八章　多选题

第三章 词汇与语法结构

一、试题分析

词汇与语法结构部分主要测试考生运用基本语法知识和词汇的能力。所占分值比例为30%，共有30小题，每小题1分。每小题是一个留有空白的不完整的英语句子。要求考生在小题下面的四个选项中，选出可以填入句中空白处的最佳项。

本部分包括词汇题和语法题两个部分内容。据初步统计，词汇题通常占历年词汇与语法结构部分的53.9%，语法题占46.1%。词汇题考试内容丰富，考点有：

(1) 单词、词组(词义、同义词)辨析。要求考生能辨析形近或意近词语的细微差别及同义词在不同语境中的应用。

(2) 固定搭配。要求考生掌握英语习惯用语、固定词语搭配、动词短语、介词短语等。

语法题考核点广，所占比例较大，但要点不变，主要考点有：非限定动词、虚拟语气、从句(名词性从句、定语从句、状语从句)、动词时态、被动语态、倒装句、强调句、主谓一致、反义疑问句等。尤其是对其常见用法和特殊用法应给予足够的重视。

二、解题技巧

1. 解题方法

解此类题时，考生应注意每道题的考点，根据考点找出线索。

(1) 顺序法：正确领悟题干内容，直接判断出最符合句子逻辑的词或词组、语法知识。

(2) 排除法：可采取语言排除、逻辑排除、语法排除或选择排除等方法。先排除较容易、较明显的错误选项，缩小范围，而后对剩余的选项进行比较分析，最后确定答案。注意词的搭配关系，特别要考虑到虚拟语气、主谓一致、非谓语动词、各种从句、倒装等一些常见考点。

做单项选择题还可用以下具体方法和技巧。

词汇题：①注意搭配；②关注空格前后的逻辑关系；③判断词组中的关键词；④判断词组中的介词或副词；⑤常识。

语法题：①自上而下——寻找题中的明显标记，如虚拟语气、倒装、主谓一致；②自下而上——对比选项共性和个性，反推考点，如时态、语态、非谓语动词、连接词(从句)。

2. 解题步骤

(1) 大致浏览所给四个选项和句子，迅速判断该题是语法题还是词汇题。如果是语法题，要通过一些标志词来判断该题涉及哪些语法内容，再进一步回想该语法内容的要点。

如果是词汇题,就要先看一下所给四个选项的词是否都认识。

(2)在第一遍的大致浏览过程中有些题很容易就可以选出肯定的答案,然后再从头开始仔细看没有选出答案的题。遵循先语法后语义的原则解题。

(3)利用暗示进行选择:注意考题设计的语境范围。平时应注重对习惯用语表达、惯用法和中英文化差别等方面知识的积累。

(4)运用排除法:可采取语言排除、逻辑排除、语法排除或选择排除等方法。先排除掉较容易、较明显的错误选项,缩小范围,而后对剩余的选项进行比较分析,最后确定答案。

三、举例分析

1. _____ a raincoat with you in case it rains.
   A. Bring   B. Fetch   C. Take   D. Hold

【翻译】带上雨衣以防下雨。

【考点】词义辨析

【解析】C。Bring(to carry something to a place):带来,拿来。Fetch(to go and bring something back):去取来。Take(to carry something from a place to another):把某物从一个地方带到另一地方。Hold(to keep something in your hand):拿住,握住。根据句意选择"Take"最合适。

2. I never expected you to _____ at the meeting. I thought you were abroad.
   A. turn on   B. turn down   C. turn off   D. turn up

【翻译】我从未想到你会出席会议,我以为你在国外呢。

【考点】词组辨析

【解析】D。turn on:打开(电灯、电视等)。turn down:拒绝;关小,调低。turn off:关掉。turn up:出现,来到。结合题意得知,D为正确答案。

3. Jack works so hard as he dreams _____ owning his own house soon.
   A. to   B. with   C. of   D. on

【翻译】杰克工作十分卖力,因为他梦想很快拥有自己的房子。

【考点】词语搭配

【解析】C。词语搭配中的"动词+介词"结构十分常见,某些动词与介词有固定搭配,如:belong to(属于),deal with(处理),consist of(构成),depend on(取决于)等。本题中dream of 是固定搭配,意为"梦想,向往"。

4. John and I _____ friends for eight years. We first got to know each other at a Christmas party. But we _____ each other a couple of times before that.
   A. had been; have seen   B. have been; have seen
   C. had been; had seen   D. have been; had seen

【翻译】我和约翰已是八年的好友,我俩第一次相识在一个圣诞晚会上,但在此以前我们曾见过几面。

【考点】谓语动词的时态

【解析】D。从时间短语 for eight years 推知,第一句的谓语动词用现在完成时。最后一句谓语动词的动作发生在第二句谓语动词动作之前，所以要选用过去完成时。

5. _____ leaves the room at last ought to turn off the lights.

   A. Anyone   B. The person   C. Whoever   D. Who

   【翻译】无论是谁最后一个离开教室都应该把灯关掉。

   【考点】名词性从句——主语从句

   【解析】C。由题意得知，选项 C 和 D 都可以引导一个名词性从句作主句的主语，但只有选项 C 的含义(无论谁)符合题意。

6. "What did the teacher say to you just now?" "She asked me _____."

   A. whether I had finished my work or not

   B. whether or not had I finished my work

   C. if my work had finished or not

   D. if or not I have finished my work

   【翻译】"刚才老师和你说了些什么？""她问我是否做完了家庭作业。"

   【考点】固定搭配、状语从句

   【解析】A。whether…or not(是否……或不)是固定搭配，引导状语从句，if 无此用法。

7. Private cars have made the traffic problems _____.

   A. the worse than before   B. worse than ever before

   C. more bad as before   D. more bad than it was

   【翻译】私人轿车造成了前所未有的交通拥挤。

   【考点】状语从句，而且只有多音节的形容词和副词在构成比较级时才用"the more +原形形容词和副词"的形式。

   【解析】B。bad 的比较级是 worse，形容词或副词比较级前不加定冠词 the，故选 B 选项。

8. His doctor advised that he _____ his job.

   A. changed   B. change   C. would   D. had changed

   【翻译】他的医生建议他换工作。

   【考点】虚拟语气

   【解析】B。在表示建议、请求、命令等意义的动词(一个坚持，insist；两道命令，order、command；三条建议，advice、suggest、propose；四点要求，ask、request、require、demand 等)引导的宾语从句中，谓语用虚拟语气 should+动词原形，而且 should 往往可以省略。

9. It is during his spare time _____ John has been studying a course in French.

   A. when   B. that   C. which   D. what

   【翻译】正是利用自己的业余时间，约翰一直在攻读法律课程。

   【考点】强调句

   【解析】B。强调句的结构是"It is/was+被强调部分+that 引导的从句"。强调句中不能出现 when、which 等词引导从句。

10. There _____ a pen and two books on the table.

A. are   B. be   C. is   D. were

【翻译】桌子上有一支笔和两本书。

【考点】主谓一致

【解析】C。在 There be 句型中，如果有两个或两个以上的主语，谓语动词通常遵循"就近原则"，即与其靠近的主语在人称和数上保持一致。

专项练习

1. ——What are you reading, Jane?
——Some books on _____ education, I'm now interested in _____ education of young people.
A. an; the   B. /; the   C. the; a;   D. an; /

2. ——You were out when I dropped in at your house yesterday.
——Oh, I _____ for a friend from Beijing at the railway station.
A. was waiting   B. had waited   C. am waiting   D. have waited

3. ——Little Jim has been eating sweets all day.
——It's no _____ he is not hungry.
A. matter   B. doubt   C. problem   D. wonder

4. Comrade Wang _____ be in Shanghai-I saw him in the company only a few minutes ago.
A. mustn't   B. can't   C. may not   D. isn't able to

5. It was not until I got home _____ I found my wallet missing.
A. that   B. when   C. where   D. which

6. The number of the people present at the concert _____ much smaller than expected. There _____ many tickets left.
A. was; was   B. were; was   C. were; were   D. was; were

7. _____ you stepped into the lab with your shoes on? You're supposed to take them off before you enter it. I told you so!
A. How come   B. How dare   C. How about   D. How long

8. They made no effort to hide their amusement _____ I produced a packet of sweets from my pocket.
A. however   B. whatever   C. whichever   D. whenever

9. _____ her work has been good, but this essay is dreadful.
A. In a word   B. In general   C. In particular   D. In total

10. She returned home from the office, only _____ the door open and something missing.
A. finding   B. to be found   C. to find   D. found

11. We should _____ ourselves assiduously and faithfully to the duties of our profession.
A. devote   B. spend   C. offer   D. provide

12. The Anti-Japanese War _____ in 1937 and it _____ eight years.

A. broke out; lasted B. broke out; was lasted
C. was broken out; lasted D. was broken out; was lasted

13. When the plane arrived, some of the detectives were waiting inside the main building _____ others were waiting on the airfield.

A. during B. where C. which D. while

14. _____ is known to everybody, Taiwan is a part of China.

A. It B. As C. That D. Which

15. ——Let's go to the zoo this Sunday. OK?

——_____. I love to see all kinds of animals.

A. I couldn't agree more B. I'm afraid not
C. I believe not D. I don't think so

16. ——What's the matter with you?

——_____ the heavy suitcase, my waist was hurt unexpectedly.

A. Having carried B. Carried C. While carrying D. While I was carrying

17. ——May I borrow your paper?

——_____.

A. By all means B. Never mind C. You are welcome D. Don't mention it

18. This bird is really lovely, and I've never seen _____ one.

A. a finer B. a finest C. the finer D. the finest

19. Since there's no more work to do, we might just _____ go home.

A. so well B. as well C. so good D. as good

20. He made _____ known to his friends that he didn't want to enter politics.

A. that B. it C. himself D. him

21. That car nearly hit me; I _____.

A. might be killed B. might have been killed
C. may be killed D. may been killed

22. A library with five thousand books _____ to the nation as a gift.

A. is offered B. has offered C. are offered D. have offered

23. She wrote a famous book, and so _____ a place in history.

A. winning B. to win C. to have won D. won

24. I'll have to change my clothes before I go out — I don't want _____ like this.

A. to see B. seeing C. to be seen D. being seen

25. We make sure we're always well stocked up with candles, just _____.

A. in case B. for certain C. in practice D. for use

26. It's hard to rescue drowning people because they _____ so much.

A. sink B. swim C. jump D. struggle

27. It has been raining for a day, but even though it hadn't rained, we _____ there by tomorrow.

A. can't get   B. won't get   C. hadn't got   D. wouldn't get

28. The little time we have together we try _____ wisely.

A. spending it   B. to spend it   C. to spend   D. spending that

29. You should put on the notices _____ all the people may see them.

A. where   B. in which   C. at   D. for them

30. She took her son, ran out of the house, _____ him in the car and drove quickly to the nearest doctor's office.

A. put   B. to put   C. putting   D. having put

31. The old house, in front of _____ there is an apple tree, is _____ I used to live.

A. that; the place   B. it; the place   C. which; where   D. what; where

32. Ten years had passed. I found she had _____.

A. a few white hairs   B. a little white hair   C. some white hair   D. more fifty hair

33. ——Hi, this way, please.

——OK. I sometimes have no sense of _____ when I arrive at the crossroad.

A. position   B. direction   C. situation   D. condition

34. Shelly had prepared carefully for her English examination so that she could be sure of passing it on her first _____.

A. intention   B. attempt   C. purpose   D. desire

35. I didn't have to work all weekend——I did it by _____.

A. chance   B. choice   C. accident   D. myself

36. "Did you get _____ to the party?" "Yes, I replied to it this morning."

A. an answer   B. an invitation   C. a question   D. a letter

37. I paid him £50 for the painting, but its true _____ must be at least £500.

A. price   B. money   C. value   D. importance

38. His letter was so confusing that I could hardly make any _____ of it.

A. explanation   B. meaning   C. sense   D. guess

39. You've just missed your _____, and you will have to wait for the next round.

A. chance   B. turn   C. time   D. part

40. ——Li Lin is very bright and studies hard as well.

——It's no _____ he always gets the first place in any examination.

A. question   B. doubt   C. problem   D. wonder

41. ——How can I use this washing machine?

——Well, just refer to the _____.

A. explanations   B. expressions   C. introductions   D. directions

42. Jim was late for two classes this morning. He said that he forgot both of the _____.

A. rooms number   B. room number   C. room's numbers   D. room numbers

43. ——Hello, I'd like to speak to Henry.

——Oh, which _____? There are two _____ in our office.

A. Henrys; Henrys   B. Henries; Henries   C. Henry; Henrys   D. Henrys; Henries

44. Electricity, like other forms of _____, has greatly increased in price in recent years.
A. pressure   B. force   C. strength   D. energy

45. ——I've got an "A" in the examination.
——That's a good _____. You will surely win a second.
A. result   B. news   C. start   D. idea

46. Dear me! Just _____ at the time! I _____ no idea it was so late.
A. look; have   B. looking; had C. look; had   D. looking; have

47. ——What's his name?
——I _____.
A. forget   B. forgot   C. had forgotten D. am forgetting

48. Your mother _____, however, say that to us that day.
A. does   B. did   C. is doing   D. was doing

49. New medicines and instruments _____ every day to extend life.
A. develop   B. are being developed
C. are developing   D. have developed

50. I _____ your last point——could you say it again?
A. didn't quite catch   B. don't quite catch
C. hadn't quite caught   D. can't quite catch

51. I feel sure I _____ her before somewhere.
A. was to meet   B. have met   C. had met   D. would meet

52. They haven't arrived yet but we _____ them at any moment.
A. are expected   B. have expected C. are expecting D. will expect

53. ——I suppose you _____ that report yet?
——I finished it yesterday, as a matter of fact.
A. didn't finish   B. haven't finished   C. hadn't finished   D. wasn't finishing

54. ——When he _____ is not known yet.
——But when he _____, he will be warmly welcomed.
A. comes; comes   B. will come; will come
C. comes; will come   D. will come; comes

55. The bridge, which _____ 1688, needs repairing.
A. is dated from   B. was dated from   C. dates from   D. dated from

56. I had hoped to see her off at the station, but I _____ too busy.
A. was   B. had been   C. would be   D. would have been

57. You _____ your turn so you'll have to wait.
A. will miss   B. have missed   C. are missing   D. had missed

58. I left my pen on the desk and now it's gone; who _____ it?
A. took   B. has taken   C. will take   D. had taken

59. You'll never guess who I met today—my old teacher! We _____ for 20 years.
    A. don't meet   B. haven't met   C. hadn't met   D. couldn't meet

60. I think you must be mistaken about seeing him at the theatre; I'm sure he _____ abroad all week.
    A. is   B. was   C. has been   D. had been

61. ——Don't put the waste on the ground.
    ——Oh, I'm very sorry. I _____ the dustbin there.
    A. don't see   B. isn't seeing   C. didn't see   D. haven't see

62. ——How is the weather in your country this summer?
    ——It _____ as much as it does now for a long time.
    A. hasn't rained   B. doesn't rain   C. wasn't raining   D. didn't rain

63. ——Does Liu Hui serve in the army?
    ——No, but he _____ in the army for three years.
    A. served   B. has served   C. is serving   D. would serve

64. ——Sorry. I _____ to post the letter for you.
    ——Never mind. _____ it myself after school.
    A. forget; I'd rather post
    B. forgot; I'll post
    C. forgot; I'm going to post
    D. forget; I'd better post

65. Unfortunately, when I dropped in, Professor Smith _____, so we only had time for a few words.
    A. has just left   B. had just left   C. just left   D. was just leaving

66. ——What were you doing when I phoned you last night?
    ——I _____ my painting and was starting to take a bath.
    A. have already finished   B. was finishing
    C. had just finished   D. was going to finish

67. You _____ television. Why not do something more active?
    A. always watch   B. are always watching
    C. have always watched   D. have always been watching

68. I have been studying computer for several years and I still _____.
    A. have   B. do   C. have been   D. am

69. Jane was disappointed that most of the guests _____ when she _____ at the party.
    A. left; had arrived   B. left; arrived
    C. had left; had arrived   D. had left; arrived

70. The pen I _____ I _____ is on my desk, right under my nose.
    A. think; lost   B. thought; had lost   C. think; had lost   D. thought; have lost

71. I told Sally how to get here, but perhaps I _____ for her.
    A. had to write it out   B. must have written it out
    C. should have written it out   D. ought to write it out

72. ——There were already five people in the car but they managed to take me as well.

——It _____ a comfortable journey.

A. can't be
B. shouldn't be
C. mustn't have been
D. couldn't have been

73. It's nearly seven o'clock. Jack _____ be here at any moment.

A. must
B. need
C. should
D. can

74. Johnny, you _____ play with the knife, you _____ hurt yourself.

A. won't; can't
B. mustn't; may
C. shouldn't; must
D. can't; shouldn't

75. The fire spread through the hotel very quickly but everyone _____ get out.

A. had to
B. would
C. could
D. was able to

76. ——When can I come for the photos? I need them tomorrow afternoon.

——They _____ be ready by 12:00.

A. can
B. should
C. might
D. need

77. ——I stayed at a hotel while in New York.

——Oh, did you? You _____ with Barbara.

A. could have stayed
B. could stay
C. would stay
D. must have stayed

78. ——Are you coming to Jeff's party?

——I'm not sure. I _____ go to the concert instead.

A. must
B. would
C. should
D. might

79. I was really anxious about you. You _____ home without a word.

A. mustn't leave
B. shouldn't have left
C. couldn't have left
D. needn't leave

80. ——Is John coming by train?

——He should, but he _____ not. He likes driving his car.

A. must
B. can
C. need
D. may

81. A left-luggage office is a place where bags _____ be left for a short time, especially at a railway station.

A. should
B. can
C. must
D. will

82. I wonder how he _____ that to the teacher.

A. dare to say
B. dare saying
C. not dare say
D. dared say

83. When he was there, he _____ go to that coffee shop at the corner after work every day.

A. would
B. should
C. had better
D. might

84. It has been announced that candidates _____ remain in their seats until all the papers have been collected.

A. can
B. will
C. may
D. shall

85. How _____ you say that you really understand the whole story if you have covered only a part of the article?

A. can
B. must
C. need
D. may

86. ——I hear you've got a set of valuable Australian coin. _____ I have a look?
    ——Yes, certainly.
    A. Do   B. May   C. Shall   D. Should

87. Water is _____ short in many big cities.
    A. running   B. flowing   C. becoming   D. moving

88. Excuse me for _____ you with such a small matter.
    A. troubling   B. taking   C. interrupting   D. making

89. This morning our water supply was _____ because of the cold weather.
    A. let down   B. cut off   C. taken up   D. brought away

90. The market was filled with salted fish, _____ the worst smell that you can imagine.
    A. sending off B. giving up   C. sending down   D. giving off

91. It was because the applicant was too proud _____ he failed in the interview.
    A. therefore   B. that   C. so that   D. so

92. Tom used to live in California, _____?
    A. used he   B. did he   C. was he   D. didn't he

93. So far there is no proof _____ people from other planets do exist.
    A. which   B. how   C. what   D. that

94. Never before _____ so highly successful in changing his surroundings.
    A. man has been B. man is   C. has man been   D. is man

95. _____ from the helicopter, the city looks very beautiful.
    A. Seeing   B. Having seen C. Seen   D. To see

96. The newspapers reported yesterday several _____ on the boundaries of these two countries.
    A. incidents   B. happenings   C. events   D. accidents

97. Some of the students in his class seem _____ to do their assignments.
    A. boring   B. interesting C. Tiring   D. unwilling

98. Let's work hard to find _____ to the problem.
    A. an answer   B. a way   C. a method   D. a solution

99. They have developed techniques which are _____ to those used in most factories.
    A. simpler   B. better   C. superior   D. greater

100. At the beginning of this term, our English teacher _____ a list of books for us to read.
    A. turned out B. made out   C. handed in   D. passed on

101. The movie is _____.
    A. success   B. a success   C. an success   D. success

102. ——I'd like _____ information about the management of your hotel, please.
    ——Well, you could have _____ word with the manager. He might be helpful.
    A. some; a   B. an; some   C. some; some   D. an; a

103. He arrives _____ the airport at ten _____ the morning.
    A. in; on   B. at; in   C. at; on   D. in; at
104. The number of the people present at the concert _____ much smaller than expected. There _____ many tickets left.
    A. was; was   B. were; was   C. were; were   D. was; were
105. Tom owns _____ larger collection of _____ books than any other student in our class.
    A. the; /   B. a; /   C. a; the   D. /; the
106. They put forward a lot of plans at the meeting, but none of _____ were carried out in their work.
    A. which   B. them   C. what   D. that
107. On _____ news today, there were _____ reports of heavy snow in that area.
    A. the; the   B. the; /   C. /; /   D. /; the
108. ——Do you regret paying ten dollars for that book?
    ——No, I would gladly have paid _____.
    A. as twice many   B. twice as many   C. twice as much   D. as twice much
109. The _____ you work, the _____ success you make.
    A. harder; greater   B. more harder; greater
    C. much harder; great   D. hardest; greatest
110. It was not until 1920 _____ regular radio broadcasts began.
    A. which   B. when   C. that   D. since
111. It will be five years _____ we meet again.
    A. since   B. until   C. before   D. when
112. I would never speak to someone like that _____ they said something unpleasant to me.
    A. even if   B. so that   C. as if   D. ever since
113. ——May I go now?
    ——_____ you've finished your work, you may go.
    A. After   B. Although   C. Now that   D. As soon as
114. Most animals have little connection with animals of a different kind, _____ they hunt them for food.
    A. if   B. while   C. unless   D. as
115. _____ he thought he was helping us with the work, he was _____ actually in the way.
    A. Although   B. Unless   C. Because   D. When
116. He left _____ London last night.
    A. to   B. for   C. from   D. with
117. _____ run faster than dogs.

A. Deer. B. Pig. C. Tiger. D. Lion

118. I have taught my sister English for one year, so she can speak _____ English.

A. little B. few C. a little D. a few

119. _____ everyone here today?

A. Be B. Are C. Is D. Am

120. Since the new technology was introduced last month, we _____ in speeding up production.

A. succeeded B. succeed C. have succeeded D. will succeed

121. They won't buy any new clothes because they _____ money to buy a new car.

A. save B. were saving C. have saved D. are saving

122. Unfortunately, when I dropped in, Professor Smith _____, so we only had time for a few words.

A. has just left B. had just left C. just left D. was just leaving

123. ——You could have asked Mr. Johnson for help. He is kind-hearted.

——I _____ that. A whole day _____ .

A. forget; wastes
B. forgot; was wasted
C. forgot; had wasted
D. forget; was wasted

124. ——Why weren't you at the meeting?

——I _____ for a long-distance call from my aunt in America.

A. waited B. was waiting C. had been waiting D. had waited

125. ——Why did you come by bus?

——My car broke down yesterday evening and I _____ it repaired.

A. didn't have B. don't have C. won't have D. haven't had

126. ——Does Liu Hui serve in the army?

——No, but he _____ in the army for three years.

A. served B. has served C. is serving D. would serve

127. Now the air pollution in this city _____ more and more serious with each passing day.

A. to become B. became C. becoming D. is becoming

128. Last week, two engineers _____ to help solve the technical problems of the project.

A. have sent B. were sent C. sent D. had sent

129. ——Did Alan enjoy seeing his old friends yesterday?

——Yes, he did. He _____ his old friends for a long time.

A. didn't see B. wouldn't see C. hasn't seen D. hadn't seen

130. ——You must have met him the other day.

——Oh, no, I _____ .

A. hadn't B. mustn't C. haven't D. didn't

131. ——Why do you look worried?

——Fred left the company half an hour ago. His work unfinished since he _____.
A. left		B. was left		C. has left		D. has been left

132. ——What's wrong with your coat?
——Just now when I wanted to get off the bus, the man next to me _____ on it.
A. sat		B. had sat		C. had been sitting		D. was sitting

133. By this time next week, the winners _____ their awards.
A. will have receive		B. will be received
C. will have received		D. will have been received

134. Even though they _____ side by side for twenty years, the two neighbors are not on good terms.
A. have been lived		B. had been living		C. had been lived		D. have been living

135. By the time your plane lands tonight, I _____ at the airport for 10 hours.
A. had waited		B. have been waited
C. had been waiting		D. will have been waiting

136. As long as you _____ the money back promptly, I'll lend it to you with pleasure.
A. return		B. will return		C. have returned		D. returned

137. No one _____ this building without the permission of the police.
A. is leaving		B. will be leaving		C. has left		D. is to leave

138. You _____ the difficulties after I explain the whole thing to you.
A. will be seen		B. will have seen		C. will see		D. see

139. ——Is it _____ that he will arrive here late?
——No, I don't think so.
A. probably		B. likely		C. possibly		D. perhaps

140. He earns quite a high _____ in his present job.
A. salary		B. bill		C. check		D. payment

141. It was because the applicant was too proud _____ he failed in the interview.
A. therefore		B. that		C. so that		D. so

142. It is because she is too inexperienced _____ she does not know how to deal with the situation.
A. that		B. this		C. so that		D. so

143. It was Japan _____ launched the war against China.
A. that		B. when		C. whom		D. which

144. _____ from the helicopter, the city looks very beautiful.
A. Seeing		B. Having seen		C. Seen		D. To see

145. If Mary had not been badly hurt in a car accident, she _____ in last month's marathon race.
A. would participate		B. might participate
C. would have participated		D. must participate

146. If I found the book, I _____ it to you.
   A. will bring
   B. would have brought
   C. would bring
   D. might have brought

147. You don't have to come in such a hurry. I'm busy now, and I would rather you _____ here tomorrow.
   A. would come   B. will come   C. came   D. have come

148. If I _____ more careful, such mistake could have been avoided.
   A. are   B. have been   C. would be   D. had been

149. The condition being _____, he may succeed.
   A. favorite   B. favorable   C. favoring   D. favored

150. Excuse me for _____ you with such a small matter.
   A. troubling   B. taking   C. interrupting   D. making

151. The market was filled with salted fish, _____ the worst smell that you can imagine.
   A. sending off   B. giving up   C. sending down   D. giving off

152. The newspapers reported yesterday several _____ on the boundaries of these two countries.
   A. incidents   B. happenings   C. events   D. accidents

153. At the beginning of this term, our English teacher _____ a list of books for us to read.
   A. turned out   B. made out   C. handed in   D. passed on

154. Tom likes _____ foreign coins.
   A. gathering   B. assembling   C. collecting   D. accumulating

155. Luckily, most sheep _____ the flood last month.
   A. endured   B. survived   C. opinion   D. passed

156. They thought about the problem for a long time but came to no _____.
   A. end   B. result   C. opinion   D. conclusion

157. The real trouble _____ their lack of confidence in their abilities.
   A. lies in   B. lies on   C. lies about   D. lie off

158. The story was so funny that everyone _____.
   A. laughed   B. interested   C. amused   D. joked

159. He _____ me by two games to one.
   A. beat   B. conquered   C. gained   D. won

160. It's almost a year since I left my mother. I'm really _____ seeing her.
   A. looking back on
   B. looking up to
   C. looking forward to
   D. looking out over

161. So far there is no proof _____ people from other planets do exist.
   A. which   B. how   C. what   D. that

162. Liquids are like solids _____ they have a definite volume.

A. in which   B. that   C. in that   D. which

163. He works too hard. That's _____ is wrong with him.

A. how   B. where   C. why   D. what

164. All _____ is peace and progress.

A. what is needed   B. which is needed   C. that is needed   D. for our needs

165. You cannot depend on _____ promise he makes.

A. whatever   B. which   C. whenever   D. whose

166. The hotel _____ we stayed was both cheap and comfortable.

A. when   B. at which   C. with which   D. since

167. Excuse me. If your call is not too urgent, do you mind _____ mine first?

A. I make   B. if I make   C. me to make   D. that I make

168. This is the longest bridge that _____ over Changjiang River.

A. is ever built   B. was ever built

C. has ever been built   D. has ever built

169. Would you please call me up later _____ they decide to go camping?

A. that   B. for   C. whether   D. when

170. David is such a good boy _____ all the teachers like.

A. that   B. who   C. as   D. whom

171. On Sundays there were a lot of children playing in the park, _____ parents seated together joking.

A. their   B. whose   C. which   D. that

172. Samuel received a training course in drawing for three years, _____ he got a good opportunity for further development.

A. after that   B. after which   C. after it   D. after this

173. Gun control is a subject _____ Americans have argued for a long time.

A. of which   B. with which   C. about which   D. into which

174. Mount Wuyi is such an attractive place of interest _____ everyone likes to visit.

A. that   B. as   C. which   D. what

175. After graduating from college, I took some time off to go travelling, _____ turned out to be a wise decision.

A. that   B. which   C. when   D. where

176. A war is so cruel that it always causes great losses, _____ has happened in Iraq.

A. what   B. as   C. that   D. one

177. It's helpful to put children in a situation _____ they can see themselves differently.

A. that   B. when   C. which   D. where

178. It is a truly delightful place, _____ looks the same as it must have done 100 years ago with its winding streets and pretty cottages.

A. as   B. where   C. that   D. which

179. Opposite is St. Paul's Church, _____ you can hear some lovely music.
A. which   B. that   C. when   D. where

180. He wrote many children's books, nearly half of _____ were published in the 1990s.
A. whom   B. which   C. them   D. that

181. I cannot but _____ the truth of your remarks, although they go against my interests.
A. to admit   B. admitting   C. admitted   D. admit

182. I forgot _____ you something that I have long meant to ask you.
A. to be asking   B. having asked   C. to ask   D. to have asked

183. ——Be careful not to drop the Ming Dynasty vase.
——Yes, we can't be _____.
A. too careful   B. very careful   C. too careless   D. careless enough

184. He began to take political science _____ only when he left school.
A. strictly   B. truly   C. carefully   D. seriously

185. He moved away from his parents and missed them _____ enjoy the exciting life in China.
A. too much to   B. very much to   C. enough to   D. much so as to

186. According to a recent U.S. survey, children spend up to 25 hours a week _____ TV.
A. to watch   B. to watching   C. watching   D. watch

187. The flu is believed _____ by viruses that like to reproduce in the cells inside the human nose and throat.
A. cause   B. being caused   C. to be caused   D. to have caused

188. It is said that in Australia there is more land than the government knows _____.
A. it what to do with   B. what to do it with
C. what to do with it   D. to do what with it

189. ——You were brave enough to raise objection at the meeting.
——Well, now I regret _____ that.
A. to do   B. to be doing   C. to have done   D. having done

190. The boy wanted to ride his bicycle in the street, but his mother told him _____.
A. not to   B. not to do   C. not do it   D. do not do

191. Paul doesn't have to be made _____. He always works hard.
A. learn   B. to learn   C. learned   D. learning

192. She looks forward every spring to _____ the flower-lined garden.
A. visit   B. paying a visit   C. walk in   D. walking in

193. His family _____ a big one. Now the family _____ watching TV.
A. is; is   B. are; are;   C. is; are;   D. are; is

194. To play basketball and to go swimming _____ useful for character-training.
A. was   B. is   C. are   D. were

195. Alice, together with the boys, _____ for having broken the rule.

A. was punished   B. punished   C. were punished   D. being punished

196. Neither Tom nor Jack and I _____ his students.

A. are   B. am   C. is   D. was

197. The number of people invited _____ fifty, but a number of them _____ absent for different reasons.

A. were; was   B. was; was;   C. were; were;   D. was; were

198. Not only I but also Rose and Mary _____ tried of having one examination after another.

A. is   B. are.   C. am   D. be

199. Jack as well as his brothers _____ Chinese in China.

A. are studying   B. have studied   C. studies   D. study

200. One third of the country _____ covered with trees and the majority of the citizens _____ black people.

A. is; are   B. is; is   C. are; are   D. are; is

201. Hiking by oneself can be fun and good for health. It may also be good for _____ building.

A. respect   B. friendship   C. character   D. reputation

202. Young kids should be taught how to get along with _____.

A. another   B. other   C. others   D. any other

203. _____ that your son is well again, you no longer have anything to worry about.

A. When   B. After   C. Before   D. Now

204. After the busy day I've had, I need a _____ drink.

A. heavy   B. sharp   C. strong   D. powerful

205. If you _____ come earlier, you would have caught the bus.

A. have   B. had   C. will have   D. would have

206. You can't find many _____ in a hospital.

A. man nurse   B. men nurse   C. men nurses   D. man nurses

207. It is said that the math teacher seems _____ towards bright students.

A. partial   B. liable   C. beneficial   D. preferable

208. People are _____ to have more confidence in a company if they know something about it.

A. like   B. liking   C. likely   D. unlike

209. After school, he helped his mother pick _____ in the field.

A. cotton   B. a cotton   C. cottons   D. some cottons

210. Tom and me had a long telephone _____ yesterday morning.

A. dialogue   B. conversation   C. talk   D. speech

211. When you're ready, I'll take you to _____ airport.

A. /   B. the   C. a   D. an

212. Tony is studying _____ mathematics.
A. ／   B. the   C. a   D. an

213. Many a student _____ the same questions by the teacher in yesterday's class.
A. asks   B. ask   C. was asked   D. were asked

214. We had a long way to go so we decided to _____ early.
A. set on   B. put on   C. set off   D. put off

215. One of the strongest hurricanes _____ was the Florida Keys Storm of 1935, during which 500 people were killed.
A. to record   B. recorded   C. recording   D. being recorded

216. I saw _____ man going into the office. I don't know who _____ man was.
A. ／; the   B. the; a   C. a; the   D. a; a

217. I won't pay them _____ they work harder.
A. if   B. in case   C. unless   D. lest

218. It _____ have rained last night, for the ground is wet.
A. will   B. must   C. can   D. should

219. Neither John nor his parents _____ at home.
A. is   B. has   C. are   D. was

220. ——How much did this bookcase cost?
——I forget _____.
A. how much it costs
B. how much did it cost
C. how much it cost
D. how much does it cost

221. _____ of the two girls is interested in painting.
A. Both   B. None   C. No one   D. Neither

222. Are those your books? I need to borrow some good _____.
A. one   B. ones   C. others   D. one's

223. Not only you but also he _____ sick.
A. is   B. are   C. has   D. have

224. Mr. Zhang as well as you _____ going to make a speech.
A. is   B. are   C. has been   D. have been

225. _____ clever the boy is!
A. What   B. What a   C. What an   D. How

226. This exercise is so difficult that only _____ students can do it.
A. a little   B. a few   C. little   D. few

227. Over _____ of China's inhabitants belong to the Han nationality.
A. nine-tenths   B. nine-tenth   C. ninth-ten   D. ninths-ten

228. _____ of September is my mother's birthday.
A. The twenty-one   B. Twenty-one   C. The twenty-first   D. Twenty-first

229. The carpet has so many stains on it that it needs _____.

A. replace　　　B. to replace　　　C. being replaced　　　D. to be replaced
230. The soldiers marched down the street, _____ their flags.
A. waved　　　B. waving　　　C. being waved　　　D. wave
231. _____ wonderful music it is! I like it very much.
A. What　　　B. What a　　　C. What an　　　D. How
232. He seldom uses computer, _____?
A. is he　　　B. isn't he　　　C. does he　　　D. doesn't he
233. Let us have a look at your essay, _____?
A. shall we　　　B. will you　　　C. do we　　　D. don't we
234. She says that you did it, _____?
A. did you　　　B. didn't you　　　C. does she　　　D. doesn't she
235. Is this the museum _____ you visited yesterday?
A. what　　　B. where　　　C. that　　　D. when
236. Are you _____ with your present salary?
A. satisfying　　　B. glad　　　C. happy　　　D. content
237. Only after a year _____ to see the result of my experiment.
A. I began　　　B. I had begun　　　C. have I begun　　　D. did I begin
238. He was disappointed so often that he became _____.
A. hopelessness　　　B. hopelessly　　　C. hopeful　　　D. hopeless
239. He suggested that we should take a notebook, _____?
A. did he　　　B. didn't he　　　C. should we　　　D. shouldn't we
240. I suppose that he's serious, _____?
A. isn't he　　　B. is he　　　C. don't I　　　D. do I
241. I didn't think he has been here, _____?
A. did I　　　B. didn't I　　　C. has he　　　D. hasn't he
242. My daughter runs faster than _____ in her class. She runs the fastest.
A. a boy　　　B. any boy　　　C. some boys　　　D. most boys
243. Everyone has finished the task _____ him.
A. but　　　B. but for　　　C. besides　　　D. except
244. This photo frame is _____ wood.
A. made up　　　B. made of　　　C. made from　　　D. made by
245. Once you enter the society, you are mostly _____ your own.
A. on　　　B. in　　　C. of　　　D. to
246. The chairman as well as any other people _____ present.
A. is　　　B. are　　　C. will　　　D. should
247. Emily _____ down and soon fell asleep.
A. lied　　　B. lay　　　C. laid　　　D. lain
248. She racked her brains trying to _____ the difficult problems.

A. work up B. work down C. work out D. work off

249. He _____ to his mother that he got A in the math exam.
A. lied B. lie C. lay D. lain

250. Einstein liked Bose's paper so much that he _____ his own work and translated it into German.
A. gave off B. turned down C. took over D. set aside

251. What did the teacher _____ you to do at home?
A. distribute B. assign C. divide D. point

252. She earns a high _____ as a doctor.
A. salary B. wages C. money D. payment

253. Lucy _____ to find a suitable house for some time.
A. was tried B. goes to try C. has been trying D. is trying

254. You _____ me because I didn't say that.
A. must have misunderstood B. must misunderstand
C. must be misunderstood D. had to misunderstand

255. The song had a melody that _____ like this.
A. was gone B. went C. is to go D. had went

256. If she _____ harder, she would have been enrolled in a better university.
A. works B. worked C. had worked D. would have worked

257. If there _____ a heavy snow next Sunday, we would not go skating.
A. is B. was C. are D. were

258. If you _____ him yesterday, you _____ what to do now.
A. had asked; would know B. had asked; will know
C. asked; would know D. asked; know

259. Before becoming President in 1928, Herbert Hoover _____ as Secretary of Commerce.
A. has served B. was served C. had served D. serving

260. To make the dessert _____ nice, she put in more butter and vanilla sauce.
A. taste B. to taste C. tasted D. tasting

261. I heard that Rose _____ here his weekend. Do you know when she _____?
A. will come; would arrive B. would come; will arrive
C. has come; comes D. had come; came

262. Thanks for your invitation, I'd be _____ to come.
A. delight B. delightsome C. delighted D. delightful

263. She wished she _____ Chuck before.
A. knows B. is knowing C. knew D. had known

264. It is suggested that we _____ a meeting next week.
A. hold B. held C. will hold D. are holding

265. It was recommended that we _____ the job as soon as possible.
A. did   B. do   C. would do   D. must do

266. You must have seen the show last week, _____?
A. must you   B. mustn't you   C. didn't you   D. haven't you

267. He must have been well informed of it, _____?
A. mustn't he   B. didn't he   C. needn't he   D. wasn't he

268. The boy in blue said he _____ play basketball.
A. didn't use to   B. didn't used to   C. usedn't   D. usen't to

269. I enjoyed the movie very much. I wish I _____ the book from which it was made.
A. have read   B. had read   C. should have read   D. are reading

270. He was very busy yesterday; otherwise, he _____ to the meeting.
A. would come   B. came   C. would have come   D. will come

271. You _____ to the discussion tomorrow if you have something more urgent to do.
A. don't need come   B. needn't come
C. needn't to come   D. don't need coming

272. _____ to speak, I shall start making preparation tomorrow.
A. Having invited   B. Having been invited
C. Inviting   D. Be invited

273. I learned a lot _____ out the experiment.
A. carrying   B. while carrying   C. when carried   D. to carry

274. The little boy longed _____ himself _____.
A. making; understood   B. to make; understand
C. to make; understood   D. to make; to understand

275. Nuclear science should be developed to benefit people _____ harm them.
A. rather than   B. better than   C. other than   D. more than

276. I don't regret _____ even if it might have upset her.
A. to tell her what I thought   B. to have told her that I thought
C. telling what I thought   D. telling her what I thought

277. When Mary paid her bill she was given a _____ for her money.
A. cheque   B. receipt   C. ticket   D. label

278. She says she'd rather he _____ tomorrow instead of today.
A. leaves   B. left   C. leave   D. would leave

279. I don't know him very well, _____ I have met him socially on a couple of occasions.
A. so that   B. when   C. although   D. since

280. She looked at me _____ I were a stranger.
A. even if   B. as if   C. lest   D. so that

281. I hope the stove will _____ enough heat to warm the room.
A. get over   B. give in   C. get out   D. give off

282. _____ wants to may attend the lecture on Sunday night.
A. One B. Whomever C. Whoever D. Whatever

283. _____ progress helps to relieve scarcities is a fact accepted by economics.
A. Although technological B. There is technological
C. Technological D. That technological

284. Is there anyone _____ can answer this question?
A. who B. which C. that D. whom

285. He is the tallest man _____ has ever lived here.
A. who B. which C. that D. whom

286. There is nothing _____ can be done now.
A. which B. that C. what D. who

287. The first English novel _____ I read was *A Tale of Two Cities* by Charles Dickens.
A. which B. that C. what D. who

288. There are many children and adolescents _____ behavior is generally unacceptable.
A. who B. whom C. whose D. that

289. He sent her a letter, _____ he said that he was sorry for what he had done to her.
A. which B. in which C. that D. whom

290. They want to know _____ do to help us.
A. what can they B. what they can C. how can they D. how they can

291. The government is believed to be considering _____ a law making it a crime to import any kind of weapon.
A. to pass B. passed C. have passed D. passing

292. That field _____ a good crop of potatoes last year.
A. planted B. grew C. raised D. yielded

293. _____ all his weak points, he at the same has many strong points.
A. Regardless of B. Although C. Despite D. No matter

294. Rarely _____ his lab those days.
A. Tom left B. did Tom leave C. is Tom leaving D. didn't Tom leave

295. He didn't say anything. _____.
A. So did Mary B. So Mary did C. Neither did Mary D. Neither Mary did

296. Richard can speak Spanish. _____.
A. So can his sister B. So his sister can
C. Neither can his sister D. Neither his sister can

297. It was essential that the application forms _____ back before the deadline.
A. be sent B. must be sent C. were sent D. would be sent

298. We were _____ for half an hour in the traffic and so we arrived late.
A. kept off B. held up C. put back D. broken down

299. _____ a reply, he decided to write again.

A. Not receiving B. Not having received
C. Having not received D. Not received
300. Everyone in the room remained _____.
A. happily and friendly B. orderly and kindly
C. happily and kindly D. orderly and friendly

第四章 完形填空

一、试题分析

完形填空测试学生各个层面上的语言理解能力及语言运用能力。短文长度为150~200个词，内容是学生所熟悉的题材。本部分所占分值比例为10%，共10小题，每小题1分。

完形填空部分的短文有10个空白处，空白处所删去的词既有实词也有虚词，每个空白处为一题，每题有四个选项。要求考生在全面理解文章内容的基础上选出一个最佳答案，使短文的意思和语言结构恢复完整。主要有以下4个考点。

（1）词义辨析：旨在测试考生对词汇的掌握程度和词语的运用能力，包括对词义的正确释义和理解，辨别同义词或反义词，以及辨别词形相近、意义不同的词等。

（2）词语搭配：旨在测试考生对常用词语搭配关系的掌握程度，包括词语的固定搭配和习惯用语，动词词组、形容词和介词的固定搭配和语义搭配，以及介词短语的固定用法等。

（3）语法结构：旨在测试考生正确运用语法知识的能力，包括动词的时态、语态和语气的用法，主谓一致，非谓语动词的用法和时态，基本句型和句子分类，以及强调句、倒装句和省略句。

（4）逻辑推理：旨在测试考生的综合分析能力，包括语篇知识和推断能力。考生应对文章进行全局性理解，分析句子之间、段落之间内在的逻辑关系。

二、解题技巧

1. 搭配判断法

根据对以往试题的分析，搭配型试题在完形填空题中占的比例最高。搭配型试题主要测试考生对常见搭配的熟练掌握程度，如哪些词要搭配不定式、动名词或某种从句，哪些词必须与某个介词搭配。在复习时要特别注意短语动词和介词的固定搭配。

2. 结构判断法

结构型试题主要包括句型、句式、连接词的选择等，解题时要运用句法知识，把握关键词，从而做出迅速正确的判断。完形填空题中有很多是利用语法的正确性与逻辑的排斥性间的矛盾来设计的。因此，考生应结合上下文的合理性及意义关系的逻辑性选择最佳答案。完形填空中常考的逻辑关系主要有4种。

（1）转折、让步关系：这种关系表明后一种观点或事实与前一种观点或事实相比有些出乎意料。

常见的表示转折、让步的词或词组有：but、still、yet、however、though、although、even if 等。

(2)因果关系：这种关系表明事物或现象之间的一种内在必然联系，即一个事件/现象（即"因"）引起第二个事件/现象（即"果"）。

表示原因的连词或词组有：because（of）、due to、owing to、thanks to、since、for、as 等。

表示结果的连词或词组有：so、therefore、then、as a result、in consequence、consequently、thus 等。

(3)递进、补充关系：这种关系表示对前一事实或观点做进一步阐述。

常用的表示递进、补充的词或词组有：moreover、likewise、besides、in addition、also、too、not only…but also、apart from、what's more 等。

(4)对比、比较关系：这种关系表明对观点或事物间的差异性和同一性进行对比和比较。

表示对比的词或词组有：in contrast、by contrast、on the contrary、conversely、unlike、oppositely 等。

表示比较的词或词组有：like、in comparison、compare…with、as、just、as 等。

3. 解题注意事项

(1)切记不要拿题就做，不看全文。

(2)注意通篇文章的关联度，切记不要把每个填空割裂开来做。

(3)切记不要把时间和精力消耗在翻译文章上，遇到不认识的词和不明白的句子，除非是影响到填空选项的选择，否则可以放在一边。

三、举例分析

There have been many great (1)_____. The first great invention was one that is still very important today—the wheel. This made it easier to carry (2)_____ things and to travel long distances.

In the early 1800s the world (3)_____ to change. There was little unknown land left in the world. People did not have to explore much any more. They began to work instead to make life better.

In the second half of the 19th century many great inventions were made. Among them were the camera, the electric light and the radio. These all became a big part (4)_____ our life today.

The first part of the 20th century saw more great inventions: the helicopter in 1909, movies with sound in 1926, the computer in 1928, and jet planes in 1930. This was also a time (5)_____ a new material was first made. Nylon came out in 1935. It changed the kind of clothes people wore.

The middle part of the 20th century brought new ways to help people (6)_____ disease. They worked very well. They made people healthier and let them live (7)_____ lives. By the 1960's most people could expect to live to be at least 60.

By this time most people had a very good life. Of course new inventions continued to be made. Man began (8) _____ ways to go into space. Russia made the first step. Then the United States took a step. Since then other countries, including China and Japan, have made their steps into space.

In 1969 man took his biggest step away from earth. Americans first walked on the moon. This is certainly just a (9) _____ though. New inventions will someday allow us to do things we have never yet (10) _____.

(1) A. discoveries   B. creations   C. invention   D. inventions
(2) A. heavy   B. light   C. clumsy   D. smart
(3) A. begin   B. open   C. started   D. start
(4) A. in   B. for   C. to   D. of
(5) A. while   B. when   C. where   D. at
(6) A. over   B. come   C. get over   D. get back
(7) A. longer   B. shorter   C. long   D. short
(8) A. going by   B. liking   C. looking for D. studying
(9) A. begin   B. beginning   C. began   D. starting
(10) A. dreamed   B. dreaming   C. to dream of D. dreamed of

参考答案：
(1)-(5). DADBC；(6)-(10). CACBD
(1) 此题为逻辑思维题。
(2) 此题为固定搭配题。
(3) 此题为固定搭配题。
(4) 此题为语法中的定语从句。
(5) 此题为近义词辨析。
(6) 此题为固定搭配题。
(7) 此题为语篇衔接。
(8) 此题为词义辨析。
(9) 此题为近义词辨析。
(10) 此题为固定搭配题。

专项练习

Passage 1（改编自 2014 年成人高考英语真题）

The Nobel Prizes are awards that are given each year for special things that people or groups of people have achieved. They are awarded in six (1) _____ : physics, chemistry, medicine, literature, peace and economics.

The prizes come from (2) _____ that was created by the Swedish inventor Alfred Nobel. He wanted to use some of his money to help make the world a (3) _____ place to live in.

Many organizations, chosen by Alfred Nobel himself, (4) _____ who receives the prizes.

Each award (5)_____ a gold medal, a diploma and a lot of money. Prizes can only be given to (6)_____ of all races, countries and religions. Only the Peace Prize can (7)_____ be given to a group.

The first Nobel Prizes were handed out (8)_____ December 10, 1901—five years after Alfred Nobel's death. Nobel was a chemist, engineer and inventor (9)_____ most famous invention, dynamite(炸药), made him a (10)_____ man. Although he gave the world such a deadly weapon, Nobel was always against wars and violence. He therefore left a lot of money that was to go to those who did a lot for the peace of mankind.

Officials at first handed out only five prizes a year. The prize for economics was first awarded in 1969. In some years prizes were not awarded because there were no worthy candidates.

All prizes are presented in Stockholm, Sweden, with the exception of the Peace Prize, which is awarded in Oslo, Norway.

(1) A. parts   B. district   C. regions   D. areas
(2) A. a bond   B. a fund   C. a scholarship   D. an investment
(3) A. better   B. richer   C. cleaner   D. bigger
(4) A. declare   B. conclude   C. determine   D. announce
(5) A. makes up   B. focuses on   C. refers to   D. consists of
(6) A. organizations   B. singles   C. institutions   D. individuals
(7) A. yet   B. also   C. still   D. ever
(8) A. on   B. in   C. at   D. by
(9) A. who   B. which   C. whose   D. whom
(10) A. humorous   B. rich   C. serious   D. smart

Passage 2

If you were to begin a new job tomorrow, you would bring with you some basic strengths and weakness. Success or (1)_____ in your work would depend, to a great extent, (2)_____ your ability to use your strengths and weaknesses to the best advantage. (3)_____ the utmost importance is your attitude. A person (4)_____ begins a job convinced that he isn't going to like it or is (5)_____ that he is going to ail is exhibiting a weakness which can only hinder his success. On the other hand, a person who is secure (6)_____ his belief that he is probably as capable (7)_____ doing the work as anyone else and who is willing to make a cheerful attempt (8)_____ it possesses a certain strength of purpose.

The chances are that he will do well. Having the prerequisite skills for a particular job is strength. Lacking those skills is obviously a (9)_____. A bookkeeper who can't add or a carpenter who can't cut a straight line with a saw is hopeless cases. This book has been designed to help you capitalize on the strength and overcome the weakness that you bring to the job of learning. But in groups to measure your development, you must first take stock of where you stand bow. As we get further along in the book, we'll be dealing in some details with specific processes for developing and strengthening learning skills. (10)_____, to begin with, you should pause to examine your present strengths and weaknesses in three areas that are critical to your success or failure in school: your attitude, your reading and communication kills, and your study habits.

(1) A. failure   B. victory   C. improvement   D. achievement
(2) A. in   B. on   C. of   D. to
(3) A. Out of   B. of   C. To   D. Into
(4) A. who   B. what   C. that   D. which
(5) A. ensure   B. certain   C. sure   D. surely
(6) A. onto   B. to   C. off   D. in
(7) A. to   B. at   C. of   D. for
(8) A. near   B. on   C. by   D. at
(9) A. idea   B. weakness   C. strenth   D. advantage
(10) A. However   B. And   C. When   D. For

Passage 3（改编自2015年成人高考英语真题）

Where do cars get their energy from? For most cars, the answer is petrol. (1)_____ some cars use electricity. These cars have (2)_____ motors that get their power from large batteries.

In (3)_____, there are even cars that have (4)_____ an electric motor and a petrol motor. These types of cars are (5)_____ hybrid(混合) cars.

Most people tend to think of electric cars as a new (6)_____, but they have been around for a long time. In the (7)_____ 19th and early 20th centuries electric cars were common because the technology for petrol engines was not very advanced.

But (8)_____ the petrol engine became easier to make and more powerful, this type of engines became the most popular Interest in electric cars was high in the 1970s and 1980s because oil became very expensive.

Recently, electric cars have again become well-liked because people want cars that pollute (9)_____. Electric cars are better than petrol cars in several ways. The biggest benefit is reduced pollution.

In areas (10)_____ there is a high percentage of electric cars, pollution is not that serious. The second benefit of electric cars is a education in the dependence on foreign oil.

Several countries don't want to rely on oil from other countries. Since electric cars can run on electricity from coal or nuclear power stations, there is less need to import oil.

(1) A. Or   B. And   C. Nor   D. But
(2) A. special   B. same   C. common   D. traditional
(3) A. time   B. addition   C. detail   D. summary
(4) A. either   B. neither   C. both   D. all
(5) A. said   B. known   C. regarded   D. called
(6) A. instrument   B. intention   C. influence   D. invention

(7) A. recent   B. late   C. beginning   D. last
(8) A. before   B. until   C. after   D. unless
(9) A. less   B. few   C. more   D. much
(10) A. what   B. which   C. where   D. when

Passage 4

At one time Einstein traveled all over the United States giving a lecture. He traveled by car, and soon became quite friendly with the driver. The driver always listened to Einstein's lecture, (1)_____ the great scientist gave again and again. One day, he told Einstein that he knew (2)_____ so well that he was sure he (3)_____ it himself. Einstein smiled and said, "Why don't you give the lecture for me next time?" The driver agreed.

That evening, both of them went along to the lecture hall. Nobody there (4)_____ Einstein before. As the driver (5)_____ his place on the stage everyone clapped. Then he began the lecture. Sure enough, he did not make a single mistake. It was a great success, and when it was over, people clapped and clapped. Then he started to leave, shaking (6)_____ with everybody, (7)_____ by Einstein quietly a few steps behind.

Just before they got to the door, a man stopped them and asked the driver a very difficult question. The driver listened carefully. Of course, he did not understand a thing, but he nodded his head as if he (8)_____. When the man stopped (9)_____, the driver said that he thought the question was very interesting but really very simple, in fact, (10) show how simple the question really was, he would ask his driver to answer it.

(1) A. that   B. this   C. which   D. it
(2) A. a lecture   B. the lecture   C. lecture   D. the lectures
(3) A. could give   B. must give   C. can give   D. would give
(4) A. had seen   B. saw   C. have seen   D. would see
(5) A. made   B. took   C. sat   D. stood
(6) A. hands   B. hand   C. the hands   D. his hand
(7) A. following   B. follow   C. followed   D. to follow
(8) A. did   B. could   C. would   D. might
(9) A. to talk   B. talked   C. talk   D. talking
(10) A. in order that B. so that   C. in order to   D. so as to

Passage 5

It was the late spring of 1979, a hot Saturday afternoon. Hundreds of us sat (1)_____, side by side, in rows of wooden chairs on the main campus lawn (校园草坪). We (2)_____ blue robes (毕业生长袍). We listened carefully to long (3)_____. When the ceremony (典礼) was (4)_____, we threw our caps in the air, and we were officially graduated from college. After that, I found Morrie Schwartz, my (5)_____ professor, and introduced him to my (6)_____. He was a small man who took small steps, as if a (7)_____ wind could; at

· 142 ·

any time, (8)_____ him up into the clouds! His teeth were in good shape. When he smiled it was as if you had just (9)_____ him the funniest joke on earth.

He told my parents how I (10)_____ every class he taught. He told them, "You have a special boy here. He helped me a lot." Shy but pleased, I looked at my feet. Before we left, I handed Mr. Schwartz a present, a briefcase with his name on the front. I didn't want to forget him. And I didn't want him to forget me. He asked if I would keep in touch, and without hesitation(犹豫) I said, "Of course." When he turned around, I saw tears in his eyes.

(1) A. along   B. around   C. beside   D. together
(2) A. took   B. wore   C. put on   D. got in
(3) A. lectures   B. dialogues   C. speeches   D. reports
(4) A. on   B. up   C. over   D. away
(5) A. lovely   B. precious   C. happy   D. favorite
(6) A. parents   B. elder brother C. girl friend   D. friends
(7) A. strong   B. north   C. warm   D. cold
(8) A. beat   B. pull   C. blow   D. wipe
(9) A. made   B. told   C. played   D. given
(10) A. left   B. reached   C. missed   D. took

Passage 6

A long time ago, a little boy loved to play around an apple tree. After eating some apples, he took a nap under the (1)_____. He and the tree loved each other. When the boy grew up, he (2)_____ played around the tree.

One day, the boy came back to the (3)_____. The tree (4)_____ the boy to play with him. "I am no longer a kid, I don't play around trees any more." The boy replied, "I want (5)_____. I need money to buy them." "Sorry, but I don't have money, but you can sell all my apples and have money to buy." The boy was so (6)_____ that he picked all the apples and (7)_____ happily. The boy never came back after he picked the apples. The tree was (8)_____.

Later, the boy needed a house for shelter, so he turned (9)_____ the tree. And the tree asked him to cut off all his branches. So the boy did. The tree was glad to see him happy but the boy never came back (10)_____ then. The tree was again lonely and sad.

(1) A. sunshine   B. screen   C. shadow   D. shelf
(2) A. no longer   B. no more   C. no wonder   D. no doubt
(3) A. top   B. area   C. tree   D. village
(4) A. developed   B. told   C. inspired   D. asked
(5) A. pleasure   B. honor   C. toys   D. fruits
(6) A. shamed   B. excited   C. embarrassed   D. knew
(7) A. chose   B. sang   C. rang   D. left
(8) A. sad   B. painful   C. angry   D. shame

(9) A. to   B. from   C. in   D. on
(10) A. afterwards   B. before   C. later   D. since

Passage 7

One day while a girl was walking in the woods she found two starving songbirds. She took them home and put them in a small (1)_____. She cared them and felt great love for the birds.

One day the (2)_____ and stronger of the two birds flew from the cage. Therefore, (3)_____ he flew close, she grasped him (4)_____. She felt glad, but suddenly she felt the bird go limp. She opened her hand and (5)_____ in horror at the dead bird.

She noticed the other bird moving back and (6)_____ on the edge of the cage. She could feel his great need for freedom. She lifted him from the cage and (7)_____ him softly into the air. The bird circled once, twice, three times.

The girl watched delightedly at the bird's enjoyment. Her heart was no longer (8)_____ with her loss. Suddenly the bird flew closer and (9)_____ softly on her shoulder. It sang the sweetest melody that she had ever heard.

The fastest way to (10)_____ love is to hold on it too tightly, the best way to keep love is to give it WINGS!

(1) A. cage   B. room   C. place   D. box
(2) A. weaker   B. taller   C. higher   D. longer
(3) A. Because   B. So   C. As   D. Since
(4) A. gently   B. slowly   C. toughly   D. wildly
(5) A. shouted   B. cried   C. glanced   D. stared
(6) A. forth   B. backwards   C. alert   D. rightwards
(7) A. fell   B. pushed   C. pulled   D. tossed
(8) A. touched   B. concerned   C. marked   D. cared
(9) A. landed   B. sat   C. slept   D. stood
(10) A. get   B. give   C. lose   D. find

Passage 8

Who doesn't love sitting (1)_____ a fire on a cold winter night? Fire is one of the man's greatest friends, but also one of the greatest enemies. Many big fires are caused by carelessness. A lighted cigarette thrown (2)_____ a car or a train window or a broken bottle lying on dry grass can (3)_____ a fire. Sometimes a fire can start on its own. Wet hay can begin burning of itself. This is (4)_____ it happens: the hay starts to rot and begins to (5)_____ heat which is trapped inside it. Finally, it bursts into flames. That is why farmers cut and store their hay when it's dry.

Fires have destroyed (6)_____ cities. In the 17th century, a small fire which (7)_____ in a shop burnt down nearly every building in London. Moscow was set fire to during the war against Napoleon. This fire (8)_____ burning for seven days. Even today, in spite of modern fire-fighting (9)_____, fire causes a great deal of damage each year both in our cities and in the countryside. It has been widely (10)_____ that fire is a good servant but a very bad master.

(1) A. beside   B. from   C. in   D. on
(2) A. into   B. out of   C. from   D. over
(3) A. happen   B. light   C. make   D. start
(4) A. what   B. why   C. how   D. because
(5) A. give off   B. get out   C. break out   D. make out
(6) A. no   B. many   C. small   D. big
(7) A. was   B. is   C. start   D. began
(8) A. lasted   B. continued   C. stopped   D. began
(9) A. methods   B. researches   C. studies   D. engines
(10) A. written   B. asked   C. forgotten   D. said

Passage 9

In the dinning room of my grandfather's house stood a heavy grandfather's clock. Meals in the dinning room were a (1)_____ for our four generations to become one. The grandfather's clock always stood like a trusted old family friend, (2)_____ us playing jokes and telling stories, which was already a (3)_____ of our life.

As a child, the old clock interested me. I watched and listened to it during (4)_____. I was surprised how at (5)_____ times of the day, the clock would strike three times, six times or more, with a wonderful great (6)_____ that echoed throughout the house. The clock chimed year after year, a part of my (7)_____, a part of my heart.

Even more (8)_____ to me was my grandfather's special action each day. He meticulously (9)_____ the clock with a special key each day. The key was magic to me. It (10)_____ our family's magnificent clock ticking and striking all year round.

(1) A. time   B. possibility   C. problem   D. pleasure
(2) A. seeing   B. hearing   C. watching   D. looking
(3) A. start   B. part   C. signal   D. mark
(4) A. stories   B. jokes   C. periods   D. meals
(5) A. busy   B. urgent   C. happy   D. different
(6) A. shock   B. sound   C. song   D. music
(7) A. memories   B. minds   C. comfort   D. information
(8) A. comfortable   B. hopeful   C. wonderful   D. skillful
(9) A. opened   B. wound   C. turned   D. started
(10) A. made   B. controlled   C. kept   D. fixed

Passage 10（高中英语完形填空改编）

I could have easily gone through life without getting to know one of the most romantic feelings—love for a dog.

For at least ten years my (1)_____ had been suggesting that we get a dog. There were several reasons why the idea (2)_____. We had noticed that, on our block, couples with no children as a rule (3)_____ one large or two small dogs. So we got one puppy (4)_____ we too had no children.

He flew into the house with thespeed of a Formula 1（一级方程式赛车）. In several minutes he ran over all the house, jumped from my shoulder onto the bed, and ended up in the bathroom, where my wife washed him with motherly care. From that day on, the invisible(看不见的) (5)_____ for the love of the new member of our household began at my home.

He seemed to (6)_____ that at once. Most of the meals that my wife had 46 for him with greater care than those for me—he didn't even look at.

Every evening I went out walking with him. I could not know who was walking whom (7)_____ one evening, when, tired from work, I (8)_____ the walk. The dog was very angry and dragged me out.

Last night our dog pulled me by the ear with his teeth, woke me up in my dream, and dragged me into the kitchen to make me turn off the light which had disturbed(干扰) his sleep. I meekly(乖乖地) admitted that I had forgotten to switch off the light, but that was not (9)_____. He looked at me like a teacher at a pupil who repeatedly makes mistakes.

Now we finally know who's the (10)_____ at home, and for twenty years we had seriously argued whether it was my wife or I.

(1) A. wife　　　　　B. son　　　　　　C. husband　　　　D. daughter
(2) A. came up with　B. came out　　　　C. came up　　　　D. came on
(3) A. kept　　　　　B. rose　　　　　　C. carried　　　　　D. invited
(4) A. if　　　　　　B. unless　　　　　 C. since　　　　　　D. before
(5) A. signal　　　　B. war　　　　　　C. work　　　　　　D. truth
(6) A. doubt　　　　B. understand　　　C. wonder　　　　　D. dislike
(7) A. while　　　　B. so　　　　　　　C. until　　　　　　D. because
(8) A. gave in　　　 B. gave up　　　　　C. gave away　　　　D. gave out
(9) A. bad　　　　　B. good　　　　　　C. enough　　　　　D. true
(10) A. boss　　　　B. member　　　　　C. adult　　　　　　D. child

第五章 阅读理解

一、大纲解析

阅读理解题主要考查考生综合运用各类语言知识和理解不同篇章的能力。题型为选择题，共 15 小题。本题向考生提供 3~4 段短文，总阅读量不少于 1000 个词。短文题材涉及日常生活、史地、文化、人物传记等。体裁有记叙文、说明文、应用文等。每篇短文后有数量不等的问题或不完整的句子。要求考生在仔细阅读短文以后，从给出的四个选项中选出可以用来回答问题或补全句子的最佳选项。要求考生能通过阅读掌握短文的主旨大意、主要事实、有关细节以及上下文的逻辑关系等，既能看懂字面意思，又能推论出隐含意思，既能回答就文章局部细节提出的问题，又能回答有关文章总体内容的问题。

二、解题方法与技巧

阅读理解是重要的语言技能，考查的要点在于是否理解文章的主旨、作者的意图和能否理解文章中心思想的重要论据、具体信息，能否做出简单、合理的判断与推理，能否根据上下文猜到生词的含义。

1. 审题

一定要仔细审阅文章的标题，它能给予考生启示，帮助考生抓住文章的主题，有利于对文章的理解。

2. 快速阅读全文

理解文章大意、中心和作者意图。重点阅读第一段和结尾句，因为它们通常是文章中心段落的概括和总结，对正确理解全文提供了重要信息，有利于抓住文章的梗概与中心。

3. 阅读文章后的问题

了解都有什么问题，以抓住阅读要点。如果文章长，可先读问题，然后带着问题去读文章，更容易抓住要点。

(1) 有的问题能从文章的一句话中找到正确答案。
(2) 有的问题能从文章的一段话中找到答案。
(3) 有的问题需要从整篇文章的中心思想来进行逻辑推理寻求答案。

4. 细读文章

根据问题，注意了解人物、事件、时间、地点、原因和过程，注意连接词及一些关键词，以分清层次，判断作者态度及观点，更好地了解文章主旨。

5. 遇到生词不要急,可用以下方法处理

(1)利用构词法的知识来猜测词义。

(2)人名、地名等专用名词,不影响阅读理解,不必弄清其含义。

(3)有些生词的含义,可根据标点如破折号、逗号、冒号等,或一些连词如 and、but、or 等,进行判断。

(4)有些生词可根据上下文来判断词义。

6. 选答案

灵活运用对应法、排除法、归纳法、比较法、抓关键词等方法,找出答案。

(1)排除法是用得比较多的一种方法。用排除法时,可排除以下选项:

①与文中的陈述事实相反的选项。

②文中完全没有提到的内容的选项。

③不合情理或荒谬的选项。

(2)对于考查作者的主导思想、情绪、倾向等方面的问题应注意:

①准确把握字里行间的意思,切忌用自己的主观想法或自己的观点代替文章作者的思想观点。

②特别注意那些描写环境和气氛的语言,以及表达感情、态度和观点的词语。

(3)结合平时积累的有关英语语言国家的文化传统、风俗习惯等背景知识来识别和评价。

7. 核查答案

用全文的主题思想统率各问题,在观点、方式、态度上存在不一致或自相矛盾的选项要重新考虑答案,与主题思想不符的要重新进行审核。

三、考题类型及示例

在阅读理解测试中,一般都要求考生理解所读材料的大意,掌握主要事实和有关的具体细节,辨别作者的基本态度和观点,根据有关信息进行一定的推理、判断或引申。阅读理解的题型可分为以下四种:主旨大意题,词语理解题,事实细节题,推理判断题。

1. 主旨大意题

主旨大意题考查的主要内容包括主题思想、写作意图、标题。这类题型中常见的问题方式有:

Which of the following is the main idea of the passage?

The main idea of the passage is…

The major point discussed in the passage is…

The best title for this passage would be…

The author's purpose in writing the passage is…

The passage is mainly about …

主旨大意题的答案要从主题句或主题词得出,所以主旨大意题的命题点也就是主题句经常出现的地方。例如:文章的首句、各段首句和段尾句;语义转折处,尤其是句首语义转折处;特殊标点符号(破折号、问号),尤其是句首的特殊标点符号之后的内容;表达强烈观点处，强烈对比处。

例：The Egyptian kingdom was not self-contained but traded widely with the outside world, using the enormous surpluses of wheat grown on rich valley to profit from high prices resulting from famine in various parts of the Mediterranean world. Relations with the neighboring and in some way similar civilization of Mesopotamia were always close, though often hostile. Syria and Palestine suffered much in biblical times from the competition of the two world powers of the day. For a long time, Egypt ruled over Syria but gradually its power declined and it was itself conquered, first by the Assyrians(663 B.C.) and then for a longer term by the Persians(525-332 B.C.)

This passage is mainly about (　　).

A. The early history of Egypt

B. Wheat trade between Egypt and its neighbors

C. The fall of Egypt

D. Famine in the Mediterranean word

【解析】A。本段无明显主题句，主题思想并非直接由一两个句子表述，而是在文中间接暗示的，这就需要根据文中细节进行概括与归纳。B、C、D均与细节有关。

2. 词语理解题

词语理解题考查学生通过上下文线索理解某些词语甚至句子的能力。这类题型常见的提问方式有：

By "…" the author mean_____.

The phrase "…" in the passage most properly mean_____.

The sentence "…" in Para. X can be best replaced by_____.

The word "…" in Para. X is closest in meaning to_____.

词语理解题旨在考查学生正确理解文章的词语信息，根据上下文猜测词义的能力。词语理解题的正确选项必然能够对所考查词汇或短语进行替换，不能替换原文的是干扰项。考生必须通过大量阅读扩大英语词汇量，同时还要学习和掌握一些基本的猜词方法。构词法推测词义是常见的一种方法，除此之外，还可以运用语篇分析，通过上下文的逻辑推测词义。

3. 事实细节题

事实细节题的目的是考查考生正确把握文中信息的能力。一般来说，这类试题难度不大，只要考生稍加注意，读懂原文，就能迅速在文中找出所需的信息。但是考生要注意，在查找信息时，一定要认真理解题意，准确找出问题信息的出处，否则就有可能给出错误的答案。事实细节题在阅读理解中占的比例较大，其试题的问题方式也没有固定的模式，这一点需要考生在日常学习中多加注意。

这类题型常见的提问方式有：

The author mentions…

Which of the following does the author discuss?

Whose suggestion was adopted at the meeting?

How did the man carry out the experiment?

Which of the following statements is not true(correct)?

According to the passage…where(when, why, how, what, which, etc.)…

4. 推理判断题

推理判断题要求考生通过字里行间，根据文章的内容或结构做出合乎逻辑的推论。这种题型有一定的难度，它考查的内容包括考生对作者观点的理解、态度的判断，对修辞、语气、隐含知识等的了解，要求考生根据常识做出合乎逻辑的推断。这种题中干扰项对答案颇具干扰力，这是造成考生难以取得高分的主要原因。推理判断题测试考生的逻辑推理能力、数字推测能力、语言分析能力、综合归纳能力等，其主要提问方式有：

It can be inferred from the passage that…

The passage implies/suggest that…

It can be concluded from the passage that…

What can we learn from the passage?

Which of the following might be discussed after the passage?

When would this passage most probably appear?

四、范例

A

Generation of Americans have been brought up to believe that a good breakfast is one of the essentials. Eating breakfast at the start of the day, we have all been told, is as necessary as the gasoline in the family car before starting a trip.

But for many people the thought of food first thing in the morning is by no means a pleasure despite all the efforts, they still take no breakfast. Between 1977 and 1983, the latest years the figures are available, the number of people who didn't have breakfast increased by 33 percent 8.8 million to 11.7 million-according to the Chicago-based Market Research Corporation of America.

For those who feel pain or guilt about not eating breakfast, however, there is some good news. Several studies in the last few years indicate that, for adults especially, there may be nothing wrong with omitting breakfast. "Going without breakfast does not affect performance." Said Arnold E. Bender, the former professor of nutrition at Queen Elizabeth College in London, "nor does giving people breakfast improve performance."

Scientific evidence linking breakfast to better health or performance is surprisingly inadequate, and most of the recent work involves children, not adults. "The literature," says one researcher, Dr. Emes to Pollitt at the University of Texas, "is poor."

【内容提要】尽管人们长期以来一直认为不吃早餐对人们的健康不利，但最近的研究成果表明：是否吃早餐对人的健康、工作并无大碍。

1. The passage is mainly concerned with _____.

A. a study of the Chicago-based Market Research Corporation

B. one of life's essentials

C. latest figures of people who don't eat breakfast

D. breakfast and human health

【考点】主旨大意题

【解析】D。题干的大意是：本文主要关注的是_____。本文的关键词是 breakfast、health、performance。全文的主旨大意就是"早餐与健康"。

2. For those who do not take breakfast, the good news is that _____.

A. several studies have been done in the past few years

B. not eating breakfast does no harm to one's health

C. adults have especially made studies in this field

D. eating little in the morning may be good for health

【考点】事实细节题

【解析】B。题干的大意是：对于那些不吃早餐的人来说，好消息是_____。从文中第三段的第二句"Several studies in the last few years indicate that, for adult especially, there may be nothing wrong with omitting breakfast."（最近几年的研究成果表明，尤其是对成年人来说，不吃早餐并没有什么不对的。）可以找到 B 为正确选项。

3. In the third paragraph, "nor does giving people breakfast improve performance" means _____.

A. anyone without breakfast does improves his performance

B. not giving people breakfast improves performance

C. people having breakfast do improve their performance

D. having breakfast does not improve performance, either

【考点】事实细节题

【解析】D。题干的大意是：第三段中"人们吃早餐也不会改善他们的工作表现"，意思是_____。本题应与前一句结合起来理解，"Going without breakfast does not affect performance."Said Arnold E. Bender, the former professor of nutrition at Queen Elizabeth College in London, "nor does giving people breakfast improve performance."（不吃早餐就上班不影响工作表现……而吃了早餐也不会改善其工作表现。）由此可知其与选项 D 同义。

4. The word "literature" in the last sentence refers to _____.

A. stories about breakfast

B. written works on a particular subject

C. any printed material

D. the modern novels of American

【考点】词语理解题

【解析】A。题干的大意是：最后一句中的"literature"这个词指的是_____。英语中 literature 有很多意思，其中有选项 B（关于某一课题的书面作品），还有选项 C（印刷品，宣传品），另外还有"文学作品，文献"等意思。但根据上下文来看，此处只能指"人们对于早餐的看法及证据"（即选项 A）。

5. What is implied but not stated by the author is that _____.

A. not eating breakfast might affect the health of children

B. breakfast does not affect performance

C. Professor Bender once taught college courses in nutrition in London

D. people who don't eat breakfast have increased

【考点】推理判断题

【解析】A。题干的大意是：作者暗示而未指明的是_____。从文中最后一段所提供的信息推断出选项 A "不吃早餐可能会影响儿童的健康" 为最佳答案。

B

Concern with money, and then more money, in order to buy the conveniences and luxuries of modern life, has brought great changes to the lives of most Frenchmen. More people are working than ever before in France. In the cities the traditional leisurely midday meal is disappearing. Offices, shops, and factories are discovering the greater efficiency of a short lunch hour in company lunch rooms. In almost all lines of work emphasis now falls on ever-increasing output. Thus the "typical" Frenchman produces more, earns more, and buys more consumer goods than his counterpart of only a generation ago. He gains in creature comforts and ease of life. What he loses to some extent is his sense of personal uniqueness, or individuality.

Some say that France has been Americanized. This is because the United States is a world symbol of the technological society and its consumer products. The so-called Americanization of France has its critics. They fear that "assembly-life" will lead to the disappearance of the pleasures of the more graceful and leisurely (but less productive) old French style. What will happen, they ask, to taste the elegance, and the cultivation of the good things in life—to joy in the smell of a freshly picked apple, a stroll(散步) by the river, or just happy hours of conversation in a local cafe?

Since the late 1950s life in France has indeed taken on qualities of rush, tension, and the pursuit of material gain. Some of the strongest critics of the new way of life are the young, especially university students. They are concerned with the future, and they fear that France is threatened by the triumph of this competitive, goods-oriented culture. Occasionally, they have reacted against the trend with considerable violence.

In spite of the critics, however, countless Frenchmen are committed to keeping France in the forefront of the modern economic world. They find that the present life brings more rewards, conveniences, and pleasures than that of the past. They believe that a modem, industrial France is preferable to the old.

1. Which of the following is a feature of the old French way of life?

A. Leisure, elegance and efficiency

B. Elegance, efficiency and taste

C. Leisure, elegance and taste

D. Elegance, efficiency and leisure

【考点】推理判断题

【解析】C。根据第二段"They fear that 'assembly-life'…in a local cafe"得知法国人以前的生活方式是优雅、休闲和有品位的,因此C项为此题答案。

2. Which of the following is NOT true about Frenchmen?

A. Many of them prefer the modern life style

B. They actually enjoy working at the assembly line

C. They are more concerned with money than before

D. They are more competitive than the older generation

【考点】事实细节题

【解析】B。从最后一段可知A项说法正确,从第一、第二段可知C、D两项说法也正确。从文章中可知,由于法国人更关心钱,他们的生活节奏加快,工作效率提高,但文中并没有指出他们很喜欢这种流水线的工作,而且有些人对这种变化持反对态度,因此B项为此题答案。

3. The passage suggests that _____.

A. in pursuing material gains the French are suffering losses elsewhere

B. it's now unlikely to see a Frenchman enjoying a stroll by the river

C. the French are fed up with the smell of freshly picked apples

D. great changes have occurred in the life style of all Frenchmen

【考点】主旨大意题

【解析】A。从第一段的最后可知A项说法正确。B、C、D三项说法过于片面,过于绝对,故不对。

4. Which of the following is true about the critics?

A. Critics are greater in number than people enjoying the new way of life

B. Student critics are greater in number than critics in other fields

C. Student critics have, on occasion, resorted to violent means against the trend

D. Critics are concerned solely with the present and not the future

【考点】事实细节题

【解析】C。第三段第三、第四句指出,学生关心未来,担心法国受到这种充满竞争的商品化文化的威胁。偶尔,他们用相当的暴力来反对这种趋势。可见,C项说法与此一致,D项不对。从最后一段中可知A、B两项均不对。因此C项为正确答案。

5. Which of the following best states the main idea of the passage?

A. Changes in French way of life

B. Criticism of the new life style

C. The Americanization of France

D. Features of the new way of life

【考点】主旨大意题

【解析】A。文章主要是讲述法国生活方式的变化,作者的态度是客观的,没有对这种变化发表个人看法,没有带任何主观色彩。因此A项为正确答案。

专项练习

Passage 1

On my way home from work one day in 1994, I stopped at supermarket for shopping. I was behind two customers. The person checking out was a young mother with her little girl. As the clerk was scanning the things she had chosen, the young lady was carefully counting her money, worried. After the last thing was scanned, the clerk told the young mother the total.

The young mother's expression turned to embarrassment as she realized she did not have enough money. She started to see which things to put back, and trying to look sympathetic—I had been in situation where I did not have enough money plenty of times. Finally, the young mother gave something back to the clerk, and asked for new total.

At that moment, the woman in front of me asked the clerk to wait a moment. She took out $5 and handed it to the clerk to pay what the young mother was short of. When the clerk tried to give the woman the fifty cents change, she pointed to the little girl and told the clerk to give it to her. The little girl smiled and ran to one of the machines to spend the money. Naturally, the young mother was thankful and said so. The woman smiled and told her she was welcome.

I will never forget the look on that little girl's face-not when she was given the money, but when she realized that a perfect stranger cared enough to help them. From the way she looked at the woman. You could tell that she learned something valuable that day some people do care.

That woman taught me several things with that one little deed. There are many situations in which we can help other people. It doesn't take much money. A few dollars to someone like me was something quite different to that mother.

1. Why was the young mother carefully counting her money?

A. She was afraid that she didn't have enough money

B. To know how much would be left after payment

C. To see if she could buy more things

D. She got ready to pay for what she had taken

2. Why did the author try to show to the young mother by smiling to her?

A. He had seen her before

B. He was willing to help her

C. He was surprised at her embarrassment

D. He understood what happened to her

3. The woman in front of the author handed five dollars to _____.

A. the author   B. the mother

C. the clerk   D. the girl

4. What is the text trying to teach us?

A. Woman and children should be helped

B. A little care can bring about great happiness

C. There are always people who are in trouble

D. A friend in need is a friend indeed

Passage 2

Although education is compulsory in the United States, it is not compulsory for all children to get their education at school. A number of parents believe that they can provide a better education for their children at home. Children who are educated at home are known as "home-schoolers". There are about 300,000 home-schoolers in the United States today. Some parents prefer teaching their children at home because they do not believe that state schools teach the correct religious values; others believe they can provide a better educational experience for their children themselves. Interestingly, results show that home-schooled children tend to do better than average on national tests in reading and maths.

David Guterson is an American writer. He and his wife teach their three children themselves. Guterson says that his children learn very differently from children in regular school. Learning starts with the children's interests and questions. For example, when there is heavy snowfall on a winter's day, it may, start a discussion or reading about climate, Alaska, polar bears and winter, tourism. Or a spring evening, when the family is watching the stars, is a good time to ask questions about satellites and the space program.

Although home schooling offers an experience that is often more interesting than regular schools, critics also point out that home-schoolers miss out on many important things. The home-schooler is an outsider who, because he or she never attended school, might be uncomfortable mixing with other people in adult life. Critics also say that most parents are not well qualified to teach their own children. However, most parents don't have the time or desire to teach their children at home, so schools will continue to be where most children get their formal education.

1. Some parents decide to teach their children at home mainly because _____.

   A. education in the United States is not yet completely compulsory

   B. they think they are better teachers than those who teach in the state schools

   C. they believe they can provide better education than the state schools

   D. programs and subjects in the state schools don't contain something about religion

2. What will David Guterson probably teach his children when the Brazilian rain forests are on the news?

   A. sports and physical exercise

   B. desert and the greenhouse effect

   C. art and literature

   D. computer and information technology

3. Some critics may object to the idea that _____.

   A. home schooling is often more interesting than the regular school

B. home-schoolers may feel uncomfortable when meeting others in the future

C. many parents are not good enough to teach their children

D. home will gradually become the main place where children receive their education

4. The best title of this passage might be _____.

A. Home-schoolers
B. Home Schooling
C. Learning, with Interests
D. Regular Schooling vs Home Schooling

Passage 3

A happy life and a meaningful life are not the same. Leading a happy life is associated with being a "taker", while leading a meaningful life corresponds with being a "giver".

Happiness is about feeling good and getting what we want. People who are happy tend to think that life is easy. They are in good physical health and able to buy the things that they need and want. Happiness is about satisfying our needs and desires. The pursuit of happiness is often associated with selfish behavior. Animals have needs and desires and they can feel happy too. What sets human beings apart from animals is not the pursuit of happiness, but also the pursuit of meaning, which is unique to humans.

We can often find meaning in helping others or marking a sacrifice for a "greater good". Meaning often comes at the expense of happiness. When people have invested themselves in something bigger than themselves, they worry more and have higher levels of stress and anxiety in their lives than happy people. Volunteering in rural schools, for example, is meaningful but also involves hardship.

Happiness, like any emotion, is felt in here and now—it eventually fades away. However, meaning is enduring. It connects the past to the present to the future.

1. What is the main idea of the passage?

A. A happy life is basically different from a meaningful life.

B. Leading a happy life is connected with being a "taker".

C. Happiness is about feeling good and getting what we want.

D. Meaning connected the past to the present to the future.

2. Paragraph 2 tells us that the pursuit of happiness is that _____.

A. sets humans apart from animals

B. is associated with selfish behavior

C. means to give up what one has

D. is unique to human being

3. From paragraph 3 we know that _____.

A. helping others can make our life meaningful

B. meaning comes together with happiness

C. happy people have higher levels of anxiety

D. volunteering in rural schools makes a happy life

4. It is implied in paragraph 4 that _____.

A. meaning will disappear sooner or later

B. living a happy life means to be a "giver"

C. happiness lasts a relatively short period of time

D. making a sacrifice for a "greater good" brings us happiness

Passage 4

When we conduct foreign trade, the importance of understanding the language of a country cannot be underestimated. The successful marketer must achieve export communication which requires a thorough understanding of the language as well as the ability to speak it. Those who deal with advertising should be concerned less with obvious differences between languages and more with the exact meanings expressed.

A dictionary translation is not the same as an idiomatic interpretation, and seldom will the dictionary translation meet the needs. A nation producer of soft drinks had the company's brand name impressed in Chinese characters which were phonically accurate. It was discovered later, however, that the translation's literal meaning was "female horse fattened with wax", hardly the image the company sought to describe. So carelessly translated advertising statements not only lose their intended meaning but can suggest something very different including something offensive or ridiculous. Sometimes, what was translated was not an image the companies had in mind for their products. Many people believe that to fully appreciate the true meaning of a language it is necessary to live with the language for years. Whether or not is the case, foreign marketers should never take it for granted that they are effectively communicating in another language.

1. Which of the following is the best topic of the passage?

   A. Idiomatic meanings of language

   B. Language problems in foreign trade

   C. Translation failures in foreign trade

   D. Culture differences between language

2. To an advertiser, which one should they pay more attention to?

   A. understanding of a language

   B. ability to speak a language

   C. obvious differences between language

   D. the different idiomatic expressions between languages

3. What is the main idea of the second paragraph?

   A. Best translation should be the intent of the original statement

   B. A dictionary translation may not convey the true meaning of an idiom

   C. A dictionary will meet the needs

   D. Both A and C

4. In terms of communication in another language, marketers should not be too _____.

   A. proud   B. modest   C. self-confident   D. happy

Passage 5

Common sense would tell us that physically active children may be more likely to become active and healthy adults. In the United States, elementary and middle schools are advised to give students two and a half hours of physical activity a week. That is what the Centers for Disease Control and Prevention and the American Heart Association recommend. They say high schools should provide about four hours of physical activity each week. Yet many schools across the country have reduced their physical education programs. Criticism of the cuts has led in some places to efforts to give students more time for exercise, not less.

The future health of Americans may depend on it. A study reported that life expectancy has fallen or is no longer increasing in some parts of the United States. The situation is the worst among poor people in the southern states, and especially women. Public health researchers say it is largely the result of increases in obesity, smoking and high blood pressure. They also blame differences in health services around the country.

In 2006, a study found that only four percent of elementary schools provided daily physical education all year for all grades. This was true of eight percent of middle schools and two percent of high schools. The study also found that 22 percent of all schools did not require students to take any P. E.

Charlene Burgeson is the executive director of the National Association for Sport and Physical Education. She says one problem for P. E. teachers is that schools are under pressure to put more time into academic subjects. Also, parents may agree that children need exercise in school. Yet many parents today still have bad memories of being chosen last for teams because teachers favored the good athletes in class.

But experts say P. E. classes have changed. They say the goal has moved away from competition and toward personal performances, as a way to build a lifetime of activity. These days, teachers often lead activities like weight training and yoga. Some parents like the idea of avoiding competitive sports in P. E. class. Yet others surely dislike that idea. In the end, schools may find themselves in a no-win situation.

1. Why are schools recommended to give students certain time for sports?

A. Because different schools set up different physical education programs

B. Because the physical activity of children will influence their health in adulthood

C. Because nowadays children spend too much time on their studies

D. Because only four percent of elementary schools provided daily physical education

2. All the following factors may have caused fallen life expectancy in some parts of the United States EXCEPT that _____.

A. more and more people are getting fat

B. an increasing number of people smoke

C. some places don't provide adequate health services

D. a lot of people don't take regular exercise

3. Today the goal of P. E. classes is to _____.

A. help all the students exercise

B. create competition among students

C. produce good athletes

D. avoid competitive sports

4. We can infer from the passage that _____.

A. parents all agree with the idea of avoiding competitive sports

B. parents enjoyed their P. E. classes when they were students

C. a lot of attention is paid to students' academic subjects

D. a lot of schools don't have enough P. E. Teachers

Passage 6

People who talk and sing to plants are not crazy, according to ArnoldBraymar, a government agriculture expert. "In fact, singing and talking to plants make them grow better," says Braymar. The reason is quite simple-when we sing or talk to plants, we exhale carbon dioxide which plants need to survive and thrive. Plants absorb the carbon dioxide through their pores during the sunlight hours and produce oxygen which people need to survive. Singing and talking is effective, however, only during the daytime. Bedtime lullabies(摇篮曲) will not help plants to sleep better or grow faster.

1. Which sentence best expresses the main idea?

A. Plants and flowers should not be left in bedrooms at night

B. Plants do not prosper when placed away from people

C. The practice of talking to plants can be defended scientifically

D. Doctor are worried about people who communicate with nature

2. The point of the paragraph is that singing and talking to plants can be _____.

A. proved dangerous by science

B. personally gratifying for most people

C. socially embarrassing for some people

D. helpful to people and plants

3. The paragraph could be entitled _____.

A. Tell Me More　　　　　　B. Carbon Dioxide, Please

C. People Are Funny　　　　　D. Let's Clear the Air

Passage 7

Researchers have found that REM (rapid eye movement) sleep is important to human beings. This type of sleep generally occurs four or five times during one night of sleep lasting five minutes to forty minutes for each occurrence. The deeper a person's sleep becomes the longer the periods of rapid eye movement.

There are physical charges in the body to show that a person has changed from NREM(non-rapid eye movement) to REM sleep. Breathing becomes faster, the heart rate increases, and, as the name implies, the eyes begin to move quickly.

Accompanying these physical changes in the body is a very important characteristic of REM sleep. It is during REM sleep that a person dreams.

1. According to the passage, how often does REM sleep occur in one night?
   A. Once   B. Twice
   C. Four or five times D. Forty times
2. The word "deeper" in Paragraph 1 is closest in meaning to which of the following?
   A. heavier   B. louder   C. stronger   D. happier
3. Which of the following shows that a person is NOT dreaming in his sleep?
   A. His eyes begin to move   B. His breathing-becomes faster
   C. His heart rate increases   D. His eyes stop moving
4. The subject of this passage is _____.
   A. why people sleep
   B. the human need for REM sleep
   C. the characteristic of REM sleep
   D. physical changes in the human body

Passage 8

Even plants can run a fever, especially when they're under attack by insects or disease. But unlike humans, plants can have their temperature taken from 3,000 feet away straight up. A decade ago, adapting the infrared (红外线) scanning technology developed for military purposes and other satellites, physicist Stephen Paley came up with a quick way to take the temperature of crops to determine which ones are under stress. The goal was to let farmers precisely target pesticide (杀虫剂) spraying rather than rain poison on a whole field, which invariably includes plants that don't have pest (害虫) problems.

Even better, Paley's Remote Scanning Services Company could detect crop problems before they became visible to the eye. Mounted on a plane flown at 3,000 feet at night, an infrared scanner measured the heat emitted by crops. The data were transformed into a color-code map showing where plants were running "fevers". Farmers could then spot-spray, using 50 to 70 percent less pesticide than they otherwise would.

The bad news is that Paley's company closed down in 1984, after only three years. Farmers resisted the new technology and long-term backers were hard to find. But with the renewed concern about pesticides on produce, and refinements in infrared scanning, Paley hopes to get back into operation. Agriculture experts have no doubt the technology works—"This technique can be used on 75 percent of agricultural land in the United States", says George Oerther of Texas A&M. Ray Jackson, who recently retired from the Department of Agriculture, thinks remote infrared crop scanning could be adopted by the end of the decade. But only if Paley finds the financial backing which he failed to obtain 10 years ago.

1. In order to apply pesticide spraying precisely, we can use infrared scanning to _____.

A. locate the problem areas

B. drew a color-ceded map

C. measure the size of the affected area

D. estimate the damage to the crops

2. Farmers can save a considerable amount of pesticide by _____ .

A. transforming poisoned rain

B. consulting infrared scanning experts

C. resorting to spot-spraying

D. detecting crop problems at an early date

3. Plants will emit an increased amount of heat when they are _____ .

A. sprayed with pesticides

B. in poor physical condition

C. facing an infrared scanner

D. exposed to excessive sun rays

4. The application of infrared scanning technology to agriculture met with some difficulties due to _____ .

A. the lack of official support

B. its high cost

C. its failure to help increase production

D. the lack of financial support

Passage 9

In 99 cases out of 100, insomnia(失眠) is caused by a disturbance of the natural sleep rhythm. The reasons why the rhythm has been disturbed are many and they range from drugs that are being taken to treat a separate medical condition to anxiety. A sudden change in lifestyle or climate could do it, or just that you've fallen into the habit of dozing off(打瞌睡) in front of the television.

Certainly the body must have enough sleep. Tests that deprived people of sleep have proved lack of it can cause fairly rapid physical and mental deterioration(恶化). But on the other hand, it doesn't need too much. So if you're sleeping in front of the TV, you won't sleep soundly at night. Similarly, if you're holidaying in Spain, and spending your days sleeping on the beach, chances are that you'll be wide awake at bedtime.

Of course, the problem for my summer insomniacs is that, despite an almost overwhelming urge to put their heads down on their desks in the afternoons, they aren't getting any extra sleep to compensate for their wakeful nights. For the worst sufferers I sometimes prescribe a mild sleeping pill which, after a few nights, reestablishes the body's natural sleep rhythm, conditioning it to accept the heat.

1. From the passage, insomnia results from _____.

A. the interrupting of the ordinary sleep pattern

B. being unable to sleep

C. keeping awake at night

D. drugs to treat a special disease

2. Lack of sleep will lead to _____.

A. a sudden change in lifestyle

B. a good condition in body

C. the habit of being sleep in front of the television

D. a quick drop in both body and mind condition

3. A mild sleeping pill can help a person well _____.

A. spend time sleeping

B. recover their normal sleep

C. keep awake at night

D. compensate for their missing sleep

4. The problem for the author's insomniacs is that they _____.

A. can't make up for the sleepless nights

B. sleep in the afternoon

C. can have extra sleep at night

D. can never sleep well

Passage 10

Vitamins are important to our health. Different vitamins are found in different foods—grains, vegetables and fruits, fish and meat, eggs and milk products. So which foods should be eaten to get enough of the vitamins our bodies need? Let us look at some important vitamins for the answer.

Vitamin A helps prevent skin and other tissues from becoming dry. People who do not eat enough Vitamin A cannot see well in darkness. They may develop a condition that dries the eyes. This can result in infections and lead to blindness. Vitamin A is found in fish liver oil. It is also in the yellow part of eggs. Sweet potatoes, carrots and other darkly colored fruits and vegetables contain substances that the body can change into Vitamin A.

Vitamin B_1 is also called thiamine(硫胺). Thiamine changes starchy foods into energy. It also helps the heart and nervous system work smoothly. Without it, we would be weak and would not grow. We also might develop beriberi(脚气病). Thiamine is found not just in whole grains like brown rice, but also in other foods. These include beans and peas, nuts, and meat and fish.

Vitamin C is needed for strong bones and teeth, and for healthy blood passages. It also helps wounds heal quickly. They body stores little Vitamin C. So we must get it every day in foods such as citrus(柑橘类) fruits, tomatoes, and uncooked cabbage.

Vitamin D increases levels of the element calcium in the blood. Calcium is needed for nerve and muscle cells to work normally. It is also needed to build strong bones. Vitamin D prevents the children's bone disease rickets(佝偻病). Ultraviolet light from the sun changes a substance in the skin into Vitamin D. Fish liver oil also contains Vitamin D. In some countries, milk products add Vitamin D to milk so children will get enough.

Vitamin K is needed for healthy blood. It thickens the blood around a cut, to stop bleeding. Bacteria in the intestines normally produce vitamin K. It can also be found in pork products, liver and in vegetables like cabbage, kale(羽衣甘蓝) and spinach(菠菜).

1. Lack of Vitamin A will lead to _____.

 A. night blindness   B. heart disease   C. beriberi   D. rickets

2. _____ is able to change rice and wheat into energy.

 A. Vitamin C   B. Vitamin K   C. Pork products   D. Vitamin B_1

3. Every day we must eat certain _____ to get Vitamin C.

 A. meat and fish   B. rice and milk

 C. fruit and vegetables   D. eggs and bones

4. It can be inferred from the passage that _____.

 A. vitamins are sometimes not necessary to our health

 B. it is important to eat a mixture of foods every day

 C. one food only contains one vitamin

 D. fruits contain more vitamin than vegetables

Passage 11

This is not a diet(减肥食谱) or a hard exercise program. Nobody can stick to those for long. Instead, it's a simple way to make weight loss a natural part of the life you already live. And guess what? It's fun! You don't have to give up the foods you love or do regular exercises. It's about balancing calories(平衡卡路里) in tiny ways that add up to big benefits(好处). You just use some tricks the "naturally thin" people do. Pick the ones you like, stick with them, and you'll lose weight and be strong!

Talk it up every time you pick up the phone, stand up and walk around. Heavy people sit on average two and half hours more every day than thin people, according to a study.

Get face time. We use e-mail so much that we've forgotten what our colleagues look like. Pick a colleague or two who sit farthest from you: and deliver 10 of those daily messages in person. And go out of your way: go to a bathroom or a copy machine on another floor and take the stairs, of course.

Think about your drink Consider beer or wine instead of a frozen drink: A glass of regular beer has 140 calories and a serving of wine has 126 calories, while a strawberry daiquiri has about 300 and amargarita 340.

Reduce a total of 100 calories each day and you'll be able to lose about 10 pounds in a year. This is really not difficult to do.

1. What is mainly talked about in the passage?

 A. How to do exercises daily

 B. How to lose weight easily

 C. How to work comfortably

 D. How to eat and drink regularly

2. Which of the following statements is TRUE according to the passage?

A. Thin people sit fewer hours daily than heavy people

B. People deliver messages to their colleagues in person

C. More people walk around when they talk on the phone

D. Heavy people make longer phone calls than thin people

3. What does the writer mean by "face time" in Paragraph 3?

A. Time for getting to know each other

B. Time for sharing ideas face to face

C. Time for doing small jobs

D. Time for sharing ideas face to face

4. Which of the following probably has the most calories?

A. Strawberry daiquiri   B. Regular beer

C. Margarita   D. Wine

Passage 12

With the large number of dogs roaring through our communities, people need to know the facts about rabies (狂犬病), a fatal disease caused by animal bites. Despite vaccination (接种疫苗) programs, rabies is still very prevalent, and will continue to be a serious public health problem for many years to come.

Rabies strikes the central nervous system and brings on choking, convulsions (抽搐) and inability to swallow liquids. It can even cause death. If you or anyone in your family is bitten by dog, cat or other animal, you should not panic, but thoroughly wash the wound with plenty of soap and water and rush to nearby hospital for immediate treatment. If you own the animal which did the biting, you should immediately call a veterinarian for advice and make sure the public health authorities know when and where the biting took place and who was bitten.

1. Rabies is a kind of disease which _____.

A. causes heart attack

B. hurt one's legs

C. causes nerve-centre problem and breathing problem

D. strikes one's brain

2. If a person is bitten by some kind of animal, you _____.

A. should be panic

B. should take him (her) to a big hospital right away

C. should help to clean the wound and ask the patient to have a good rest at home

D. should help to clean the wound and then take him (her) to a nearby hospital quickly as possible

3. Which is the best title of the passage?

A. What a Rabies?   B. The Horrible Rabies

C. What Are Animal Bites?   D. How to Control Rabies

Passage 13

Students enrolled at least half time may borrow up to $3,000 form the government over a two-year period. Repayment of the loan begins six months after the student leaves school. These loans carry on interest until this time. The current interest rate is 5 percent. Students may borrow up to $4,500 annually from a bank, credit union, savings and loan association or other eligible lender. Repayment on these loans usually begins six months after the student leaves school. These loans carry no interest until this time. This current interest rate is 9 percent. Parents may borrow up to $300 annually for each dependent college. Repayment begins forty-five days after receiving the loan, and the interest rate is 12 percent.

1. Which of the following is the main purpose?

A. To remind students and their families to repay their loan

B. To compare interest rates

C. To inform students and parents of the various loans available

D. To show that government loans charge the least interest

2. The highest interest rate is charged to _____.

A. full-time students

B. parents

C. students borrowing from a credit union

D. half-time students

3. If parents had three children in college how much could they borrow annually?

A. $900   B. $3,000   C. $300   D. $9,000

4. According to the passage which of the following is true.

A. The government lends students enrolled at least half time up to 3,000 annually.

B. Students may borrow up to $4,500 annually from four sources.

C. Students enrolled less than half time may borrow money.

D. The current interest rate from banks is 5 percent.

5. It can be inferred from the passage that _____.

A. the student's school determines who is an eligible lender

B. money is available for student loans

C. students need not be enrolled half time to borrow money

D. the interest rate on student loans is increasing

Passage 14

Lantern Festival, which was celebrated on Saturday this year, marked the final day of the Chinese Lunar New Year. It has been an important festival since the Western Han Dynasty (206 BC-AD 24).

In ancient China, marriage was often decided by parents or even the government. During some periods, like the Jin Dynasty (265-420), marriage policies went to extremes. Single women had to get married by a certain age. If a female was still single at 17, there would be a forced marriage with local administrators' involvement.

However extreme policies to force people to get married were rare, and young people still had certain freedoms to get married with people they liked, rather than being completely manipulated by their parents or government. Ancient Chinese had milder ways to encourage people to find a spouse, such as fairs and meetings during festivals.

Lantern Festival is one of the festivals that provided ancient Chinese single young men and women a chance to meet and get to know each other. On the night of that day, unmarried men and women would meet at the flower fair and lantern-decorated street. Romance often happened, although not all of these stories ended happily.

Ouyang Xiu, a famous poet from the Song Dynasty, depicted a woman's longing for the man she met during Lantern Festival in his poem Yuan Xi. It goes like this: "Last lantern festival, the flowers fair, decorated with lights were daylight bright. We met after dusk when the moon rose behind willow trees. This year the moon and lanterns are still the same, yet you are not here anymore. I am sad, with tears shed on the sleeves of my spring coat."

1. Lantern Festival (is) _____.

A. marked the first day of the Chinese New Year

B. celebrated on Saturday last year

C. an important festival

D. celebrated by foreigners

2. What does this passage mainly discuss?

A. How do people celebrate Lantern Festival

B. A poem of Lantern Festival

C. The forced marriage of young people

D. Lantern Festival provides opportunities for romance

3. What is the author's attitude towards the marriage in ancient China?

A. neutral   B. objective   C. negative   D. doubtful

4. What can we infer from the passage?

A. In ancient China, a female can be unmarried at 20

B. Young people hardly had freedom to find a person they liked

C. Young people look forward to Lantern Festival

D. Every couple is happy after meeting in Lantern Festival

Passage 15

The Mongolians' nomadic way of life determined their diet, which traditionally consisted mainly of the meat, milk and other dairy products provided by the livestock which they tended. This included mutton, beef and goat, as well as milk and other dairy products from cattle and goats.

Today, the diet of the Mongolians has been expanded to include vegetables as well as pasta and rice, the former in recognition of the sad fact that the traditional Mongolian diet often leads to struma, or an abnormally enlarged thyroid gland leading to a "swollen" neck, a medical condition caused by the lack of iodine in one's diet, and the latter in order to provide a more carbohydrate-rich diet and perhaps to supplement meat, which is not always as plentiful as one might wish.

1. What is not included in Mongolian's diet?

A. pork B. milk C. beef D. mutton

2. The Mongolian's way of life is _____.

A. settled B. unchangeable C. migratory D. dangerous

3. What is the cause of "swollen" neck?

A. have no access to vegetables

B. lack of iodine in the diet

C. eat too much meat

D. drink milk

4. Today, the diet of Mongolians offers more _____.

A. protein B. vitamin C. carbohydrate D. sugar

Passage 16

Stress may be defined as the response of the body to any demand. Whenever people experience something pleasant or unpleasant, we say they are under stress. We call pleasant kind "eustress", the unpleasant kind "distress".

People sometimes compare our lives with that of the cave man, who didn't have to worry about the stock market or the atomic bomb. They forget that the cave man worried about being eaten by a bear or about dying of hunger—things that few people worry about today. It's not that people suffer more stress today; it's just that they think they do.

It is inconceivable that anyone should have no stress at all. Most people who are ambitious and want to accomplish something live on stress. They need it. But excessive stress is by all means harmful. Worse, chronic exposure to stress over a long time may cause more serious disease and may actually shorten your life.

The most frequent causes of distress in man are psychological—lack of adaptability, not having a code of behavior. So the secret of cooping with stress is not to avoid it but to do what you like to do and what you were made to do, at your own rate. For most people, it is really a matter of learning how to behave in various situations. The most important thing is to have a code of life, to know how to live.

1. The modern man is suffering _____.

A. more stress than the cave man

B. less stress than the cave man

C. different stress from the cave man

D. same stress as the cave man

2. Which of the following is not an example that causes distress?

A. Lacking in adaptability and code of life

B. Killing a bear in hunting

C. The failure to pass final examinations

D. Having an economic problem

3. According to the passage, which of the following statement is NOT true?

A. Every one will suffer certain kinds of stress in his life

B. Chronic exposure to stress may shorten your life

C. Excessive stress is especially harmful to health

D. Most people can learn to avoid stress

4. According to the passage, one should _____.

A. try to avoid as much as stress as possible

B. cope with stress in different ways

C. learn to do things at his own rate

D. have the response of the body to any demand

Passage 17

Life expectancy is rising in much of the world. But doctors are seeing another trend that is disturbing. Some people are choosing lifestyles that result in early death. A new US study looks at four lifestyles choices that prevent people from staying healthy and living longer.

It used to be rare for people to live to 100. But babies born in the US today can hope to live that long. In the 20th century, life expectancy in wealthy nations increased by as much as 30 years. Average life expectancy for Americans is 78. But doctors are seeing people adopt bad habits that can cut their life short, such as eating too much or eating too much junk food, exercising too little and smoking cigarettes. These habits increase the risk for cancer, heart disease and stroke.

Researchers at Harvard University and the University of Washington wanted to find out how many years are lost with these lifestyle choices. "What we found was that high blood pressure, smoking, overweight account for five years of loss of life expectancy in men and about four years in women at the national level." Goodarz Danaei, one of the principal researchers said. The researchers broke down the data into race, income and location, and they found even greater bad habits and the best health. "They are not getting heart disease because of low blood pressure. They are not getting cancer because they have low risk factors for cancer, including smoking." Danaei said.

1. Some people's early death is the result of their _____.

A. life expectancy   B. genes   C. lifestyles   D. hobbies

2. Babies born nowadays in the US can be expected to _____.

A. live to 100   B. live less than 100   C. live 30 years longer   D. live to 78

3. What will be the result of exercising too little and smoking cigarettes?

A. They cut people's life short B. They do not harm to people's health
C. They certainly lead to cancer D. They certainly lead to heart disease
4. Compared with Asian-Americans, middle-income whites have _____
A. fewer bad habits B. better health
C. better blood pressure D. lower risk of cancer

Passage 18

The SUBWAY company is committed to providing a wide range of great tasting, healthier food choices while reducing our environmental footprint and creating a positive influence in the communities we serve around the world. Whatever you're in the mood for, SUBWAY stores have a huge range of Subs, salads, treats and drinks to choose from. "Eat Fresh, Live Green" is our way of letting you know we are committed to healthy food and environmental living. At the SUBWAY chain, we don't just serve food; we serve fresh, healthy food—we train you to become a sandwich artist. We don't cook with any oils, so when you go home, your clothes don't smell; the work environment is fun and supportive and offers job variety with flexible working hours. If you want to join us, fill in the online application form. A SUBWAY chain representative will get in touch with you shortly after.

1. What type of company SUBWAY is?
A. transport   B. food   C. environment protection   D. advertising
2. What products are provided in SUBWAY EXCEPT?
A. salads   B. treats   C. toys   D. drinks
3. What can be inferred from this passage?
A. People who are crazy about junk food may not accept SUBWAY
B. Staff's clothes could smell when they go home
C. Staff has to work in a fixed working time
D. Staff has to work all the time
4. This passage aims to _____.
A. sell products
B. advertise the company and recruit new members
C. tell people how to protect the environment
D. tell people how to make a sandwich

Passage 19

Grandma Moses is among the most famous twentieth-century painters of the United States, yet she had only just begun painting in her late seventies. As she once said of herself: "I would never sit back in a rocking-chair, waiting for someone to help me."

She was born on a farm in New York State. At twelve she left home and was in a service until at twenty-seven, she married Thomas Moses, the tenant of hers. They farmed most of their lives. She had ten children, of whom five survived; her husband died in 1928.

Grandma Moses painted a little as a child and made embroidery pictures as a hobby, but only changed to oils in old age because her hands had become too stiff to sew and she wanted to keep busy and pass the time. Her pictures were first sold at an exhibition, and were soon noticed by a businessman who bought everything she painted. Three of the pictures were shown in the Museum of Modern Art, and in 1940 she had her first exhibition in New York. Between the 1930's and her death she produced some 2,000 pictures: careful and lively pictures of the country life she had known, with a wonderful sense of color and form.

1. Which of the following would be the best title for the passage?

A. Grandma Moses

B. The Children of Grandma Moses

C. Grandma Moses: Her Best Pictures

D. Grandma Moses and Her First Exhibition

2. From Grandma Moses's words of herself in the first paragraph, it can be inferred that she was _____.

A. independent   B. pretty   C. rich   D. alone

3. Grandma Moses began to paint because she wanted to _____.

A. make her home beautiful   B. keep active

C. improve her salary   D. gain an international fame

4. Grandma Moses spent most of their life _____.

A. nursing   B. painting   C. farming   D. embroidering

Passage 20

In the fall of 1924 Thomas Wolfe, fresh from his courses in play writing at Harvard joined the eight or ten of us who were teaching English composition in New York University. I had never before seen a man so tall as he, and so ugly. I pitied him and went out of my way to help him with his work and make him feel at home.

His students soon let me know that he had no need of my protectiveness. They spoke of his ability to explain a poem in such a manner as to have them shouting with laughter or struggling to keep back their tears of his readiness to quote in detail from any poet they could name.

Indeed, his students made so much of his power of observation that I decided to make a little test and see for myself. My chance came one morning when the students were slowly gathering for nine o'clock classes.

Upon arriving at the university that day, I found Wolfe alone in the large room which served all the English composition teachers as an office. He did not say anything when I asked him to come with me out into the hall, and he only smiled when we reached a classroom door and I told him to enter alone and look around.

He stepped in, remained no more than thirty seconds and then came out. "Tell me what you see." I said as I took his place in the room, leaving him in the hall with his back to the door. Without the least hesitation and without a single error, he gave the number of seats in the room, pointed out those which were taken by boys and those occupied by girls, named the colors each student was wearing, pointed out the Latin verb written on the blackboard, spoke of the chalk marks which the cleaner had failed to wash from the floor, and pictured in detail the view of Washington Square from the window.

As I rejoined Wolfe, I was speechless with surprise. He, on the contrary, was wholly calm as he said, "The worst thing about it is that I'll remember it all."

1. What is the passage mainly discussing?
A. Thomas Wolfe's teaching work
B. Thomas Wolfe's course in playwriting
C. Thomas Wolfe's ability of explaining
D. Thomas Wolfe's genius

2. Which of the following is NOT said in the passage?
A. Wolfe's students praised Wolfe's power of observation
B. The author made an experiment on Wolfe's ability
C. Wolfe's students asked the author to have a test of their ability
D. Wolfe did not feel angry when he was tested

3. What do we learn about Wolfe from the passage?
A. He tried hard to remember what was in the classroom
B. He stayed in the classroom for a short time
C. He stayed drew a picture of Washington Square
D. He followed the author into the classroom

4. What can be inferred from the passage?
A. The author was happy to see the test result
B. What the students said was hardly true
C. Wolfe would remember forever what the author had done
D. Wolfe felt joyful after he had been tested

Passage 21

When I was about 12 I had an enemy, a girl who liked to point out my shortcomings. Week by week her list grew: I was skinny, I wasn't a good student, I was boyish, I talked too loud, and so on. I put up with her as long as I could. At last, with great anger, I ran to my father in tears.

He listened to my outburst quietly. Then he asked, "Are the things she says true or not?"

True? I wanted to know how to strike back. What did truth have to do with it?

"Mary, didn't you ever wonder what you are really like? Well, you now have that girl's opinion. Go and make a list of everything she said and mark the points that are true. Pay no attention to the other things she said."

I did as he directed and discovered to my surprise that about half the things were true. Some of them I couldn't change (like being skinny), but a good number I could and suddenly wanted to change.

For the first time in my life I got a fairly clear picture of myself.

I brought the list back to Daddy. He refused to take it.

"That's just for you," he said, "You know better than anybody else the truth about yourself, once you hear it. But you've got to learn to listen, not to close your ears in anger or hurt. When something said about you is true you'll know it. You'll find that it will echo inside you."

Daddy's advice has returned to me at many important moments.

1. What did the girl's enemy like to do?

    A. Talking with her   B. Pointing out her weak points

    C. Reporting to the teacher D. Quarreling with her

2. What did the girl do when she could no longer bear her enemy?

    A. She turned to her father   B. She cried to her heart's content

    C. She tried to put up with her again D. She tried to be her friend

3. Why did the girl's father ask her to make the list?

    A. He wanted to keep the list at home

    B. He didn't know what the girl's enemy had said

    C. He wanted the girl to talk back

    D. He wanted her to check if she really had these weak points

4. What can we infer from reading the passage?

    A. The girl benefited from her father's advice

    B. The girl was very often angry with her father

    C. The girl's father loved other people's advice

    D. The girl was easily hurt by her father

Passage 22

There was once a young man who suffered from cancer. He was 18 years old and he could die anytime. He never went outside; but he was sick of staying home and wanted to go out for once. So he asked his mother and she gave him permission.

He walked down his block and found a lot of stores. He passed a CD store and saw a beautiful girl about his age and he knew it was love at first sight. He opened the door and walked in.

She looked up and asked, "Can I help you?"

He said, "Uh…Yeah…Umm…I would like to buy a CD."

He picked one out and gave her money for it.

"Would you like me to wrap it for you?" She asked, smiling her cute smile.

He nodded and she went to the back. She came back with the wrapped CD and gave it to him. He took it and walked out of the store.

He went home and from then on, he went to that store every day and bought a CD, and she wrapped it for him. He took the CD home and put it in his closet. He was still too shy to ask her out. His mother found out about this and told him to just ask her. So the next day, he took all his courage and went to the store as usual. He bought a CD like he did every day and once again she went to the back of the store and came back with it wrapped. He took it and when she wasn't looking, he left his phone number on the desk and ran out.

One day the phone rang, and the mother picked it up and said, "Hello?"

It was the girl!!! The mother started to cry and said, "You don't know? He passed away yesterday…"

Later in the day, the mother went into the boy's room because she wanted to remember him. She thought she would start by looking at his clothes. So she opened the closet.

She was to face to face with piles and piles of unopened CDs. She was surprised to find all these CDs and she picked one up and sat down on the bed and she started to open one. Inside, there was a CD and as she took it out of the wrapper, out fell a piece of paper. The mother picked it up and started to read it. It said: Hi…I think you're really cute. Do you wanna go out with me? Love, Jocelyn.

The mother was deeply moved and opened another CD…

Again there was a piece of paper. It said: Hi…I think you're really cute. Do you wanna go out with me? Love, Jocelyn.

1. Why did the boy go to the CD store everyday and buy a CD?

A. He loved the girl

B. He loved music

C. He loved collecting CDs

D. He was sick of staying home and wanted to go out

2. What did the girl in the CD store feel about the boy?

A. It was not mentioned

B. She was not interested in the boy

C. She felt sorry for the boy

D. She liked the boy

3. Who was Jocelyn?

A. The boy

B. The girl in the CD store

C. The boy's mother

D. A total stranger

4. What did the passage try to tell us?

A. The boy was too shy to ask the girl out

B. The boy loved music so much

C. There was love at first sight

D. Both the boy and the girl missed their love

Passage 23

Gina was surprised to find that it was not raining in London. She stepped down from the train that had brought her from Dover to Victoria Station and put her two heavy suitcases on the platform. People were hurrying everywhere: through the entrances and exits, up and down the steps, along the other platforms and over to the ticket counters where there were already queues forming. The porters all seemed to be occupied with other passengers.

In Milan everyone told her that it was always raining in England. Today, however, they were wrong. It was warm and dusty—just like at home. She could even hear someone speaking her native language somewhere near the station bookstall. She walked slowly towards the gate at the end of the platform where a railway official was collecting the tickets. She handed him her ticket and walked through. She looked up at the station clock. Its hands were pointing to 3: 15 p.m.

A young woman was sitting on a bench reading an English magazine. She looked friendly, so Gina went up to her.

"Excuse me," she said. The young woman glanced up with a simile. "Can you tell me how to get to the circus?"

"The circus?" The young woman looked puzzled. "What circus do you mean?"

Gina shook her head. "I'm sorry. I have just arrived from Italy to attend a school for overseas students in London. It is near the circus."

"Do you have a letter with the school's address on it?" Asked the young woman.

"Oh yes. Now I remember." Gina opened her handbag and found a postcard with a British stamp on it.

"Ah," said the young woman. "It's Oxford Circus that you want. It's the name of an area in the middle of London. You must go down those steps and take the Tube. Follow the colors. That's the easiest way." She showed Gina on the colored map of the underground railway the route from Victoria to Oxford Circus.

"Good luck," she said. "And by the way, I come from Italy too!"

1. Gina is _____.
   A. expecting a friend to meet her
   B. attending a school matters
   C. going to study English
   D. late for her students

2. "Her native language" means _____.
   A. the language of her own country
   B. her natural way of speaking
   C. the language she had come to learn
   D. the language of a foreign country

3. The woman was puzzled because she _____.
   A. had never been to a circus
   B. did not know the word "circus"
   C. did not know what circus Gina was referring to
   D. did not know where Oxford Circus was

4. Gina made the woman understand by _____.
   A. showing her a letter
   B. opening her handbag
   C. showing her an address
   D. showing her on the map

Passage 24

Man's first real invention, and one of the most important inventions in history, was the wheel. All transportation and every machine in the world depend on it. The wheel is the simplest yet perhaps the most remarkable of all inventions, because there are no wheels in nature-no living thing was ever created with wheels. How, then, did man come to invent the wheel? Perhaps some early hunters found that they could roll the carcass of a heavy animal through the forest on logs more easily than they could carry it. However, the logs themselves weighed a lot.

It must have taken a great prehistoric thinker to imagine two thin slices of log connected, at their centers by a string stick. This would roll along just as the logs did, yet be much lighter and easier to handle. Thus the wheel and axle came into being and with them the first carts.

1. The wheel is important because _____.
   A. it was man's first real invention B. all transportation depends on it
   C. every machine depends on it D. both B and C

2. The wheel is called _____.
   A. simple   B. complicated   C. strange   D. unusual

3. It was remarkable of man to invent the wheel because _____.
   A. it led to many other inventions B. man had no use for it then
   C. there were no wheels in nature D. all of the above

4. The wheel was probably invented by _____.
   A. a group of early hunters B. the first men on earth
   C. a great prehistoric thinker D. the man who made the first cart

Passage 25

The large part which war played in English affairs in the Middle Ages, the fact that the control of the army and navy was in the hands of those that spoke French, and the circumstances that much of English fighting was done in France all resulted in the introduction into English of a number of French military terms. The art of war has undergone such changes since the battles of Hastings, Lewes and Agincourt that many words once common are now only in historical use. Their places have been taken by later borrowings, often like wise from French, many of them being words acquired by the French in the course of their wars in Italy during the sixteenth century. Yet we still use French words of the Middle Ages when we speak of the army and the navy, of peace, enemy, battle, soldier, guard and spy, and we have kept the names of officers such as captain and sergeant. Some of the French terms were introduced into English because they were needed to express a new object or a new idea. In other cases a French and a native English word for the same thing existed side by side. Sometimes one or the other has since been lost from the language; but sometimes both the borrowed and the native word have been still in common use.

1. The main idea of this passage is that _____.
   A. most of today's common English military terms dated from the sixteenth century or later

B. a study of the English vocabulary shows the important part which war has played in the history of England

C. many French words borrowed into English during the Middle Ages have since disappeared from the language

D. many military terms used in English were originally borrowed from French, some as early as the Middle Age

2. All of the following have something to do with the introduction into English of many French military terms except that _____.

A. war played an important part in English affairs in the Middle Ages

B. the English army and navy were controlled by those who spoke French in the war between England and France

C. France invaded England in the Middle Ages and many battles were fought in England

D. much of English fighting was done in France in the war between England and France

3. The art of war has undergone such changes that _____.

A. we no longer use any French words of the Middle Ages

B. many words once common are not used any longer and they are replaced by Italian words

C. French military terms have disappeared from the English language

D. many words once common are now only in historical use and their places have been taken by the newly-borrowed words

4. Which of the following is not the French word borrowed into English during the Middle Ages?

A. sergeant　　　B. battle　　　C. spy　　　D. fight

5. The writer takes the words "battle" and "fight" as an example to show _____.

A. French words are needed to express something new

B. a French and a native word for the same thing have been still in common use side by side

C. French word or the other has been lost from the English language

D. "battle" is the borrowed word and "fight" is the native one

Passage 26

Sand is in high demand. In some parts of the world, people are going to increasingly great lengths to get their hands on the golden grains. Sand is easily the most mined material in the world. According to the UN Environment Program (UNEP), sand and gravel account for up to 85% of everything mined globally each year.

Modern cities are built with, and often on, sand. Most of it is used in the construction industry to make concrete and asphalt. No surprise, then, that Asia is the biggest consumer of sand. China alone accounts for half of the world's demand. Sand also has industrial uses: it is used to make glass, electronics, and to help extract oil in the fracking industry(水力压裂行业), which is to extract oil by using high-pressure water and sand. And large quantities of sand tend to be dumped into the sea to reclaim land: Singapore, for example, has expanded its land area by over 20% since the 1960s in this way. The Maldives and Kiribati have used sand to shore up their islands against rising sea levels. The UN forecasts that, by 2030, there will be over 40 "megacities" home to more than 10m inhabitants (up from 31 in 2016), which means more housing and infrastructure will need to be built. And sea levels will continue to rise. So sand will only become more useful.

But why is there a shortage, when sand seems so abundant? Desert sand is too smooth, and so cannot be used for most commercial purposes. In any case, the proximity of sand to construction sites is generally important too: because sand is relatively cheap, it tends to be uneconomical to transport across long distances. Most countries also have rules in place about where, and how much, sand can be mined. But voracious demand has sparked a profitable illegal trade in many rapidly developing countries. The result is that existing deposits are being mined more quickly than they can be naturally filled, which is damaging the environment. Dredging causes pollution and harms local biodiversity. Thinning coastlines affect beaches' capacity to absorb stormy weather.

1. Which of the following cannot be inferred from the passage?

   A. Sand is easily the most mined material in the world

   B. All sand is used in the construction industry to make concrete and asphalt

   C. Singapore has enlarged its area since the 1960s

   D. Desert sand is not suitable for most commercial area

2. What is the meaning of "magacities"?

   A. An Industrial country   B. A Desert

   C. A Huge city   D. A Small city

3. According to the paragraph 3, what is the reason of the shortage of sand?

   A. Sand is relatively cheap

   B. Voracious demand has sparked a profitable illegal trade in many rapidly developing countries

   C. Desert sand is too smooth, and so cannot be used for most commercial purposes

   D. Thinning coastlines affect beaches' capacity to absorb stormy weather

4. What is the best title of this passage?

   A. The use of sand   B. The sand in Maldives

   C. Desert   D. Demand and shortage of sand

Passage 27

The great ship, Titanic, sailed for New York from Southampton on April 10th, 1912. She was carrying 1316 passengers and a crew of 891. Even by modern standards, the 46,000 ton Titanic was a colossal ship. At that time, however, she was not only the largest ship that had ever been built, but was regarded as unsinkable, for she had sixteen water-tight compartments. Even if two of these were flooded, she would still be able to float. The tragic sinking of this great liner will always be remembered, for she went down on her first voyage with heavy loss of life.

Four days after setting out, while the Titanic was sailing across the icy waters of the North

Atlantic, a huge iceberg was suddenly spotted by a look-out. After the alarm had been given, the great ship turned sharply to avoid a direct collision. The Titanic turned just in time, narrowly missing the immense wall of ice which rose over 100 feet out of the water beside her. Suddenly, there was a slight trembling sound from below, and the captain went down to see what had happened. The noise had been so faint that no one thought that the ship had been damaged. Below, the captain realized to his horror that the Titanic was sinking rapidly, for five of her sixteen water-tight compartments had already been flooded! The order to abandon ship was given and hundreds of people plunged into the icy water. As there were not enough life-boats for everybody, 1500 lives were lost.

1. According to the passage, Titanic was thought to be except _____.

A. great   B. floatable   C. unsinkable   D. tragic

2. What can be inferred from the passage?

A. The ship would be able to float if three of the sixteen water-tight compartments had been flooded

B. The great ship collided with the iceberg directly

C. If there were enough life-boats for everybody, more lives could be saved

D. Nearly all the crew lost their lives

3. In the first paragraph, "colossal" means _____.

A. huge   B. unsinkable   C. modern   D. wonderful

4. The best title for this passage is _____.

A. The Loss of Titanic   B. The Structure of Titanic

C. A Great Ship   D. An Iceberg

Passage 28

Boxing matches were very popular in England two hundred years ago. In those days, boxers fought with bare fists for Prize money. Because of this, they were known as "prize-fighters". However, boxing was very crude, for there were no rules and a prize-fighter could be seriously injured or even killed during a match.

One of the most colorful figures in boxing history was Daniel Mendoza who was born in 1764. The use of gloves was not introduced until 1860 when the Marquis of Queensberry drew up the first set of rules. Though he was technically a prize-fighter, Mendoza did much to change crude prize-fighting into a sport, for he brought science to the game. In his day, Mendoza enjoyed tremendous popularity. He was adored by rich and poor alike. Mendoza rose to fame swiftly after a boxing-match when he was only fourteen years old. This attracted the attention of Richard Humphries who was then the most eminent boxer in England. He offered to train Mendoza and his young pupil was quick to learn. In fact, Mendoza soon became so successful that Humphries turned against him. The two men quarreled bitterly and it was clear that the argument could only be settled by a fight. A match was held at Stilton where both men fought for an hour. The public bet a great deal of money on Mendoza, but he was defeated. Mendoza met Humphries in the ring on a later occasion and he lost for a second time. It was not until his third match in 1790 that he finally beat Humphries and became Champion of England. Meanwhile, he founded a highly successful Academy and even Lord Byron became one of his pupils. He earned enormous sums of money and was paid as much as $100 for a single appearance. Despite this, he was so extravagant that he was always in debt. After he was defeated by a boxer called Gentleman Jackson, he was quickly forgotten. He was sent to prison for failing to pay his debts and died in poverty in 1836.

1. Boxing is a match _____.

   A. which was popular three hundred years ago

   B. which was not formed the first set of rules until 1860

   C. which asked boxers to wear gloves

   D. which attracted few people to watch

2. What does the underlined sentence mean?

   A. He was very welcome   B. He enjoyed his life happily

   C. He had a lot of money   D. He enjoyed boxing

3. What happened between Richard Humphries and Mendoza?

   A. Richard was the first teacher who taught Mendoza how to do boxing

   B. Richard was jealous of Mendoza's success so he turned against Mendoza

   C. They started a fight directly

   D. Richard was lost twice in the fight with Mendoza

4. What is the author's attitude towards the life of Mendoza?

   A. negative   B. positive   C. objective   D. doubtful

Passage 29

Seeing a volcano erupt is a wonderful experience, and you can really feel the heat by climbing to the summit of Pacaya for a close-up view. There are guided tours every day up this highly active volcano from Antigua, giving travelers a chance to see Mother Nature at her most powerful.

Pacaya is an easy drive from Antigua, a beautiful city with many colorful houses along its old streets that are turned into art-works during its Holy Week festival. No matter when you come to Antigua, you won't miss the Pacaya-tour companies.

But climbing Pacaya is no easy job: it is 2,560 metres high, and reaching the summit takes two to three hours seemingly one-step-forward and two-step-back movements. As you climb, you hear the dull sounds of eruptions high above. Steaming, hot remains from recent eruptions begin to line the path as you near the active summit: the McKenney Cone. Just as though you were going to walk over to the edge of the cone, the road turns to the left and up to the relative safety of the old, inactive summit.

Many tours are timed so that you arrive at the cone of the volcano in plenty of time for sunset and the full contrast between the erupting red lava and the darkening sky. On a good day the view from the summit is extremely exciting. The active mouth boils, sending red lava over its sides, and once in a while shoots hot streams up to 100 metres into the air. There is a strong bad smell in the air even if you take care to be upwind of the cone. As evening turns deeper into the night, the burning lava quietly falls down the side of the volcano. For you, too, it is time to get down.

1. What is the main purpose of this passage?

A. To attract tourists to Pacaya

B. To describe the beauty of Pacaya

C. To introduce guided tours to Pacaya

D. To explain the power of nature at Pacaya

2. Antigua is a city _____.

A. where people can enjoy cultural festivals

B. where the daring Pacaya tour starts

C. that gives a close-up view of Pacaya

D. that is famous for its tour companies

3. Climbing to McKenney Cone, people will _____.

A. walk directly to the active summit

B. hear the continuous loud noise from above

C. make greater efforts than to other summits

D. see a path lined with remains of earlier eruptions

4. Many tours are timed for people to _____.

A. get down the mountain in time when night falls

B. avoid the smell from the upwind direction of the cone

C. enjoy the fantastic eruption against the darkening sky

D. appreciate the scenery of the 2560-metre-high mountain

Passage 30

Do you want to know something about the history of weather? Don't look at the sky. Don't look for old weather reports. Looking at tree rings is more important. Correct weather reports date back only one century, but some trees can provide an exact record of the weather even further back.

It is natural that a tree would grow best in a climate with plenty of sunlight and rainfall. It is also expected that little sunlight or rainfall would limit the grow of a tree. The change from a favorable to an unfavorable climate can be determined by reading the pattern of rings in a tree trunk. To find out the weather of ten years ago, count the rings of the tree trunk from the outside to the inside. If the tenth ring is far from the other rings, when it is certain that plenty of sunny and rainy weather occurred. If the rings are closing together, then the climate was bad for the tree.

Studying tree rings is important not only for the history of weather, but also for the history of man. In a region of New Mexico you can find only sand—no trees and no people. However, many centuries ago a large population lived there. They left suddenly. Why?

A scientist studied patterns of dead tree rings which had grown there. They decided that the people had to leave because they had cut down all the trees. Trees were necessary to make fires and buildings. So, after the people destroyed the trees, they had to move.

In this instance studying tree rings uncovered an exciting fact about the history of man.

1. It is understood that in a favorable climate _____.

A. tree rings grow close together

B. tree rings grow far apart

C. trees in New Mexico will grow big and tall

D. people can cut down most of the trees in New Mexico

2. Why did ancient people usually live where there were plenty of trees?

A. trees provided them with shades

B. trees indicated plenty of sunlight and rainfall

C. trees were material for building houses and burning

D. trees provided them with fruit and food

3. The scientists are interested in studying tree rings because they can tell _____.

A. whether in that area the climate was healthy or not

B. whether a particular tree was healthy or not

C. whether people took good care of the trees or not

D. how old the trees were

4. The people had to leave the region of New Mexico because _____.

A. they had cut down all the trees

B. there were many trees there

C. they had no water

D. bad weather stopped the growth of the trees

Passage 31

The oldest stone buildings in the world are the pyramids. They have stood for nearly 5,000 years, and it seems likely that they will continue to stand for thousands of years yet. There are over eighty of them scattered along the banks of the Nile, some of which are different in shape from the true pyramids. The most famous of these are the "Step" pyramid and the "Bent" pyramid.

Some of the pyramids still look as mush alike as they must have been when they were built thousands of years ago. Most of the damage suffered by the others has been at the hands of men who were looking for treasure or, more often, for stone to use in modern buildings. The dry climate of Egypt has helped to keep the pyramids in good condition, and their very shape has made them less likely to fall into ruin. These are good reasons why they can still be seen today, but perhaps the most important is that they were planned to last forever.

The "Step" pyramid had to be on the west side of the Nile, the side on which the sun set. This was for spiritual reasons. It also had to stand well above the level of the river to protect it against the regular floods. It could not be too far from the Nile, however, as the stones to build it needed to be carried in boats down the river to the nearest point. Water transport was, of course, much easier than land transport. The builders also had to find a rock base, which was not likely to crack under the great weight of the pyramid. Finally, it had to be near the capital, or better still, near the king's palace so that he could visit it easily to personally check the progress being made on the final resting place for his body.

1. According to the passage, the "Step" pyramid _____.

A. is unlikely to fall into ruin in the near future

B. was built on the sands along the Nile

C. is one that was built later than the true pyramids

D. is the most famous of the true pyramids

2. The most important reason why some pyramids remain in good condition is that _____.

A. people have taken care of them

B. it doesn't rain often in Egypt

C. they were well designed

D. the government has protected them from damage

3. Most of the damage to the pyramids has been caused by _____.

A. the regular floods

B. the dry climate of Egypt

C. people searching for gold

D. people in search of building materials

4. The Egyptians built the pyramids along the banks of the Nile because _____.

A. they believed in their god

B. it was difficult to find a large rock base far from the Nile

C. the river helped a lot in the transport of building materials

D. it was not easy to choose a suitable place for the pyramids

Passage 32

People living more than three thousand meters above sea level find it difficult to raise vegetables all year long. People living in the highlands of Peru and Bolivia, for example, cannot grow vegetables outdoors during the months of May through September. It is very cold in the highlands at that time of year. If traditional farming methods are used, vegetables will not survive.

However, there is another way to grow vegetables throughout the year in cold areas. It is a method of gardening developed by a private agency called World Neighbors. The method uses "hot houses" build below ground. A hot house is a building covered with plastic or glass in which vegetables or flowers are grown. The traditional hot house is built above ground.

The air temperature is cold in the highlands of Peru and Bolivia during the winter. But, the winter sun is hot. So, World Neighbors advises farmers there to build hot houses below ground. The design is simple. The material does not cost much. Here is how World Neighbors says to built it: dig a hole two and one-half meters wide and six meters long. Make it about two meters deep. Build wall with a door in one end of the hole. Dig steps from the ground down to the door.

Now, build a wall along the top edge of the hole. Make it about one-half meters tall. Earth bricks work fine. Build two shorter walls on the ends. These will be uneven; one side will be as high as the existing wall. The other side will be at ground level. Leave a small opening in each of these sloping walls. This prevents the hot house from becoming too hot. Now, make the roof. Build a wood frame. Cover it with clear plastic. Connect it to the brick walls.

The underground hot house we have described is large enough for two raised vegetables beds. Each is one meter wide and six meters long. Each is seeded and watered just as if it were in a garden above ground.

The dirt walls protect the growing plants from the cold. The clear plastic roof permits the sun's heat to enter. At night, the roof should be covered with straw. This helps prevent cold air from entering. An under ground hot house this size will provide enough vegetables for one family. Groups needing more vegetables can make it bigger.

1. If you lived in Peru, you _____.

A. should raise the special kinds of vegetables that can endure cold

B. could not plant at all

C. had to work out some new unusual plants

D. would not have many vegetables to eat

2. To our surprise, the "hot houses" invented by World Neighbors are _____.

A. covered with a transparent plastic ceiling

B. built under ground

C. quiet small

D. hotter than traditional ones

3. The hot house can be kept warm by using _____.

A. a big oven

B. an electricity heater

C. the heat of the earth's interior

D. the sun shine

4. The measure to prevent the hot house from becoming too hot is to _____.

A. make the roof sloped

B. dig holes on the walls

C. make the wall not vertical

D. make the walls shorter than the ground

第六章 翻 译

一、试题分析

翻译(Part IV Translation)部分共 10 小题，考试时间为 20 分钟。这一部分包括两节。

A 节(Section A)为英语译汉语，有 5 小题，要求将阅读理解材料中标号的 5 个画线句子译成汉语。本节考查学生对常用句型和词语的综合理解和运用能力。

B 节(Section B)为汉语译英语，给出 5 个单句或包含 5 个句子的短文。本节考查学生实际运用语言的综合能力。

试题特点：结构简单、题材广泛、重点词汇及句型突出，考查英语语言运用的基本能力。

二、解题技巧

做好翻译题的关键在于了解英汉两种语言的差异，把握两种语言不同用语习惯，按照忠实、通顺两大原则，使译文尽可能多地反映原文信息。

1. 英译汉

将英语译为汉语，需要注意两个层面：一个是词汇，另一个是句法，而句法着重于从句。

(1)词汇选择：根据上下文关系和自身搭配，选择正确的词汇。例如：

①词义的引申。delicate skin(娇嫩的皮肤)；delicate porcelain(精致的瓷器)；delicate health(虚弱的健康)；delicate living(奢侈的生活)；delicate stomach(容易吃坏的胃)。

②词义的转换。英语在表达上多用名词、形容词、介词，而汉语多用动词、副词。例如：

英：The very sight of him makes me nervous.

汉：一看到他，我就感到紧张。

英：Independent thinking is an absolute necessity in study.

汉：学习中必须进行独立思考。

(2)句法翻译：在翻译长句时，首先要对句子进行分析，弄清句子的结构和层次，抓住句子的中心内容，分清各句子成分之间的语法关系和内在联系，然后根据汉语表达的需要重新安排结构，使用相应的翻译技巧译出。

①主语从句：主语从句包含的信息为重要信息，位于句首。例如：

英：What he told me was only half-truth.

汉：他告诉我的只是半真半假的东西而已。

形式主语 It 与 accept、agree、argue、claim、report、say、suggest 等动词连用，一般增补主语，或译为无主句。例如：

英：It is generally accepted that the experiences of the child in his first years largely determined his character and later personality.

汉：人们普遍认为，孩子早年的经历很大程度上决定了他们的性格和未来的人品。

②宾语和表语从句：一般直译。例如：

英：I understand that he is well qualified, but I feel that he needs more experience.

汉：我知道他很符合条件，但是我觉得他还需经验。

英：Things are not always as they seem to be.

汉：事物并不总是如其表象

③同位语从句：一般直译。

英：She had no idea why she thought of him suddenly.

汉：她不明白自己为什么突然想起他来。

④状语从句：一般包括时间、地点、原因、条件、让步、目的、结果。英译汉时多放于句首，结果状语除外。例如：

英：Now that all of us are here, let's start our meeting.

汉：既然大家都到了，我们开始开会吧。

英：She sat behind me so that I could not see the expression on her face.

汉：她坐在我身后，所以我看不到她的表情。

2. 汉译英

(1)确定主语：

①以原句主语作为译文主语。例如：

汉：我们的房子是一百多年前建造的。

英：Our house was built over a hundred years ago.

②重新确定主语：可以是句子中其他词语，也可以是句外词语。例如：

汉：人不可貌相。

英：It is impossible to judge people from their appearance.

③增补主语。例如：

汉：用劳动实现自己的理想，用理想指导自己的劳动。

英：You realize your ideals through labor and you guide your labor by ideals.

(2)确定谓语：选择谓语时必须考虑英语句法规范，遵循"主谓一致"原则，保证谓语和主语在人称和数上一致，动词时态、语态正确。鉴于此，强化语法意识、增强句法观念至关重要。

(3)调整语序：

①状语的位置：灵活。一般按照动词—方式—地点—时间的顺序。例如：

汉：他每晚都在图书馆用心读书。

英：He reads hard in the library every evening.

②定语位置：单词作定语放在中心词前，较长定语如词组或句子则放在中心词之后。

例如：

汉：举世闻名的万里长城。

英：the world famous Great Wall.

汉：山东曲阜是中国古代著名的思想家、教育家孔子的故乡。

英：Qufu, Shandong Province, is the birthplace of Confucious, a well-known ancient Chinese thinker and teacher.

最后，在答题时应注意书写工整，不要犯低级错误。例如：首字母要大写，词语拼写无误，男、女性别要正确等。

三、举例分析历年真题

（一）英译汉

1. He never went outside; but he was sick of staying home and wanted to go out for once.

【解析】never：从不，从没有过。be sick of doing：厌倦做某。for once：一次。

【翻译】他从来没出去过，但他厌倦了待在家里，想出去一次透透气。

2. How men first learned to invent words is unknown, in other words, the origin of language is a mystery.

【解析】How引导的主语从句，表示方式"怎样、如何"。in other words：换句话说。origin：起源。mystery：迷。

【翻译】人们最初如何发明了词语还不为人知，也就是说，语言的起源还是个谜。

3. In addition, 75% of the world's mail is written in English; 60% of the world's radio stations now broadcast in English.

【解析】in addition：此外，另外。in English：用英语。

【翻译】此外，世界邮件的75%是用英语写的，世界广播电台的60%用英语播音。

（二）汉译英

1. 处理这些问题全凭经验

【解析】处理：deal with。凭借可转换为依靠、依赖：depend on。经验：experience，通常可以加"s"使用。研究句子结构可知无主语，故用"It"作为形式主语。

【翻译】It all depends on experiences to deal with these problems.

2. 请你帮我在纽约预定一个四星级宾馆的房间好吗？

【解析】"你能帮我……吗？"为固定句式：Could you please help me to +动词原形？地点由小及大的表示：用介词in 首先引出宾馆再引出纽约。

【翻译】Could you please help me to book a room in a four-star hotel in New York?

3. 整套设备可以在几个小时内安装完毕。

【解析】整套设备作为主语放在句首直译为：The complete set of equipment。可以：can/could。某段时间内用介词：within。安装：设备为被安装，故用被动语态。此外，阅读全句可知为规律性动作，故采用一般现在时。再结合被动语态故采用 can be done。

【翻译】The complete set of equipment can be fixed within several hours.

专项练习

（一）英译汉

1. How men first learned to invent words is unknown, in other words, the origin of language is a mystery.

2. Success relies not only on one's ability but also a willingness to cooperate.

3. In spite of all the difficulties, they are determined to carry out their promises.

4. Educate a man and you educate an individual, but educate a woman and you educate a whole family.

5. Scientists have done countless experiments to show that praise is far more effective than criticism in improving human behavior.

6. Jim used to think that the more time he spent on his studies, the better grades he would receive. But now he has realized that it is not always the case.

7. In Britain today women make up 44% of the workforce, and nearly half the mothers with children are in paid work.

8. It is useful to be able to predict the extent to which a price change will affect supply and demand.

9. We love peace, yet we are not the kind of people to yield to any military threat.

10. Whenever circumstances permitted, they would come and lend us a helping hand.

11. It won't make much difference whether you leave or stay.

12. Where our motherland needs me, I will respond to her call.

13. It's obvious that the development of science and technology is vital to the modernization of china.

14. She refused to hand over the car keys to her husband until he had promised to wear his

safety belt.

15. Quite a few young people nowadays have the habit of listening to background music while doing their homework.

16. As far as the method itself is concerned, it is worth trying.

17. Whether we like it or not, the world we live in has changed a great deal in the last hundred years.

18. The key to our room is attached to a large plastic block with the room number on it.

19. As I viewed these once familiar surroundings, images of myself as a child there came to my mind.

20. Over years, I have written extensively about animal-intelligence experiments.

21. You'd better open a savings account at the bank near the university.

22. A friend in need is a friend indeed.

23. This idea sounds good, but will it work in practice?

24. It is estimated that about 80% of the world's population cannot afford to proper food, housing or medical care.

25. Americans often say that there are only two things a person can be sure of in life: death and taxes.

26. We know that a cat, whose eyes can take in many more rays of light than ours, can see clearly at night.

27. Practice should go hand in hand with theory.

28. Closely related to our daily life are goods prices.

29. One who makes no investigation has no right to speak.

30. Individual freedom does not in any way mean that you can do what you like at your free will.

（二）汉译英

1. 长城是中国的历史文化符号之一。

2. 无论生活多难，我都不会失去信心。

3. 物体离我们越远，看起来就越小。

4. 政府已经采取积极措施防止空气污染。

5. 建设和谐校园的关键在于让每个学生都能积极参与进来。

6. 他们已经十年没见面了。

7. 在我看来，讨论是解决问题的好方法。

8. 你应该利用课外一切机会学英语。

9. 她对知识有强烈的渴望，但不知道如何求知。

10. 人们只有生病了才知道健康的价值。

11. 他一直全身心地扑在工作上。

12. 一天，苏珊(Susan)在浏览书籍时，被一个真实故事吸引住了。

13. 和远方的朋友保持联系不是一件容易的事。

14. 邻居们都不能容忍他那样对年迈的父亲说话。

15. 李大伯自己虽不富裕，但在别人需要帮助时，他从不犹豫。

16. 在中国，随着经济发展，旅游越来越受到人们的欢迎。

17. 他的演讲激励我们比以往任何时候都更加努力工作。

18. 不管他们说什么，做你认为正确的事。

19. 一个人要想健康，每天锻炼身体是非常必要的。

20. 他试了好几次，但试验还是以失败告终。

21. 就是在这间小屋里，他们勤奋地工作着。

22. 如果我们不努力的话，就学不好英语。

23. 一个人的学习能力是无限的。

24. 人和动物的区别之一在于人能学习并使用语言。

25. 萨姆买不起他极想要的那种照相机，因为那相机太贵了。

26. 学好一门外语是非常重要的。

27. 他用了大约半年的时间才完成这篇论文。

28. 你让我做的事情我都已经做完了。

29. 一旦他适应了新环境，他就会取得更大的进步。

30. 无论贫富，人人都有接受教育的权利。

第七章 词义辨析

一、试题解析

词义辨析主要考查学生对词汇的掌握以及同义词和近义词的运用。本题所占分值比例为20%，共10小题，每小题2分。每题会有一个划线词，划线词可以是名词、动词、形容词、副词、动词短语等。提供四个选项，要求考生根据划线词的含义从四个选项中选出一个含义相近的同义词。

二、解题技巧

1. 语境推测法

根据所给句子推测出划线词的含义，掌握每个选项词的含义，并根据上下文的逻辑来选择恰当的词语。

2. 排除法

把握每个选项词的真正内涵，并从用法、使用场合、搭配结构上进行一一排除，最终留下恰当的词语。

三、试题示例

1. I can't let you into the building without security clearance.
   A. surface   B. safety   C. situation   D. sense

   【题目解析】B。题干意思为"没有通过安全检查我是不能让你进入这栋楼的"。划线词security指"保安措施，安全工作"。选项A，surface指"表面"，不符合句意；选项B，safety指"安全"，符合句意；选项C，situation指"情况、形势"，不符合句意；选项D，sense指"感觉"，不符合句意。

2. The pressure of city life forced him to move to the country.
   A. stress   B. standard   C. education   D. cost

   【题目解析】A。题干意思为"城市生活的压力迫使他搬到了乡下"。划线词pressure指"压力"。选项A，stress指"压力"，符合句意；选项B，standard指"标准"，不符合句意；选项C，education指"教育"，不符合句意；选项D，cost指"花费、费用"，不符合句意。

3. If we shift the furniture against the walls, we will have more space to dance.
   A. change   B. lift   C. move   D. put

【题目解析】C。题干意思为"如果我们把家具移到墙边，我们就会有更宽的空间来跳舞"。划线词 shift 指"移动、转移"。选项 A，change 指"改变、变化"，形容某物变得和原来不一样了，不符合句意；选项 B，lift 指"举起、抬起"，不符合句意；选项 C，move 指"移动、改变位置"，符合句意；选项 D，put 指"放置"，不是划线词的同义词。

4. When she saw the clouds, she went back to the house to <u>fetch</u> her umbrella.
   A. teach　　　B. come　　　C. get　　　D. stand

【题目解析】C。题干意思为"当她看到乌云，她回家去拿伞"。划线词 fetch 指"（去）拿来"。选项 A，teach 指"讲授、教导"，不符合句意；选项 B，come 指"来"，不符合句意；选项 C，get 指"去取、去拿、得到"，符合句意；选项 D，stand 指"站立"，不符合句意。

5. I'm sure that your letter will get <u>immediate</u> attention. They know you're waiting for the reply.
   A. continued　　B. instant　　C. careful　　D. general

【题目解析】B。题干意思为"我相信你的信会得到立刻关注。他们知道你在等待回复"。划线词 immediate 指"立即的、立刻的"。选项 A，continued 指"连续的、反复的"，不符合句意；选项 B，instant 指"立刻的、马上的"，符合句意；选项 C，careful 指"仔细的、小心的"，不符合句意；选项 D，general 指"大体的、总体的"，不符合句意。

6. Frank put the medicine in a top drawer to make sure it would not be <u>accessible</u> to the kids.
   A. reachable　　B. relative　　C. acceptable　　D. sensitive

【题目解析】A。题干意思为"Frank 把药放到顶层的抽屉中，以确保孩子够不到。"划线词 accessible 指"可得到的、可接近的"。选项 A，reachable 指"可得到的"，符合句意；选项 B，relative 指"相关的"，不符合句意；选项 C，acceptable 指"可接受的"，不符合句意；选项 D，sensitive 指"敏感的"，不符合句意。

7. She <u>gradually</u> realized that he was not telling the truth.
   A. fortunately　　B. slowly　　C. recently　　D. immediately

【题目解析】B。题干意思为"她逐渐意识到他没有说实话"。划线词 gradually 指"逐渐地、逐步地"。选项 A，fortunately 指"幸运地"，不符合句意；选项 B，slowly 指"慢慢地"，符合句意；选项 C，recently 指"最近"，不符合句意；选项 D，immediately 指"立刻、马上"，不符合句意。

8. It seems that living green is <u>surprisingly</u> easy and affordable. A small step makes a big difference.
   A. exactly　　B. fortunately　　C. amazingly　　D. hardly

【题目解析】C。题干意思为"看起来绿色生活是惊人地容易，并且人们承受得了。小小的行动就能产生很大的改变"。划线词 surprisingly 指"出人意料地"。选项 A，exactly 指"确切地"，不符合句意；选项 B，fortunately 指"幸运地"，不符合句意；选项 C，amazingly 指"令人惊讶地"，符合句意；选项 D，hardly 指"几乎不、简直不"，不符合句意。

9. Don't <u>stare</u> at people like that, you might upset them.
   A. look at　　B. work at　　C. throw at　　D. marvel at

【题目解析】A。题干意思为"不要像那样盯着别人看，你会使他们感到不安"。划线词

stare at 指"凝视、目不转睛地看"。选项 A, look at 指"看、盯"；选项 B, work at 指"从事于……，致力于……"；选项 C, throw at 指"投向、向……投去"；选项 D, marvel at 指"对……惊奇"。根据词义辨析，选项 A 符合句意。

10. The incomes of skilled workers went up. Meanwhile, unskilled workers saw their earnings fall.

  A. Moreover   B. Therefore   C. At the same time   D. Otherwise

【题目解析】C。题干意思为"技术熟练的工人工资增加了，同时技术不熟练的工人工资在下降"。划线词 meanwhile 指"同时"。选项 A, moreover 指"再者、而且"；选项 B, therefore 指"因此"；选项 C, at the same time 指"同时"；选项 D, otherwise 指"否则"。根据词义辨析，选项 C 符合句意。

专项练习

1. He had been miraculously healed of his illness.
  A. treated   B. cured   C. examined   D. prescribed

2. The investigation into the fire accident was carried out by two policemen.
  A. question   B. doubt   C. number   D. research

3. If you leave the club, you will not be admitted in.
  A. received   B. turned   C. allowed   D. moved

4. The questionnaire takes approximately ten to fifteen minutes to complete.
  A. nearly   B. mainly   C. punctually   D. precisely

5. He says that my new car is a dissipation of money.
  A. lack   B. question   C. waste   D. load

6. The earthquake caused great destruction in that region.
  A. change   B. addition   C. reason   D. damage

7. Just as Professor Scotti often puts it, success is ninety-nine percent mental attitude.
  A. makes   B. says   C. gets   D. means

8. Even after I washed the coat it still had some faint marks on it.
  A. powerful   B. much   C. light   D. easy

9. I'm trying to break the custom of getting up too late.
  A. habit   B. tradition   C. convenience   D. leisure

10. Ms. Watson is remarkably beautiful and very talented.
  A. basically   B. outstandingly   C. perfectly   D. actively

11. We should set off at once, otherwise we will miss the bus.
  A. send out   B. make out   C. give out   D. set out

12. The performance lasted nearly three hours.
  A. continued   B. covered   C. reached   D. played

13. The young man made a commitment to his parents that he would try to earn his own living after graduation.

A. prediction B. plan C. promise D. contribution

14. There were alternative methods of travel available.
A. impressive B. selective C. active D. creative

15. Despite the adverse conditions, the road was finished in one year.
A. native B. negative C. wonderful D. helpful

16. The good thing about children is that they adjust very easily to new environments.
A. appeal B. attach C. apply D. adapt

17. As the applause trailed off, the curtain on the stage dropped slowly.
A. took off B. passed out C. died down D. stayed up

18. Public expenditure on the Health Service is out of hand.
A. cost B. experience C. equipment D. transportation

19. His mind is perfect tranquility.
A. imagination B. shape C. calm D. thinking

20. The first thing is to identify local crime problems.
A. appreciate B. watch C. benefit D. recognize

21. This wine glass looks very fragile.
A. slow B. weak C. pretty D. common

22. She discreetly organized the meeting for her department.
A. carefully B. bravely C. usually D. rarely

23. The general marshaled his forces for a major offensive.
A. marked B. gathered C. took D. shouted

24. John was elevated as the manager of the branch office.
A. classified B. spotted C. assured D. promoted

25. Students on a part-time course are not eligible for a loan.
A. responsible B. reliable C. applicable D. desirable

26. We need to ensure the credibility of the market.
A. authenticity B. ability C. possibility D. difficulty

27. The chairman asked me to express our appreciation to all your hard work.
A. happiness B. thankfulness C. explanation D. emotion

28. Did you participate in any of the activities that were on offer at he hotel?
A. break in B. run in C. put in D. take part in

29. The purchase will account for 39.5% of the whole shares.
A. make up B. take up C. set up D. break up

30. The play was dramatically interesting, so many people went to watch it.
A. usually B. remarkably C. briefly D. directly

31. A successful businessman has to be aggressive.
A. attractive B. outgoing C. ambitious D. effective

32. Her rough, red hands reflected a life of hard physical work.

A. recalled B. returned C. showed D. reacted

33. The actual cost of the building was much higher than our original estimate.
A. plan B. evaluation C. consideration D. ticket

34. Developers use the images to sell to prospective customers.
A. potential B. present C. past D. private

35. Finally, you need to cope with the variations.
A. go with B. agree with C. deal with D. meet with

36. Generally speaking, a lot of patience is required to look after a sick patient.
A. agreed B. regarded C. decided D. needed

37. Nancy accidentally knocked the glass off.
A. unexpectedly B. frankly C. carefully D. rightly

38. All his friends remarked on the change in him since his marriage.
A. complained about B. thought about
C. brought about D. talked about

39. The formerly robust economy has begun to weaken.
A. rapid B. fast C. strong D. hard

40. Stan initially wanted to go to medical school.
A. obviously B. firstly C. lastly D. surprisingly

41. You can have a spiritual dimension to your life without being religious.
A. interest B. aspect C. habit D. dream

42. Her interest in art was stimulated by her father.
A. encouraged B. offered C. loaded D. remained

43. You'd better sort out the business affairs before going.
A. give up B. hurry up C. turn up D. clear up

44. How do you implement this practice?
A. fulfill B. impact C. press D. check

45. The government had granted them permission to leave the country.
A. gained B. denied C. scanned D. allowed

46. You can trust our product as we have strict control over its quality.
A. rigid B. standard C. various D. deep

47. Owners of personal computers now are springing up.
A. running out B. coming out C. working out D. breaking out

48. Some early doctors, notably Hippocrates, thought that diet was important.
A. especially B. significantly C. relatively D. originally

49. The British were not prepared to make any concessions.
A. promises B. schedules C. yieldings D. strategies

50. What recommendations do you have for other applicants?
A. exceptions B. relations C. suggestions D. transactions

第八章 多选题

一、试题分析

2018年专升本考试中多选题型发生了变化，由传统的考查语法、词汇知识运用改为着重考查常用词汇的拼写，以考查学生对常用英语词汇的掌握情况。专升本英语多选题考查范围较广，有名词、动词、形容词和副词等。学生需从被调换字母顺序或少字母的四个单词中选出拼写错误的单词。错选或漏选不得分。

二、解题技巧

需要学生平时积累词汇，并牢记单词的正确拼写，总结常见的单词拼写规律。

三、举例分析

找出下列单词拼写错误的选项：

1. A. absolutte   B. accessible   C. adaptetion   D. adequte   （   ）

【答案】A C D

【解析】A选项的单词多了一个字母"t"，应为absolute；C选项的单词字母"a"错写成"e"，应为adaptation；D选项漏写了字母"a"，应为adequate。

2. A. applicastion   B. beddings   C. developement   D. discount   （   ）

【答案】A B C

【解析】A选项的单词多了字母"s"，应为application；B选项的单词少了字母"d"，重读闭音节结尾，且末尾仅有一个辅音字母的单词在变ing形式时要双写最后一个辅音字母，应为beddings；C选项多了字母"e"，应为development。

专项练习

找出下列单词拼写错误的选项：

1. A. distingush   B. earthqueke   C. electricity   D. fery   （   ）
2. A. flixeble   B. fragile   C. harmoney   D. garage   （   ）
3. A. identify   B. incidant   C. instaed   D. jugement   （   ）
4. A. liberti   B. licence   C. mediem   D. nervuos   （   ）
5. A. occupation   B. padle   C. particular   D. passive   （   ）
6. A. pursuade   B. restuarant   C. rigid   D. salute   （   ）

7. A. satelite	B. separation	C. southren	D. spray	( )
8. A. sorrow	B. vertion	C. vocabulery	D. wisper	( )
9. A. controvertial	B. benifet	C. basement	D. harber	( )
10. A. hisetate	B. mountanous	C. dayli	D. scene	( )
11. A. sensitive	B. vedio	C. carpete	D. suffer	( )
12. A. wholsale	B. enthusiastic	C. energatic	D. disguesting	( )
13. A. dynamic	B. hallwey	C. impression	D. contredict	( )
14. A. concerte	B. bravery	C. accompanny	D. buffett	( )
15. A. programe	B. suspention	C. sunny	D. against	( )
16. A. commitment	B. allternative	C. humerous	D. prefer	( )
17. A. pronounciation	B. sence	C. unbaerable	D. ugly	( )
18. A. vacation	B. urgente	C. monitore	D. merry	( )
19. A. discourege	B. probably	C. questionaire	D. queeu	( )
20. A. quarter	B. sking	C. negotiatte	D. stuborn	( )

参 考 文 献

薄冰,1990. 高级英语语法[M]. 北京:高等教育出版社.
薄冰,1998. 薄冰英语语法[M]. 北京:开明出版社.
孙胜忠,2010. 专升本入学考试专用教材英语[M]. 北京:知识出版社.
文秋芳,1996. 英语学习策略[M]. 上海:上海外语教育出版社.
熊婧竹,2014. 简析辽宁省专升本英语考试试题解题技巧及应对策略[J]. 教育教学论坛(39):248-250.
云南省普通高校专升本招生考试命题研究组,云南省普通高等学校专升本招生考试命题研究中心,2008. 2013年云南省普通高等学校专升本招生考试应试教材——英语[M]. 北京:光明出版社.
张道真,1979. 实用英语语法[M]. 北京:商务印书馆.
张鑫,2014. 专升本英语试卷分析与解题备考策略[J]. 语文学刊:外语教育教学(7):148-194.
周良元,1992. 英语测试与应试技巧[M]. 武汉:武汉工业大学出版社.

附录 专升本英语词汇表

A

ability n. 1. 能力，本领 2. 才能，才干
absent adj. (from)缺席的，不在场的
absolute adj. 绝对的，完全的
absorb vt. 吸收(液体，知识) [be absorbed in 专心于]
accent n. 口音，腔调
accomplish vt. 完成；实现
according adj. 相符的，一致的
achieve vt. 完成，达到，实现
acquire vt. 获得，取得；学到
activity n. 活动；活性，活力
actual adj. 现实的，实际的
addition n. 1. 加法，加起来 2. 增加物
adequate adj. 足够的
administration n. 管理，经营；行政部门
admire vt. 赞美，赞赏，钦佩
admission n. 1. 准许进入，准许 2. 承认；招认
admit vt. 1. 许可进入，准许进入 2. 承认，供认
adopt vt. 1. 采取，采用 2. 收养
advanced adj. 高级的；年老的；先进的
advantage n. 1. 优势，长处 2. 利益，便利
adventure n. 奇遇；冒险
advertisement n. 广告(= ad)
affair n. 事务，事情，事件
agency n. 代理，代办；机构，(党、政)机关，厅
agriculture n. 农业
altitude n. (尤指海拔)高度，高处
altogether adv. 完全地，全然；总共；总之
amaze vt. 使惊奇，使吃惊

amuse vt. 使欢乐，逗……笑
analysis n. 分析，分解
ancient adj. 古代的
anger n. 愤怒，怒气
angle n. 角，角度；观点，看法
announce vt. 发表，宣布
annoy vt. 使苦恼，骚扰
annual adj. 每年的，一年一次的
anxious adj. 忧虑的，焦虑的，不安的
apartment n. 房间，单元住宅，公寓住
apologize/-ise vi. 道歉，谢罪
apparent adj. 明显的，显而易见的
appearance n. 出现，露面；外貌，外观
application n. 请求，申请；应用
apply vt. 应用，运用 vi. 请求，申请；适用
appoint vt. 任命，委派；指定
approximately adv. 近似地，大约
argue v. 辩论，说服
arise vi. 出现，发生
arrange v. 排列，整理，安排
arrest vt. 逮捕 n. 逮捕，拘留
arrow n. 箭；箭头，记号
ash n. 灰，灰烬
ashamed adj. 羞愧的，惭愧的
assistant n. 助手，助教 adj. 辅助的
associate vt. 使发生联系，使联合
assume vt. 假定，设想，假设；采取，呈现
astonish vt. 使惊讶，使吃惊
atmosphere n. 大气，空气；气氛，环境
attach vt. 缚上，系上，贴上
attack vt. 进攻，攻击，抨击；动手处理(某事)
attempt vt. 尝试，企图 n. 努力，尝试
attitude n. 姿势，态度，看法

attract　vt. 吸引　vi. 有吸引力
authority　n. 权威，权力威信
awful　adj. 可怕的，威严的；极度的

B

balance　n. 秤，天平；平衡　v. (使)平衡
bare　adj. 1. 赤裸的，无遮蔽的　2. 稀少的
bargain　n. 1. 廉价物　2. 交易　v. 议价
base　n. 1. 底部，基础　2. 根据地，基地
battery　n. 电池
battle　n. 战役，战争，战斗　v. 搏斗，斗争
beam　n. 1. 梁，桁条　2 (光线的)束，柱
beast　n. 兽，牲畜
behavior　n. 1. 举止，行为　2. (机器的)特性
bench　n. 长凳
bend　v. 弯曲，专心于，屈服　n. 弯曲
beneath　prep. 在下边
benefit　n. 利益，好处　vt. 有益于，有助于
bet　v. 1. 赌，打赌　2. 敢说，肯定
bind　v. 绑，捆
biology　n. 生物学
bitter　adj. 1. 苦的　2. 痛苦的，怀恨的
blame　v. 指责，责备　vt. 责备，指责
blank　adj. 1. 空白的，空着的　2. 失色的
blanket　n. 毯子
blind　adj. 1. 瞎的　2. 盲目的　vt. 使失明，缺乏眼光或判断力
board　n. 1. 木板　2. 船舷　vt. 上(船、飞机等)
bold　adj. 1. 大胆的　2. 粗体的
border　n. 边界，国界；边，边沿，边境　vt. 1. 与……接壤　2. 接近
bore　n. 令人讨厌的人　vt. 使烦扰　v. 钻孔
bottom　n. 基础，根基；底部
boundary　n. 边界，分界线
bow　n. 弓　v. 鞠躬，点头
brain　n. 脑，头脑；(常 pl.)脑力，智能
branch　n. 1. 枝，分枝；分部，分店　2. 支流，支脉，支线
brand　n. 商标，牌子
breath　n. 呼吸，气息
brick　n. 砖
brief　adj. 简短的，短暂的　vt. 简短介绍，简要汇报
brilliant　adj. 1. 灿烂的，闪耀的　2. 有才气的
bunch　n. 串，束
burden　n. 担子，负担
burn　v. 烧，烧焦，点(灯)，使感觉烧热　n. 烧伤，灼伤
burst　v. 爆裂，炸破　n. 突然破裂，爆发
bury　vt. 埋葬；掩埋，隐藏
button　n. 纽扣，按钮　v. 扣住，扣紧

C

cable　n. 电报；缆，索，钢丝绳；电缆
calculate　v. 计算　vt. 计划，打算
camera　n. 照相机
camp　n. 露营地，阵营　vi. 露营，扎营
campaign　n. 战役，(政治或商业性)活动
campus　n. (大学)校园
canal　n. 运河，沟渠
cancel　vt. 1. 取消　2. 删去
cancer　n. 癌，毒瘤
candle　n. 蜡烛
capable　adj. 有能力的，有才能的[be capable of 能……的，可以……的]
capacity　n. 1. 容量　2. 能力
capital　n. 首都，首府　adj. 首位的，重要的
captain　n. 队长，首领；船长
capture　vt. 俘获，捕获，夺取
carbon　n. 碳
carpenter　n. 木匠
carpet　n. 地毯
castle　n. 城堡
cave　n. 洞穴，窑洞
cease　v. 停止，终了
ceiling　n. 天花板，最高限度
celebrate　v. 庆祝
cell　n. 细胞
ceremony　n. 1. 典礼，仪式　2. 礼节
certificate　n. 证书，证明书
chain　n. 1. 链(条)；镣铐　2. 连锁店
challenge　n. 挑战　vt. 向……挑战
champion　n. 冠军，胜利者
channel　n. 海峡；频道；路线

· 200 ·

character n. 1.(事物的)特性,性质 2.(人的)品质,性格

charge v. 1.收费 2.控告 3.充电 n.(pl.)费用

chart n. 海图,图表

cheek n. 面颊

cheque n. 支票,账单

chest n. 胸腔,胸膛;箱,柜

chief n. 首领,领袖 adj. 主要的,首席的

chill n. 寒意,寒冷

chimney n. 烟囱

choice n. 选择,抉择,精选品

church n. 教堂;教会,教派

cigarette n. 纸烟

circle n. 圆周,圆形物

circumstance n.(pl.)环境,情况

citizen n. 市民,公民

civil adj. 市民的,公民的

claim n.(根据权利提出)要求;主张

classical adj. 古典的,古典文学的

clerk n. 职员,办事员;店员

climate n. 气候

clinic n. 门诊部

clue n. 线索

coast n. 海岸

code n. 1.准则,法规 2.代码,密码,编码

collar n. 1.衣领 2.环状物

colleague n. 同事,同僚

collect v. 1.收集,搜集 2.聚集,集中

combination n. 1.结合,联合,合并 2.化合,化合物

command n. 指令,命令;统帅,指挥

commander n. 司令官,指挥官

comment n. 注释,评论,意见

commercial adj. 商业的,贸易的 n. 商业广告

commit vt. 1.犯(错误),干(坏事) 2.把……交托给,提交

committee n. 委员会

common adj. 1.普通的 2.共同的,公共的

communication n. 传达,信息,交通;沟通

community n. 社区,同一地区的居民

compare v. 1.比较,相比 2.比喻

complain v. 1.(about, of)抱怨 2.投诉

complete adj. 全部的,完全的,完成的 vt. 完成,使完善

complex adj. 复杂的 n. 联合体

complicated adj. 复杂的,难解的

compose vt. 组成,构成 v. 创作

computer n. 计算机,电脑

comrade n. 朋友,同志,伙伴

concentrate v. 1.(on)集中 2.浓缩

concept n. 观念,概念

concern vt. 涉及,关系到 n. 关心,关注,担忧

conclude v. 结束,终止 vt. 推断,断定

condition n. 1.状况 2.(pl.)环境;条件

conduct n. 行为,操行 vt. 1.引导 2.管理

conference n. 会议

confess v. 承认,坦白,忏悔

confidence n. 1.(in)信任 2.信心

confirm vt. 1.证实 2.确定,确认 3.批准

conflict n. 斗争,冲突 vi. 抵触,冲突

confuse vt. 混淆,使糊涂

congratulate vt. (on)祝贺,庆贺

congress n. (代表)大会

connect v. (with)连接,联合

conquer vt. 征服,战胜,占领

conscious adj. (of)意识到的,自觉的

consequence n. 结果

consider vt. 1.认为,把……看作 2.考虑,细想

consist vi. 1.(of)由……组成 2.(in)在于

construction n. 1.建造,构造,建筑 2.建筑物

consult v. 商量,商议,请教;查阅,参考

consumer n. 消费者

contact n. 接触,联系 vt. 接触,联系

contain vt. 包含,容纳,容忍

content n. 容量;(pl.)内容,目录

continent n. 大陆,陆地

contract n. 合同,契约,婚约

contrary adj. (to)相反的,逆

contribute v. (to)贡献,有助于

conversation n. 会话,交谈

convey vt. 1.传达,表达,传递 2.运送,输送

convince vt.(of)使确信,使信服
cooperation n. 合作,协作
copper n. 铜
core n. 中心,核心
correspond vi.(with)符合,一致
courage n. 勇气,精神
court n. 法院,法官;球场,庭院
cousin n. 堂兄弟姊妹,表兄弟姊妹
crack v.(使)破裂,(使)爆裂
crash n. 碰撞,坠落,坠毁
crawl vi. 1. 爬行,蠕动 2. 徐徐行进
create vt. 1. 创造,创作 2. 引起,造成
creature n. 生物
credit n. 信用,贷款,赊欠
crime n. 犯罪,罪行,罪恶
critical adj. 1. 批评的,评论的 2. 紧要的,危急的
crude adj. 粗鲁的
curiosity n. 好奇心
current adj. 1. 流行的 2. 当前的,现在的
curse n. 诅咒,咒骂 vt. 诅咒,咒骂
curve n. 曲线;弯曲,弯曲物

D

damage v. 损害,毁坏
dare v. & aux. 敢,竟敢
dark adj. 黑暗的 n. 黑暗,暗处
dawn n. 黎明,拂晓 vi. 破晓
deaf adj. 1. 聋的 2. 不愿听的
death n. 1. 死亡 2. 毁灭
debt n. 债,债务,欠款
decade n. 十年,十年期
decide v. 1. 决定,决心 2. 解决,裁决
declare vt. 1. 断言,宣称 2. 宣布,声明
decrease v. & n. 减少,减小
defend vt. 防守,保卫
define vt. 1. 给……下定义 2. 限定,规定
definite adj. 明确的,肯定的
degree n. 1. 度,度数 2. 学位 3. 程度
delay v. & n. 耽搁,延迟
delicate adj. 精巧的,精密的
delight n. 快乐,高兴

deliver vt. 1. 递,送 2. 移交,交付
demand v. 要求,请求 n. 要求,请求
democracy n. 民主
demonstrate vt. 论证,证实;演示,说明
department n. 部,局,处,科,部门;系
depend vi. 依……而定,取决于[depend on/upon 相信,依赖;依……而定]
depth n. 1. 深,深度 2. 深奥,深刻
describe vt. 描写,记述,形容
desert n. 沙漠,不毛之地
deserve vt. 应收,值得,应得
design v. 设计,构思,绘制 n. 设计,图样
desire vt. 欲望,期望,希望 n. 愿望,心愿
despair n. 绝望 vi.(of)对……绝望
despite prep. 不管,尽管
destroy vt. 1. 破坏,毁灭 2. 消灭
determination n. 决心,决定;确定,限定
devil n. 魔鬼,恶棍
devote vt.(to)把……奉献给,把……专用于
diamond n. 金刚石,钻石;菱形
direct adj. 直接的 vt. 管理,指导,指挥 vi.(to)把……对准
director n. 指导者,主任,导演
disadvantage n. 不利,不利条件,缺点
disappear vi. 消失,不见
disappoint vt. 使失望,使受挫折
discourage vt. 使泄气,使沮丧
discovery n. 发现;发现的东西
discuss vt. 讨论,商议
disease n. 病,疾病,病害
disgust n. 厌恶 vt. 使厌恶
display vt. & n. 陈列,展览;显示
distance n. 距离,间隔[in the distance 在远处]
distinct adj. 1. 清楚的,明显的 2.(from)截然不同的,独特的
distinguish vt. 1. 区别,辨别 2. 辨认出
distribute vt. 分发,分配;散布,分布
district n. 地区,区域;区,行政区
disturb vt. 1. 弄乱,打乱 2. 打扰,扰乱
dive vi. & n. 潜水,跳水,下潜,俯冲
divide v. 1. 分,划分 2. 分开,隔开
document n. 公文,文件,文献

domestic   adj. 家庭的，家里的；本国的，国内的
dot   n. 点，圆点   vt. 在……上打点
double   adj. 双的，双重的；两倍的   vt.（使）加倍
doubt   n. 怀疑，疑问   v. 怀疑［no doubt 无疑地］
dozen   n.（一）打，十二个
draft   n. 草稿，草案，草图   vt. 起草，为……打样，设计
drag   v. 拖，拖曳
dramatic   adj. 戏剧的，剧本的，戏剧性的
dust   n. 灰尘，尘土   vt. 掸掉……上的灰尘

E

eager   adj. 热心于，渴望着［be eager to do 渴望做……］
eagle   n. 鹰，鹰状标饰
earn   vt. 赚，挣得，获得
ease   n. 安逸，安心   v. 使安心，减轻，放松
economic   adj. 经济（上）的，经济学的
economy   n. 经济，节约
edge   n. 刀口，利刃，边缘，优势   vt. 使锋利
editor   n. 编辑，编辑器，编者
educate   vt. 教育，训练，培养
education   n. 教育，训练，教育学
effect   n. 结果；效果；作用；影响   vt. 招致；实现；达到(目的等)
efficient   adj. 生效的，有效率的，能干的
effort   n. 努力，成就
elder   n. 年长者，父辈   adj. 年长的，资格老的
elect   vt. 选举，推选，选择
electric   adj. 电的，导电的，电动的
element   n. 要素，元素，成分
elevator   n.（美）电梯（英国用 lift）
emergency   n. 紧急情况，紧急事件
emotion   n. 感情，情绪，情感
emphasis   n. 强调，重点
endure   v. 耐久，忍耐
enemy   n. 敌人，仇敌
enormous   adj. 巨大的，庞大的
entertain   v. 娱乐，招待，款待
enthusiasm   n. 狂热，热心，热衷的事物

entire   adj. 全部的，完整的
entitle   v. 给……权利（或资格），给……题名，给……称号
entrance   n. 入口，门口，进入
environment   n. 环境，外界
envy   n. & vt. 羡慕，嫉妒
equal   adj. 相等的   vt. 等于，比得上
era   n. 时代，纪元，时期
essential   adj. 本质的，基本的，精华的
estimate   v. 估计，估价，评估
evidence   n. 证据，明显，迹象，根据
evil   adj. 邪恶的，有害的，诽谤的   n. 邪恶，不幸
exceed   v. 超越，胜过
excellent   adj. 卓越的，极好的
exchange   vt. 交换，兑换，交流，交易
exclaim   v. 呼喊，惊叫，大声叫
execute   vt. 执行，实行，完成，处死
exhaust   v. 用尽，耗尽，使精疲力尽，排气
exhibit   v. 展出，陈列   n. 展览品，陈列品
exhibition   n. 表现，展览会，展览品
exist   vi. 存在，生存，生活
existence   n. 存在，生活，存在物
expand   vt. 使膨胀，详述，扩张
expect   vt. 预料；预期   v. 期待，期望
explain   v. 解释，说明
explanation   n. 解释，解说，说明
explode   v. 使爆炸，爆炸，激发
explore   v. 探险，探测，探究
export   v. 输出，出口
expose   vt. 使暴露，受到，使曝光
express   vt. 表达，表示
extend   v. 延伸，伸展，扩大
extensive   adj. 广阔的，广泛的
extent   n. 广度，宽度，长度，范围
external   adj. 外部的，客观的
extra   adj. 额外的，特别的
extraordinary   adj. 非常的，特别的，异常的
extreme   adj. 极端的，极度的

F

factor   n. 因素，要素

fade vi. 1. 褪色 2. 衰减，消失
fail vi. 1. (in)失败，不及格 2. 不，未能
faint adj. 虚落地，衰弱的 vi. 昏晕，昏倒
fair adj. 公平的，合理的
faith n. 1. 信任，信用 2. 信仰，信条
familiar adj. (with, to)熟悉的，通晓的
fan n. 1. 扇子，风扇 2. 迷，狂热者 v. 扇
fare n. (车，船，飞机等的)费，票价
farewell n. 辞别，再见，再会
fashion n. 流行，风尚，时样
fasten vt. 扎牢，使固定
fate n. 命运
fault n. 1. 过错 2. 缺点，毛病
favo(u)r n. 喜爱 vt. 赞成
fear n. 害怕，担心 v. 害怕，为……担心
feather n. 羽毛
feature n. 1. 特征 2. 特色，特写
feed vt. (on, with)喂养，饲养
fellow n. 伙伴，同事
female adj. 女性的，雌的
fence n. 栅栏，篱笆
festival n. 节日，喜庆日
fetch vt. 接来，取来
fever n. 1. 发烧，发热 2. 狂热
fiber/-bre n. 纤维
field n. 1. 原野，旷野 2. 领域 3. 运动场
fierce adj. 凶猛的，残忍的
figure n. 1. 外形，体形 2. 图形，画像
financial adj. 财政的，金融的
finger n. 手指
firm n. 公司，(合伙)商号
fist n. 拳头
flag n. 旗
flame n. 1. 火焰 2. 光辉，光芒
flash n. 闪光
flat adj. 平坦的 n. 一层，公寓
flavo(u)r n. 情味，风味 vt. 加味于
flexible adj. 柔韧性，易曲的；灵活的
flight n. 飞行；飞机的航程，班机
float vi. 浮动，飘浮
flood n. 洪水 vt. 淹没 vi. 被水淹，溢出
flour n. 面粉

flow vi. 流动 n. 流动，流量
fluent adj. 流利的，流畅的
fluid n. 流体 液体 adj. 流动的，不固定的
focus n. 1. (兴趣活动等的)中心 2. 焦点[focus on 使聚焦]
fog n. 雾
fold n. 褶痕 vt. 折叠
folk n. 人们 adj. 民间的
follow v. 1. 跟随，接着 2. 领会，听得懂[as follows 如下]
fond adj. [只作表语]喜爱的，喜欢的
fool n. 愚人，白痴 vt. 愚弄，欺骗
foolish adj. 愚蠢的，傻的，笨的
footstep n. 脚步，脚步声；足迹
forbid vt. 禁止，不许
force n. 1. 力量 2. 势力，暴力 vt. 强制
in force 有效，实施中[come/go into force 生效，实施]
forecast n. 预测，预报 vt. 预想，预测
forehead n. 前额，(任何事物的)前部
foreign adj. 外国的；外来的，异质的
formal adj. 正式的；形式的
former adj. 从前的，以前的 pro. 前者
forth adv. 往前，向外
fortunate adj. 幸运的，幸福的
fortune n. 财富；运气，好运，命运
forward adj. 早的，迅速的，前进的
found v. 建立，创立
foundation n. 1. 基础，根本 2. 建立，创立
fountain n. 1. 泉水，喷泉 2. 源泉
fraction n. 小部分，片断，分数
frame n. 1. 框架，框子 2. 架，骨架
frank adj. 坦白的，率直的，老实的
freeze v. (使)结冰，(使)冷冻
freight n. 货物，船货；运费
frequency n. 频率，周率，发生次数
fresh adj. 1. 新鲜的 2. 新的，新近的
frighten vt. 使惊吓
frost n. 1. 霜 2. 霜冻，严寒
frown v. 皱眉，蹙额
fry v. 油炸，油煎
fuel n. 燃料 vt. 加燃料，供以燃料

fulfill   vt. 1. 实践，履行 2. 完成
fun   n. 娱乐，有趣的人或事物
function   n. 功能，作用
fund   n. 资金，基金
fundamental   adj. 基础的，基本的
fur   n. 毛皮，毛，软毛
furniture   n. 家具
further   adj. 更远的，更多的，深一层的
future   n. 未来，将来   adj. 未来的，将来的 [in (the) future   今后，将来]

G

gain   v. 获得，博得   n. 收益，得益
gallon   n. 加仑
gap   n. 1. 缺口，裂口，间隙 2. 差距，隔阂
garage   n. 汽车间，修车厂，车库
gas   n. 气体，煤气，毒气，汽油
gather   v. 1. 聚集，聚拢 2. 收集
gay   n. (尤指男)同性恋者
gene   n. 因子，基因
general   adj. 1. 一般的 2. 总的，大体的 [in general   通常，大体上]
generate   vt. 1. 产生，发生 2. 发电
generous   adj. 慷慨的，大方的
genius   n. 天才，天赋，天才人物
geography   n. 地理学，地理
ghost   n. 鬼，幽灵
giant   n. 巨人   adj. 庞大的，巨大的
glance   v. (at, over)扫视，匆匆一看
glimpse   n. 一瞥，一看
glove   n. 手套
glue   n. 胶，胶水   vt. 胶合，粘贴，黏合
goal   n. 1. 目的，目标 2. 球门
goat   n. 山羊
government   n. 政府，政体
grace   n. 优美，雅致
grain   n. 谷物，谷类；谷粒，细粒，颗粒
grand   adj. 1. 盛大的 2. 重大的，主要的
grant   vt. 同意，准予
graph   n. 图表，曲线图
grasp   vt. 1. 抓住，抓紧 2. 掌握，领会
grateful   adj. (to, for)感激的，感谢的

grave   n. 坟墓
gravity   n. 地心引力，重力
greedy   adj. 1. 贪吃的 2. (for)贪婪的
grey/gray   adj. 灰色的，灰白的   n. 灰色
grip   vt. 紧握，紧夹   n. 掌握，控制
grocery   n. 食品杂货(店)
guard   n. 1. 卫兵，警卫员 2. 守卫，看守
guilty   adj. 1. (of)有罪的 2. 内疚的

H

hammer   n. 铁锤，槌，锤子   v. 锤击，锤打
handle   vt. 处理，操作
hang   vt. 悬挂，绞死，垂下 [hang about   闲待着，终日无所事事]
harbo(u)r   n. 海港，避难所
hardware   n. 五金器具，硬件，部件
harm   vt. 伤害，损害   n. 伤害，损害
harvest   n. 收获，收成，成果   v. 收获
haste   n. 匆忙，草率
heap   n. 堆，大量，许多   vt. 堆，堆起，积累
heat   n. 热，热度，温度
heave   v. 举起   n. 举起，起伏
heaven   n. 天，天空，天堂
height   n. 高，高度，海拔
helicopter   n. 直升(飞)机
hence   adv. 因此，从此，以后
henceforth   adv. 自此以后，今后
hesitate   v. 1. 犹豫，踌躇 2. 不愿
hide   v. 隐藏，掩藏，隐瞒，掩饰
highway   n. 公路，大路
hint   n. 暗示，提示，线索
hire   n. 租金，工钱，租用，雇用
history   n. 历史，历史学，历史记录
hole   n. 洞，孔，突破口
honest   adj. 诚实的，正直的
hono(u)r   n. 尊敬，敬意，荣誉 [in honour of   纪念，向……表示敬意]
horizon   n. 地平线，视野
horror   n. 惊骇，恐怖，惨事
humble   adj. 卑谦的，恭顺的
humo(u)r   n. 幽默，诙谐
hunt   v. 打猎，猎取(与after, for连用)

I

ideal   n. 理想   adj. 空想的，理想的
identify   vt. 识别，鉴别
ignore   vt. 不理睬，忽视，不顾
illustrate   vt. 举例说明，阐明
image   n. 图像，肖像，形象
imagination   n. 想象，想象力
imitate   vt. 模仿，仿效，仿造
immense   adj. 广大的，无边的，巨大的
impact   n. 碰撞，冲击，影响   vt. 撞击，对……发生影响
imply   vt. 暗示，意味
import   n. 进口，输入   vt. 输入，进口
important   adj. 重要的，重大的，有地位的
impress   vt. 印，盖印，留下印象
improve   v. 改善，改进
incident   n. 事件，事变
incline   vt. 使倾向于，使倾斜
income   n. 收入，收益，所得
increase   n. 增加，增大，增长   v. 增加，加大
indeed   adv. 真正地，(加强语气)确实
indefinite   adj. 模糊的，不确定的
independent   adj. 独立的，不受约束的
indicate   vt. 指出，显示，预示，表明
indirect   adj. 间接的
individual   n. 个人   adj. 个别的，单独的
industrial   adj. 工业的，产业的
industry   n. 工业，产业，勤奋
infant   n. 婴儿，幼儿
infect   vt. 传染，感染
influence   n. 影响，感化，势力
inform   vt. 通知，告诉
information   n. 消息，情报，资料，信息
inherit   vt. 继承，遗传而得
initial   adj. 最初的，词首的，初始的
injure   vt. 损害，伤害
ink   n. 墨水
innocent   adj. 清白的，无罪的，天真的
inquire/enquire   v. 1. 问；询问   2. 调查
insect   n. 虫，昆虫，卑鄙的人
insist   v. 坚持，强调
inspect   vt. 检查，视察

inspire   vt. 鼓舞，激发，使生灵感，产生
instal(l)   vt. 安装，安置，使就职
instance   n. 实例，情况
instant   adj. 立即的，直接的，紧迫的
institute   n. 学会，学院，协会
instruction   n. 指示，用法说明(书)，指导
instrument   n. 手段，器械，仪器
insult   n. 侮辱，凌辱   vt. 侮辱，凌辱
insurance   n. 保险，保险业
intelligence   n. 智力，聪明，智能
intend   vt. 想要，打算，意指
intense   adj. 强烈的，剧烈的，热情的
intention   n. 意图，目的
interfere   vi. 干涉，干预，妨碍，打扰
intermediate   adj. 中间的
internal   adj. 内在的，国内的，内部的
international   adj. 国际的，世界的
interpret   v. 解释，说明，口译
interrupt   vt. 打断，中断，妨碍，插嘴
interview   vt. 接见，会见   n. 接见，会见
intimate   adj. 亲密的，隐私的
invade   vt. 侵略，侵袭，侵入
invent   vt. 1. 发明，创造   2. 虚构；杜撰
invest   v. 投资，投入(时间，精力等)
invisible   adj. 看不见的，无形的
invitation   n. 邀请，招待
involve   vt. 1. 卷入，陷入   2. 包含，涉及
iron   n. 铁，熨斗，烙铁   v. 烫(衣服)
isolate   vt. 使隔离，使孤立
issue   n. 出版，发行   v. 发行，颁布

J

jail   n. 监狱，看守所
jealous   adj. 1. 妒忌的   2. 羡慕的
jet   n. 喷气发动机，喷气式飞机
jewel   n. 宝石
joint   n. 1. 接头，接合处   2. 关节，骨节
journal   n. 定期刊物，杂志
judg(e)ment   n. 1. 审判，判决   2. 判断力
junior   n. 1. 年少者   2. 地位较低者，晚辈
justice   n. 公平
justify   v. 证明……是正当的

K

kettle   n. 水壶
kick   v. & n. 踢
kilogram(me)   n. [物]千克
kilometer/-tre   n. [物]千米
kingdom   n. 1. 王国   2. 领域
knee   n. 膝，膝盖
kneel   vi. 跪下
knife   n. 刀，餐刀
knit   v. 编织，结合

L

laboratory   n. 实验室（口语可简称 lab）
labo(u)r   n. 1. 劳动   2. 劳动力；劳工
ladder   n. 梯子，阶梯
landlord   n. 房东，地主
launch   vt. 1. 发射   2. 使(船)下水
laundry   n. 1. 洗衣房   2. 洗的衣服
leaf   n. 1. 叶子   2.(书刊)的一张
league   n. 1. 同盟，联盟   2. 联合会，社团
leak   v. 1. 漏，渗   2. 泄漏
lean   v. 1. 倾斜，屈身   2. 依靠，依赖
leather   n. 皮革，皮革制品
lecture   n. 演讲，讲课
legal   adj. 法律的，法定的，合法
leisure   n. 1. 空闲，闲暇   2. 悠闲，安逸
length   n. 1. 长，长度   2. 一段，一截[at length   1. 最后，终于   2. 详细地]
lens   n. 透镜，镜头
lest   conj. 唯恐，以免
liberty   n. 自由
librarian   n. 图书管理员
library   n. 图书馆，藏书室
lid   n. 盖子
lightning   n. 闪电
limit   n. 界线，限度   vt. (to) 限制，限定
limitation   n. 限制
limited   adj. 有限的
link   v. 连接，联系   n. 链接，环节
literary   adj. 文学(上)的
literature   n. 文学，文学作品，文献
load   v. 装(货)，装载   n. 装载(量)

loaf   n. 一个(面包)
loan   n. 1. 贷款   2. 出借，借给
local   adj. 地方的，本地的
locate   vt. 使…坐落于，位于
location   n. 位置，场所
lock   n. 锁   v. 锁，锁上
logic   n. 逻辑，逻辑学

M

magic   n. 魔法   adj. 魔术的，有魔力的
magnificent   adj. 华丽的，宏伟的
maintain   vt. 1. 维修，保养   2. 维持，保持
major   n. 专业，专业学生
majority   n. 多数，大多数
male   adj. 男的，雄的
manager   n. 经理，管理人
mankind   n. 人类
manner   n. 1. 方法   2. (pl.) 礼貌，规矩
manual   adj. 手的，手工的   n. 手册，指南
manufacture   vt. 制造，加工   n. 制造，产品
marriage   n. 结婚，婚姻
marvel(l)ous   adj. 奇迹般的
master   n. 硕士   vt. 精通，掌握
match   n. 火柴；比赛   v. 相配，相称
mate   n. 伙伴，同事；配偶
material   n. 材料，原料   adj. 物质的
mathematics (maths)   n. 数学
mature   adj. 1. 成熟的，熟的   2. 成年人的
maximum   n. 最大值   adj. 最高的，最大的
mayor   n. 市长
meantime   n. 其间
meanwhile   adv. 当时，同时
measure   v. 量，测量   n. (常 pl.)措施，办法
mechanical   adj. 机械的，机械制的
medal   n. 奖章，勋章，奖牌
media   n. 新闻媒体，传播媒介
medical   adj. 医学的，医疗的
medicine   n. 内服药
medium   n. 中间，媒介物，介质   adj. 中等的，适中的
melt   v. (使)融化，(使)熔化
member   n. 成员，会员
memory   n. 1. 记忆，记忆力   2. 回忆

mend vt. 修补，缝补
mental adj. 精神的，智力的
mention vt. 提及，说起 n. 提及，说起
merchant n. 商人
mercy n. 仁慈，宽恕
microphone n. 话筒
microscope n. 显微镜
mild adj. 1. 温和的，温柔的 2. 轻微的
military adj. 军事的，军用的
millimeter/-tre n. 毫米
miracle n. 奇迹，奇事
miserable adj. 痛苦的，悲惨的
mission n. 1. 使命，任务 2. 使团，代表团
mixture n. 1. 混合 2. 混合物，混合剂
model n. 1. 样式，型 2. 模范，典型
moderate adj. 中等的，适度的
modest adj. 谦虚的，谦让的
moisture n. 潮湿，湿气
monument n. 纪念碑
moral adj. 道德(上)的
motion n. 1. 运动 2. 手势，眼色，动作
motive n. 动机，目的
motor n. 发动机，电动机
mud n. 泥，泥浆
murder vi. & n. 谋杀，凶杀
muscle n. 肌肉
mystery n. 神秘，神秘的事物

N

nail n. 指甲；钉，钉子 vt. 钉，将……钉牢
naked adj. 裸体的，无遮盖的，无装饰的 [the naked eyes 肉眼]
narrow adj. 狭窄的，严密的，有限的
nation n. 国家，民族
national adj. 国家的，民族的；国立(有)的
native adj. 本国的，出生地的，本地的
natural adj. 自然的，天生的，天赋的 [natural resources 自然资源]
navy n. 海军
neat adj. 整洁的，灵巧的，优雅的
necessary adj. 1. 必需的；必要的 2. 必定的，必然的
needle n. 针，缝衣针；针叶；针状物

negative adj. 1. 否定的，否认的 2. 负的
neglect vt. 疏忽，忽视
neighbo(u)r n. 邻居，邻国
nephew n. 侄子，外甥
nerve n. 神经；勇气，魄力，胆量
nervous adj. 焦虑的，紧张不安的
nest n. 鸟巢，鸟窝；巢穴；庇护所
niece n. 侄女；外甥女
noble adj. 1. 高尚的 2. 贵族的，显贵的
nod v. 点头 n. 点头
nonsense n. 无意义的话；胡扯
noodle n. 面条(常用复数)
normal adj. 1. 正常的 2. 标准的
notice n. 1. 警告；通知，布告 2. 注意
novel n. 小说
nowadays adv. & v. 现在，现今
nowhere adv. & v. 无处；任何地方都不
nuclear adj. 1. 核心的 2. 原子核的
numerous adj. 许多的
nurse n. 护士 vt. 护理，看护，照料
nut n. 果核，坚果，果仁

O

obey vt. 服从，顺从
object n. 1. 物体 2. 对象 3. 目标
oblige vt. 迫使，责成，强迫 [be obliged to do sth. 被迫做……]
observation n. 观察，观测
observe vt. 观察，观测
obtain vt. 获得，得到
obvious adj. 明显的
occasion n. 场合，时机，机会
occupy vt. 占领，占据，占用，占，填满
occur vi. 发生，出现
ocean n. 海洋
odd adj. 奇数的
offend vt. 冒犯，触怒
offer vt. 提供，提出 n. 提议，提供
official n. 官员，行政人员
omit vt. 1. 省略，删去 2. 遗漏，疏忽
onion n. 洋葱
opera n. 歌剧 [opera house 歌剧院]
operate vt. 1. 使运转，经营 2. 动手术，开刀

opportunity   n. 机会
oppose   vt. 反对，反抗
opposite   adj. 1. 对面的，相对的   2. 相反的   n. 反义词，相反的事物
ordinary   adj. 平凡的，普通的，一般的
organ   n. 1. 器官   2. 口琴
organization/-isation   n. 1. 组织   2. 机构，团体
organize/-ise   vt. 组织，创办
origin   n. 1. 起源，开端   2. 出身，来历
output   n. 1. 产量   2. 输出，输出量
outward   adv. 向外，在外   adj. 向外的
oven   n. 炉，灶
overcome   vt. 战胜，克服
overlook   vt. 1. 忽视，忽略   2. 俯瞰，俯视
oversea(s)   adj. 海外的   adv. 在海外，去海外
owe   vt. 1. 欠（债等）   2. 把……归因于

P

pace   n. 步，步伐
pacific   adj. 1. 和平的，平静的   2. 太平洋的
paint   n. 油漆   vt. 1. 给……上油漆   2. 绘，画
palace   n. 宫殿
pale   adj. 1. 苍白的   2. 淡的，暗淡的
palm   n. 1. 手掌，掌心   2. 棕榈树
paragraph   n. 段，节
pardon   vt. 原谅，饶恕   n. 原谅，饶恕
participate   vi. (in) 参与，参加
particular   adj. 特殊的，特别的
partner   n. 1. 合作伙伴，合伙人   2. 舞伴
passive   adj. 被动的
passport   n. 护照
path   n. 1. 小路，小径   2. 路线，轨道
patience   n. 忍耐，耐心
patient   n. 病人   adj. 忍耐的，耐心的
pattern   n. 1. 图案，图样   2. 型，式样
pause   vi. & n. 中止，暂停
paw   n. （动物的）爪子，脚爪
peace   n. 1. 和平   2. 平静，安宁
peak   n. 1. 山顶，最高点   2. 高峰的，最高的
peculiar   adj. 特殊的，特有的
pepper   n. 胡椒，胡椒粉
percent   n. 百分之……
perform   vt. 1. 履行，执行   2. 表演，演出

period   n. 1. 时期   2. 学时，课时   3. 周期
permanent   adj. 永久的，持久的
permit   vt. 许可，允许   n. 许可证
persist   vi. 1. (in) 坚持   2. 持续
persuade   vt. 说服，劝导（成功）
pet   n. 宠物，宠儿
petrol   n. 汽油
physical   adj. 物质的，有形的
picnic   n. 野餐   vi. 去野餐
pigeon   n. 鸽子（一般指家鸽）
pile   n. 堆   v. (up) 堆积，堆
pill   n. 药丸
pillow   n. 枕头
pilot   n. 1. 飞行员   2. 领航员，引水员
pink   n. 粉红色，桃红色   adj. 粉红色的
pioneer   n. 先驱，倡导者
pipe   n. 1. 管子   2. 烟斗
plain   adj. 朴素的，平常的   n. 平原，旷野
planet   n. 行星
plant   n. 植物，作物
plastic   n. (常pl.) 塑料，塑料制品   adj. 可塑的，塑性的
platform   n. 1. 平台，台   2. 站台，月台
playground   n. 运动场，游乐场
pleasant   adj. 令人愉快的，舒适的
plenty   n. 丰富，大量
pocket   n. 袋子，小袋   vt. 把……装入袋内
poem   n. 诗
poet   n. 诗人
point   n. 点，小数点   v. 1. (at, to) 指向，表明   2. (out) 指出
poison   n. 毒，毒物
policy   n. 政策，方针
polish   vt. 1. 磨光，擦亮   2. 使优美，润饰
pollute   vt. 弄脏，污染
pond   n. 池塘
population   n. 人口
position   n. 1. 位置，方位   2. 职位，职务
positive   adj. 1. 积极的，肯定的   2. 正的，阳性的
possible   adj. 1. 可能的   2. 合理的，允许的
postage   n. 邮费，邮资
postcard   n. 明信片

postpone vt. 推迟，延期
pot n. 罐，壶
poverty n. 1. 贫穷；贫困 2. 缺乏；贫乏
powder n. 1. 粉末，粉 2. 火药，炸药
power n. 1. 权力，政权 2. 功率，动力
practical adj. 实际的，实践的
praise vt. 赞扬，歌颂 n. 赞扬，赞美的话
pray v. 1. 请求，恳求 2. 祈祷
precious adj. 宝贵的，珍贵的
precise adj. 精确的；准确的
predict v. 预言，预告
preparation n. 准备，预备
president n. 1. 总统 2. 会长；校长
press vt. 1. 压，揿，按 2. 压榨，压迫
pretend v. 假装，假扮
prevent vt. (from)预防，防止
previous adj. 先前的
price n. 1. 价格，价钱 2. 代价
pride n. 1. 自豪 2. 骄傲，傲慢 vt. (使)自豪，(使)自夸
primary adj. 1. 最初的，初级的 2. 首要的，主要的
principle n. 原理，原则
prison n. 监狱
private adj. 1. 私人的，个人的 2. 秘密的，私下的
prize n. 奖赏，奖金，奖品 vt. 珍视
procedure n. 过程，步骤
proceed vi. 1. 进行，继续下去 2. 前进
process n. 1. 过程，进程 2. 工序，制作法
produce v. 生产，制造 n. 产品，农产品
profession n. 职业
professor n. 教授
profit n. 1. 利润 2. 益处，得益
progress n. 前进，进步 vi. 前进，进步
project n. 1. 方案，计划 2. 工程，项目
promise vt. & n. 允诺，答应
promote vt. 1. 促进，发扬 2. 提升，提拔
pronunciation n. 发音，发音方法
proof n. 1. 证明，证据 2. 校样，样张
proper adj. 适合的，恰当的
property n. 1. 财产，资产 2. 性质，特征
proportion n. 1. 比例 2. 部分，份

proposal n. 提议，建议
propose vt. 1. 提议，建议 2. 提名，推荐
protect vt. (from)保护
protein n. 蛋白质
proud adj. 1. (of)自豪的，得意的 2. 骄傲的，妄自尊大的
prove vt. 1. 证明，证实 2. 检验，考验
provide vt. (with, for)提供，供给
province n. 省
public adj. 1. 公共的 2. 公开的 n. 公众，民众
pulse n. 脉搏，脉冲
punctual adj. 准时的，严守时刻的
punish vt. 惩罚，处罚
pupil n. 1. 学生，小学生 2. 瞳孔
purchase vt. & n. 买，购买
pure adj. 1. 纯的，纯洁的 2. 纯理论的
purple adj. 紫的 n. 紫色
purpose n. 1. 目的，意图 2. 用途，效果
pursue vt. 1. 追赶，追踪 2. 继续，从事
puzzle n. 难题，谜 v. (使)迷惑

Q

qualify vt. 1. 使合格，使具有资格 2. 证明……合格
quality n. 品质，性质；特质，特性；才能
quantity n. 量，数量
quarrel n. 争论，争辩，口角；争论的原因
quarter n. 四分之一；一刻钟，15分钟
queen n. 王后，女王
quit v. 离开，辞职，停止
quote vt. (from)引用，引证

R

rabbit n. 兔
race n. & vi. 赛跑，比赛
radar n. 雷达，无线电探测器
raise v. 上升，提出 vt. 升起，唤起，提出
range n. 范围，射程，山脉
rank n. 等级，横列，阶级，军衔
rapid adj. 迅速的，飞快的
rare adj. 稀有的，杰出的，珍贵的
rat n. 老鼠

rate n. 比率；速度，速率；等级；价格
raw adj. 生的，未加工的，原始的
ray n. 光线，闪烁 v. 射出光线
react vi. 起反应，对……有影响；起反作用
reality n. 真实，事实，现实
realize/-ise vt. 认识到，了解到，实现
recall vt. 回忆，回想
receipt n. 收到，收据
reception n. 接待，招待会，接收
recognize/-ise vt. 认出，承认，公认
recommend vt. 推荐，介绍，建议
recover vt. 重新获得，恢复；痊愈，复原
reduce vt. 减少，缩小，简化，还原
reference n. 提及，涉及；参考，参考书目
reflect v. 反射，反映，反省
refuse vt. 拒绝，谢绝
regard vt. 把……当作，考虑，尊敬
region n. 区域，地方，领域
register v. 登记，注册
regret n. & v. 遗憾，悔恨；抱歉，歉意
relate vt. 叙述；有联系；涉及，有关
relation n. 关系，联系；叙述；亲戚
release v. 释放，解放
reliable adj. 可靠的，可信赖的
rely v. 依赖，依靠；信赖，信任 [rely on/upon 依靠；信赖]
relief n. 减轻(痛苦等)；解除
remain vi. 保持，剩余，逗留
remark n. 评论，备注，注释
remind vt. 提醒，使想起
remote adj. 遥远的，偏僻的
remove adj. 移动，开除，迁移
renew v. 使更新，使恢复，使新生，复兴
replace vt. 取代，替换；把……放回原处
represent v. 代表，描绘，象征
republic n. 共和国，共和政体
rescue vt. 援救，营救 n. 援救，营救
research n. 研究，调查 vi. 研究，调查
reserve v. 保存，保留 n. 储备(物)
residence n. 居住，住处
resist vt. 抵抗，反抗
resolution n. 决心，决定，决议
resource n. 资源(常用复数)；财力

respect n. 尊敬，敬意 vt. 尊敬，尊重
respond v. 回答，响应，反应
responsibility n. 责任，职责
restore vt. 恢复，归还；修复，重建
restrict vt. 限制，约束，限定
resume vt. 再继续 n. 摘要；[美]履历
retain vt. 保持，保留
retire vi. 退休；撤退；就寝
reveal vt. 展现，显示；揭示，暴露
revolution n. 革命；旋转
reward n. 报酬，奖金 vt. 酬劳，奖赏
ribbon n. 缎带，丝带，带状物
rid vt. 使摆脱，使去掉
ripe adj. 熟的，成熟的 v. 成熟
root n. 根，根本 v. (使)生根，使固定
rough adj. 粗糙的，粗略的，粗野的
route n. 路线，航线，通道 v. 发送
routine n. 例行公事，常规，日常工作
rubbish n. 垃圾，废物，废话
ruin v. (使)破产 n. 毁灭，崩溃
rural adj. 乡下的，乡村风味的，农村生活的

S

sack n. 袋，包 vt. 解雇
sail v. 航行(于) vi. 启航，开船
sake n. 缘故，理由 [for the sake of 为了……起见]
salary n. 薪水，工资
sample n. 样品 vt. 抽样试验，抽样调查
satellite n. 卫星
satisfy vt. 1. 满足，使满意 2. 说服，使相信
sausage n. 香肠
saw n. 锯子，锯床 v. 锯，锯开
scale n. 刻度，标度
scare v. 惊吓，受惊 n. 惊恐，恐慌
scene n. 景色，景象 舞台，发生地点
schedule n. 时间表，日程安排表
scholar n. 学者
scissors n. 剪刀
scold v. 责骂，申斥
scope n. 1. 范围 2. 余地，机会
score n. 得分，分数；二十
scream v. 尖声叫 n. 尖叫声

screen n. 屏幕；帘 vt. 掩蔽，遮
screw n. 螺旋，螺钉 v. 拧，拧紧
seal n. 封铅，封条 vt. 封，密封
secondary adj. 次要的，二级的
section n. 部分；断面，剖面；部门，科
secure adj. 安全的，可靠的
seize v. 占领，抓住，逮住
select vt. 选择，挑选 adj. 精选的
selfish adj. 自私的
senior adj. 年长的
sensitive adj.（to）1. 敏感的 2. 易受伤害
separate adj.（from）分离的，分开的
series n. 1. 系列，连续 2. 丛书
servant n. 仆人
settle v. 1. 解决，决定 2. 定居，（使）安家
severe adj. 1. 严厉的 2. 剧烈的，严重的
sew v. 缝制，缝纫
shade n. 树荫，阴暗 vt. 遮蔽，遮光
shadow n. 阴影，荫，影子
shake v. & n. 1. 摇动，摇 2. 颤抖，震动
shallow adj. 浅的；浅薄的
shame n. 羞耻，羞愧
shape n. 1. 形状，外形 2. 情况，状态
sharp adj. 锋利的，锐利的
shave v. 剃，刮
shed vt. 1. 流出 2. 脱皮；落叶；褪毛
sheet n. 1.（一）片，（一）张，薄片 2. 被单
shelf n. 架子
shell n. 壳；炮弹
shelter n. 躲避处，掩蔽，保护
shiver vi. & n. 战栗，发抖
shock n. 震动 v.（使）震惊，（使）激动
shore n. 滨，岸
shortcoming n. 缺点，短处
signal n. 信号 v. 发信号，用信号通知
signature n. 签名，署名
significance n. 意义；重要性
silence n. 静，沉默 vt. 使沉默，使安静
silver n. 银 vt. 镀银
sincere adj. 诚挚的，真实的
single adj. 单人的；单一的；未婚的
sink v. 沉没，（使）下沉 n. 水槽，水池
site n. 位置，地点

slide v.（使）滑动，（使）滑行
slight adj. 轻微的，微小的
slim adj. 苗条的；薄的
slope n. 斜坡，斜面；倾斜 v.（使）倾斜
smooth adj. 光滑的，平滑的；平稳的
social adj. 社会的
society n. 社会；团体，会，社
soft adj. 软的，柔软的；温和的
soil n. 泥土，土壤 v. 弄脏，（使）变脏
solar adj. 太阳的，日光的
sole adj. 1. 单独的，唯一的 2. 独有的
solid adj. 1. 固体的 2. 实心的 3. 结实的
solution n. 解答，解决办法
solve vt. 解决，解答
sore adj. 1. 疼痛的 2. 痛心的 n. 痛处
sorrow n. 悲哀，悲痛
source n. 源，源泉；来源，出处
sow v. 播（种）
space n. 间隔，距离；空地，空间，太空
spacecraft n. 航天器，宇宙飞船
spacious adj. 广阔的，宽敞的
spare adj. 多余的 v. 节约，节省
spark n. 火星，火花
specific adj. 1. 明确的 2. 特有的，特定的
spider n. 蜘蛛
spill v. 溢出，溅出
spin v. 1. 旋转 2. 纺，纺纱 n. 旋转
spirit n. 1. 精神 2. 气概，志气
splendid adj. 壮丽的，辉煌的；极好的
spoon n. 匙，调羹
spray v. 喷，（使）溅散 n. 浪花，水花
spread v. & n. 散布，传播
spy n. 间谍 v. 当间谍；察觉，发现
square n. 1. 正方形 2. 广场 adj. 1. 正方形的
  2. 平方的
stable adj. 稳定的
stain n. 污点，瑕疵 v. 污染
standard n. 标准，规格 adj. 标准的
stare v.（at）凝视，盯着看
starve v.（使）饿死，（使）饿
statistic n. 统计数字，统计资料
steady adj. 稳固的，稳定的
steak n. 牛排，肉排，鱼排

steal   v. 偷，窃取
steam   n. 蒸汽，水汽   vi. 蒸发   vt. 蒸
steel   n. 钢
stick   n. 棍，棒，手杖   v. 粘住；贴住［stick to 坚持，坚守］
stir   vt. 搅拌，搅动
stock   n. 库存，储品   vt. 储存
stocking   n. 长袜
stomach   n. 胃，胃口
stone   n. 石，石头；宝石
stool   n. 凳子
stoop   v. 俯(身)，弯(腰)   n. 弯腰，曲背
storage   vt. 储藏，储备
storm   n. 暴风雨，暴风雪
stove   n. 炉
straight   adj. 1. 直的，笔直的   2. 正直的
strain   vt. 扭伤，损伤
strategy   n. 战略，策略
straw   n. 稻草，麦秆
stream   n. 溪，川；流   v. 流，涌
stress   n. 压力，应力；重音
strict   adj. (with)严格的，严厉的
strike   v. 1. 击，撞   2. 敲(响)
stripe   n. 条纹
struggle   n. & vi. 1. 奋斗   2. 挣扎，搏斗
stubborn   adj. 顽固的，倔强的
stuff   n. 原料，材料   vt. 塞满，填满
stupid   adj. 愚蠢的，笨的
substance   n. 1. 物质   2. 实质，主旨
suffer   vt. 遭受，蒙受；忍受，忍耐
sufficient   adj. (for)足够的，充分的
superior   adj. (to)较……多的，优于……的
supply   vt. (with, to)供给，供应
support   vt. 1. 支撑   2. 支持   n. 支持者
suppose   v. 料想，猜想   vt. 假定
supreme   adj. 1. 极度的   2. 至高的，最高的
surface   n. 表面，面；外表，外观
surround   vt. 包围，环绕
survey   vt. 1. (向公众)调查   2. 测量，勘定
survive   v. 幸免于，幸存
suspect   vt. 猜疑，怀疑   n. 嫌疑犯
swallow   v. 吞，咽   n. 1. 吞，咽   2. 燕子
symbol   n. 1. 符号，记号   2. 象征
sympathy   n. 同情，同情心
system   n. 1. 系统，体系   2. 制度，体制

T

territory   n. 领土；版图；领地
terror   n. 恐怖，惊骇
theater/-tre   n. 剧场，戏院；戏剧
theory   n. 理论，学说
thick   adj. 1. 厚的；粗的   2. 浓的；稠
thief   n. 小偷，贼，盗贼
thorough   adj. 彻底的，完全的
thread   n. 线索；脉络；思路
threat   n. 威胁，恫吓
throat   n. 咽喉，喉咙，嗓音
thrust   v. 猛推，冲，猛刺
thunder   n. 雷声，雷   v. 打雷
tobacco   n. 烟草，烟草制品，抽烟
toe   n. 脚趾，脚尖；袜子尖；鞋尖
tolerate   v. 容忍，宽容，纵容
ton   n. 吨；许多；大量
tongue   n. 1. 舌头   2. 语言；口语；话
tough   adj. 困难的，费力的
tour   n. 旅行，旅游，周游，漫游
toward(s)   prep. 1. 向；往   2. 朝，对
towel   n. 手巾，毛巾
tower   n. 塔，高楼
trace   n. 踪迹，行踪   vt. 跟踪，追踪
track   n. 足迹，痕迹   vt. 跟踪，追踪，尾随
trade   n. 贸易，生意；职业，行业
tradition   n. 惯例，规矩；传统
transfer   v. 迁移；调任；转移
transform   vi. 改变，转化，变换
translation   n. 翻译，译文，转化
transmission   n. 播送，传送，传输，转播
transport   vt. 运输，运送   n. 运输，运送
treat   v. 1. 对待，看待   2. 治疗
tremble   vi. 战栗，发抖，震动
trend   n. 倾向，趋势
triangle   n. 三角形
trick   n. 1. 诡计，骗局   2. 窍门，诀窍
trim   adj. 整齐的，整洁的   v. 修整，修剪
triumph   n. 胜利，成功，凯旋
troop   n. 军队，部队

twist　v. 1. 卷，捻，搓　2. 扭曲　3. 转动
typical　adj. 典型的，具有代表性的
tyre　n. 轮胎(英式英语)（AmE. = tire）

U

undergo　vt. 经历，遭受，忍受
underground　adv. 在地下，秘密地　n. 地铁
underline　vt. 在……下面划线，加下划线
underneath　adv. 在下面　prep. 在……的下面
understand　v. 懂，了解
undertake　vt. 承担，担任
unexpected　adj. 想不到的，未预料到
uniform　n. 制服
union　n. 联盟，协会
unique　adj. 唯一的，独特的
unite　v. 联合，团结
universe　n. 宇宙，世界，万物，领域
university　n.（综合）大学
upon　prep. 在……之上
upper　adj. 上面的，上部的
upset　vt. 扰乱，使不适，使心烦
urban　adj. 城市的，市内的
urge　vt. 1. 催促　2. 力劝
urgent　adj. 急迫的，紧急的

V

vain　adj. 徒然的，无益的
valley　n.（山）谷，流域
vanish　vi. 消失，突然不见
variety　n. 变化，多样性，品种，种类
vehicle　n. 交通工具，车辆
version　n. 译文，译本，版本
victim　n. 受害人，牺牲者，牺牲品
victory　n. 胜利，战胜
violence　n. 猛烈，强烈，暴力，暴虐，暴行
violet　n. 紫罗兰　adj. 紫罗兰色的
visible　adj. 看得见的，明显的，显著的
vital　adj. 重大的，至关重要的
vitamin　n. 维生素
volume　n. 1. 体积　2. 大量，音量
voyage　n. 航程，航空，航海记，旅行记

W

wealth　n. 财富，财产，大量
wander　vi. 漫步，徘徊
war　n. 战争
warn　vt. 警告，注意，通知
weak　adj. 弱的，虚弱的，软弱的
weapon　n. 武器
weave　vt. 编织，纺织
wedding　n. 婚礼
weed　n. 野草，杂草　v. 除草，铲除
welfare　n. 福利；福利救济
wheat　n. 小麦
wheel　n. 轮，车轮，轮子
whisper　n. & v. 耳语，低声说
whistle　n. 口哨，汽笛
wicked　adj. 坏的，邪恶的，恶劣的
widespread　adj. 分布广泛的，普遍的
wing　n. 翅，翅膀
wipe　v. 擦，揩，擦去
wisdom　n. 智慧，明智
wit　n. 智力，才智，智慧
withdraw　vt. 取（钱），取消　vi. 缩回，退出
worm　n. 虫，蠕虫
worship　vt. 崇拜，尊敬
wound　n. 创伤，伤口　vt. 伤，伤害
wrap　vt. 包装，缠绕，裹
wrist　n. 手腕

X

X-ray　n. X光，X射线

Y

yard　n. 1. 院子　2. 码（=0.914米）
yield　vi.（to）屈服，屈从　n. 产量，收益
youth　n. 1. 青春，青年时期　2. 小伙子，年轻人
　　　3. 青年(男女)

Z

zero　n. 零点，零度
zone　n. 地域，区域